A Dangerous Meeting:
In the Shadows with Mercyful Fate

MARTIN POPOFF

A Dangerous Meeting:
In the Shadows with Mercyful Fate

MARTIN POPOFF

WYMER PUBLISHING
Bedford, England

First published in Canada by Power Chord Press in January 2020
under the title *Black Funeral: Into the Coven with Mercyful Fate*.
This revised edition published in 2025 by Wymer Publishing, Bedford, England
www.wymerpublishing.co.uk Tel: 01234 326691
Wymer Publishing is a trading name of Wymer (UK) Ltd.

Copyright © 2025 Martin Popoff / Wymer Publishing.

Print edition (fully illustrated): **ISBN: 978-1-915246-85-1**

Edited by Jerry Bloom.

The Author hereby asserts his rights to be identified
as the author of this work in accordance with sections
77 to 78 of the Copyright, Designs & Patents Act 1988.

All rights reserved. No part of this publication may be
reproduced or transmitted in any form or by any means,
electronic or mechanical, including photocopying, or any
information storage and retrieval system, without written
permission from the publisher.

This publication is sold subject to the condition that it shall not,
by way of trade or otherwise, be lent, re-sold, hired out or
otherwise circulated without the publisher's prior consent in any
form of binding or cover other than that in which it is published
and without a similar condition including this condition
being imposed on the subsequent purchaser.

Printed and bound in Great Britain by CMP, Dorset.

A catalogue record for this book is available from the British Library.

eBook formatting by Lin White at Coinlea Services.
Typeset/Design by Andy Bishop / Tusseheia Creative.
Cover design: Tusseheia Creative.
Front and back cover photos: Bill O'Leary/Timeless Concert Images.

CONTENTS

Introduction		7
Chapter 1:	The Early Years *"Nuns Have No Fun"*	11
Chapter 2:	Melissa *"Please use your fame for the good of the youth."*	35
Chapter 3:	Don't Break the Oath *"When I saw the other guys' faces, I knew it was real."*	69
Chapter 4:	"Satan's Fall" *King Diamond Goes Solo*	89
Chapter 5:	In the Shadows *"God damn, this is genuine Mercyful Fate, man."*	97
Chapter 6:	Time *"Death has so many different aspects to it, but the skull is final."*	119
Chapter 7:	Into the Unknown *"You need to figure this out and get this to stop."*	143
Chapter 8:	Dead Again *"Dark imagery and nightmarish situations and ghostly things."*	165
Chapter 9:	9 *"There is nothing held back, just like the early days."*	179
Chapter 10:	An Epilogue *"Burn in Hell"*	207
Discography		233
Interviews with the Author		236
Additional Citations		236
About the Author		238
A Complete Martin Popoff Bibliography		239

INTRODUCTION

The records made by Mercyful Fate speak for themselves, each as creepy as the last, in creation of a catalogue arguably more unsettling that those of the proper black metal bands the good King Diamond inspired.

It is my near obsession with these albums that inspired a first making of this book five years ago, called *Black Funeral: Into the Coven with Mercyful Fate*, and now, this expanded and reconsidered edition you hold within your tight grasp.

As for why I care so much, let's look at history and chart the progress, because there really aren't that many examples of rock acts this devilish.

Putting aside light music witch types like Black Widow and Coven, the big one everybody knows about is Black Sabbath. But Ozzy, Tony, Geezer and Bill are downright cuddly compared to what King was conjuring a couple hard rock generations later. And besides, all one has to do is go through the lyrical canon of Geezer Butler and realise that the guy was actually fighting for the good side. He may as well have been an anti-war, anti-nukes, enviro-priest, even if the music thundering along behind his wisdoms could turn your hair white.

Next in line is Venom, who arrived on the scene a couple years before Mercyful. This was actually pretty Satanic stuff, but it was undercut, at least in comparison with what was to come out of Denmark, by the dirtiness of their sound.

If Cronos, Mantas and Abaddon had sold their souls, how come they couldn't play better? Ancillary to Venom were the likes of Demon, Witchfynde, Angel Witch and Witchfinder General, but none of them could hold a candle, capability-wise to what came next.

Enter Mercyful, who could indeed play better and indeed represented a huge leap forward. As I'm sure I touch down upon in the ensuing chapters, the debut *Melissa* album was in possession of an uneasy abundance of professionalism, especially for a debut, especially for a debut from Denmark.

I remember sitting around with my buddies and conjecturing, after hearing a few acrobatic time-changes, that the last time we felt that a band was so good that they must have traded eternal damnation for virtuosity, well, that was Judas Priest, back with *Sad Wings of Destiny*.

Same sort of thing as *Melissa*: all of a sudden, here we were listening to the new best band in the world and they are arriving alive in our lives from out of the ether. As metal-attuned as we were, nobody had ever heard of these guys (yes, I somehow whiffed on the *Nuns Have No Fun* EP), and that's because they were rookies and rookies were not supposed to be this good.

Further on this crucial comparison, sure, Judas Priest had been around in some guise since 1969, but *Sad Wings of Destiny* was their second album, and it was essentially on an indie label. And then in 1983, along comes Mercyful Fate, also on a small label, also mysteriously bubbling up from no man's land, delivering a record that sounds like it cost $300,000 to make. What's more, the lyrics were pointedly Satanic, the vocals pointedly otherworldly, as was the face of the band's lead shrieker making those bird noises.

Honestly, for us, it made for a situation where it felt like there was Mercyful Fate and then there was everybody else. And it's not that they were my absolute favourite band at any point, it's just that they were weirdly "the best." But yes, to be sure, the elements that made us think they were a bit misguided tended to make them *not* the favourite and also put them in a little bit of a box, a novelty box. Whether it was from the positives or the negatives or a mix of both, Mercyful Fate stood aside looking on and in, proposing, from way out on its own path, an experiment in human achievement.

How aware were they of their own rarefied greatness? The frustrating thing is, I've asked various Judas Priest guys on numerous occasions if they had any clue that in 1976 they were operating on an almost godly level of musical acumen not known since Deep Purple with *In Rock* and they just verbally shrugged. Actually, only recently, K.K. Downing has said some interesting things about being "progressive blues" that begin to explain it.

Pan forward seven years, and Hank and Michael and King indeed embody a comparatively larger amount of self-awareness, although there's also an endearing degree of modesty that tempers the articulation of their evident and self-evident greatness.

But yes, fact is, the mandate with Mercyful was more or less to be better than the best before them, which they all recognised as Judas Priest. That's really all you need to know when it comes to the music—King and Michael especially were a couple of record nerds who knew that the best metal so far could be experienced on *Sin After Sin* and *Stained Class*, and that if they were to be "the heaviest band in the world," they'd have to do better than that.

INTRODUCTION

The concept of King Diamond was another component altogether. As we will explore throughout this book, he will be afforded ample space to explain himself. But all the explaining in the world doesn't dispel the notion that the band's success was always going to be limited by a trio of things coming from King, and that's his devil-loving lyrics, his painted face and, above all, his profuse use of falsetto.

Now, the one that was due to cause him the most grief with potential fans probably was the latter, the high, clean singing, that top gear, that falsetto, which, let's face it, contains within its lettering, the shorter word "false."

Whatever your thoughts on this controversial vocal technique—and frankly, it's my least favourite thing about the band—there's only one King. Unarguably, Kim Bendix "King Diamond" Petersen is one of the most distinctive vocalists in all of heavy metal history.

And there's a resonance beyond as well: this idea of using vocals as an instrument of terror. In this light, King is really the most serious practitioner revolving around this abstract notion until the arrival of the black metal guys themselves, who have so much to thank Mercyful Fate for in so many ways, not least of which is an *eventual* growth toward progressive metal.

Okay, enough about that, because really, as we amble enjoyably together through all of these great records to come, these points will come up again, and at times you'll hear more from me on it, but of course also from the guys in the band.

I did want to make one other point however as to why this story was worthy of an expansion and second printing. As we all know, Mercyful Fate were briefly (magically) a band, and then they went away for nine years and then came back and put together a prolific run of five reunion studio albums.

Okay, so what I loved about doing this book is that on a pretty objective level, those five records are as good as the first two, which are a couple of the greatest albums in heavy metal history. In that respect, I'm back to the ol' cherished role of DJ—or, sure, writer, and even record label owner—who has housed within his sideline role in the music industry the fun mission of proselytising about great music that might have been forgotten or under-appreciated at the time.

This is exactly the same way I felt about my middle-years Iron Maiden book, *Holy Smoke: Iron Maiden in the '90s*. The value in that book was not, per se, the look-in at the Iron Maiden catalogue itself. Rather, it was the full and strident examination of the Bruce Dickinson solo catalogue. So yes, I'd like you to put some time and effort into giving the Mercyful Fate reunion albums the chance I think they deserve, the same way we should all be celebrating the likes of *Skunkworks, Accident of Birth* and *The Chemical Wedding*, or indeed little-known records I've celebrated in books on Montrose, Angel, Riot or Max Webster.

It's funny, I knew I loved every one of those Mercyful Fate reunion albums at the time, as much as I do now. Why? Well, as I perused the Wikipedia pages on each of them, I saw my own grades there from my old *The Collector's Guide to Heavy Metal* books... and they were indeed very high scores! It's always nice when that happens.

So, as I went through these records to bring you an analysis of each of them in detail, it was good to see that I was right all along. All the hard work that went into the likes of *In the Shadows, Time, Into The Unknown, Dead Again* and *9* made for some crushing and accomplished heavy metal, works of high fidelity and inspired yet meticulous performance, and yes, impressive conceptual substance lyrically from King time and time again, who brought us a varied suite of bittersweet dead time stories. And now it's time to get meta on you and bring you the chapters—the individual dead time stories—about King Diamond's dead time stories.

So, without further ado, pour yourself a brandy, sink into your favourite blood-red leather chair surrounded by your library of ancient texts, lift monocle to eye and let's celebrate together this uncommon—and uncommonly skilled—heavy metal export from the land of Lars.

Martin Popoff
martinp@inforamp.net; martinpopoff.com

1.
THE EARLY YEARS
"NUNS HAVE NO FUN"

My buddies and I were unacquainted with the *Nuns Have No Fun* EP—I'll admit that. But then again, hell, I'm not even sure that's true so I may be selling us short. I just remember that to be the case as I write this right now.

So, let's just say that there was no reference point, no context, for the unholy howl we heard playing *Melissa* for the first time. These would have been the ensuing months of another tough Western Canadian winter, but the eerily evolved metal magic that was *Melissa* would become the perfect pox on Christmas, led by the shrieking falsetto of King Diamond and his band of Danish brothers hell-bent on bettering Judas Priest and the New Wave of British Heavy Metal that came like a killing machine in the wake of *Killing Machine*.

We would eventually learn that there were reasons Mercyful Fate came fully formed into the metal world, plush and expensive, practiced and efficient, progressive and sumptuously captured on vinyl, ready to confound expectations.

Kim Bendix "King Diamond" Petersen, born June 14th, 1956, in a western suburb of Copenhagen, had been plying his trade in bands since 1976, moving from Brainstorm to Black Rose, where he began exploring his ghoulish and theatrical persona while his band thundered along doing their best Uriah Heep impressions.

"Alice Cooper—that's one show I will never forget," begins King, charting the path that led him first to rock 'n' roll, then to shock 'n' roll. "I saw them in '75 before I played in any band. The first band I played with, Brainstorm, was friends from school. I didn't sing; I only played guitar. That was in '76 that we started up there. I had seen Alice in '75, the *Welcome to My Nightmare* show in Copenhagen, and that show blew my mind. That was the show where I decided myself that if I ever started a band, I would use makeup. Not his style but makeup, because the makeup he used worked on me. It felt unreal; it felt like a person from another world. I was down front and reached up and touched his boot and it seems like he might have disappeared; it was magical to see. From right there I decided I'm going to use makeup. We started and wore makeup with the band called Brainstorm."

"No inspiration for the makeup," continues King, asked about what would seem an obvious touchstone, Kiss. "That's not where that came from. I definitely liked Kiss with the old, heavy albums, and that was from the beginning of Kiss that I listened to them. The show was incredible. I didn't see it as much talking about shock horror. It was more like a show. He was spitting blood and breathing fire, but it wasn't shock like I felt with Alice Cooper."

"With Alice, it was the magical things that went on, on stage. All the magician's tricks that went into it that make you go home and think, 'How the hell did they do that?' I remember from the *Welcome to My Nightmare* show there was this big screen that they were projecting a film on. I remember the song was called 'Escape,' and they were running after these four dancers they had on stage, but they were being projected up on screen running after him, chasing him. He had broken out of a coffin. Then he suddenly walked out through that screen onto the stage and disappeared on the film. And then they came out after him onto the stage, ran around chasing him, caught him, lifted him up, carried him back onto the screen. Right when they walked through that screen again, they were on film."

"Of course, he had the guillotine and he's done the electric chair. There are so many things that are more horror. His wife back then was one of the actresses on stage and there was this song called 'Only Women Bleed.' It could also have been 'I Love the Dead,' but there was one where he smacked her around. But then you realised at some point that they had some tricks with the lights and that she had switched places with a life-sized doll and when he picked up the doll and smacked it around, it wasn't until the end that you realised it's a doll. There were some amazing things he did when I saw him."

Reaching back further though, to his early teens, King says that "It was the late '60s when I first jumped on the whole thing. That's when I first heard Led Zeppelin. Jimmy Page's guitar sound is what got me started in music. I had to make that sound myself. I saved up money from my allowance and eventually had enough to get an electric guitar and knew absolutely nothing about music at that time except for listening to radio. Coming home with that guitar the first day and not getting a peep out of it was strange to me and I didn't understand it."

"There was a guy… he was younger than my parents, but he was the husband of some friends that they had. I can't remember how it was, but he was an electronics mechanic and my parents saw him with his wife's parents. He helped me build my first amp. He said, 'You need a distortion pedal' or 'I'll help you build an amp and we'll build in distortion,' and we built my first cabinet together. I remember my amp had the red button for on and off and then a black button, and that was the one for my tough sound. That was back with Black Rose when we started up. I've never had a lesson in my life; it's all been self-taught. I started teaching myself to play guitar."

This would prove to be a boon later in life when King would jump right in and compose music for both Mercyful Fate and King Diamond, on top of providing the lyrical concepts, singing it all and embodying the focus of most of the visuals.

Further on his roots, Diamond explains that "A lot of my friends were uneasy listening to the first Black Sabbath album when it first came out because he's singing about the devil and this and that. To me it was more like they are standing on a hill looking down into a little village seeing things, describing what they saw, not so much being involved themselves. So, they were in an observatory role where they were saying this and that. Of course they had, 'I turn around and I run,' when they got a little closer, but they were never involved in that way."

A DANGEROUS MEETING: IN THE SHADOWS WITH MERCYFUL FATE

"And you could see they always had their big Christian crosses around their neck. Maybe they were a little uneasy about those things themselves and wanted to have a little protection—who knows? They are big heroes of mine and they're early influences of some other people. But to scare me, I never felt scared listening to their music. I've heard a lot of our fans say the opposite. 'Oh, you scared the crap out of me the first time I heard *Abigail.*' Really? Great! I didn't get that. You can watch a horror movie and you can get some of those shocks there with the suspense we love as humans, but I never saw ourselves as giving that through an album. That was pretty amazing, when someone told me that. I wouldn't think that would be possible."

"Led Zeppelin were mood-creators, too," figures King. "All those things and stories played backwards, listening to 'Stairway to Heaven' backwards—I've done it. I did it with a friend of mine one night and it got a little creepy. I was living in an apartment that was really haunted at the time in Copenhagen. Sitting there at night, we actually recorded it by playing the vinyl backwards onto a tape deck, and then we could sit and play the tape deck over and over. We recorded it at different speeds, and we got so many lines out of it that made sense. Then you're thinking, did they really start it like that, or is it really pure coincidence? But then you hear the haunting sounds on the first Led Zeppelin album, on 'Dazed and Confused,' where he used the violin bow. He created some of those horror sounds (hums eerie notes). It's already there—you had some of those feelings. Sabbath had some of those classic chords too, in the song 'Black Sabbath.' Which I think is very inspired by classical music. I wouldn't want to do that because I want to write my own stuff, but you could take a lot of classical music and transform it, play it with heavy guitars and you'll get some real heavy, moody, complex stuff."

At this point then, King had not only his first introduction to the Satanic, but also onstage theatrics and heavy, heavy music, both in the listening and the creating, which happened as soon as he hit that black button for his "tough sound." But it was what the likes of Sabbath and Alice Cooper could achieve psychologically that was truly inspiring to the young Dane.

"I've learned over the years to try and create that kind of shock. For me, I stop before I explain things in complete detail. You have to leave the details to the listener, because the listener can scare himself the most, more than I can. I don't know exactly what kinds of fears the listener has, but there are some general things. But it's the listener that makes up all these things that are the worst for him. So, I give a lot of suggestions. Of course there's a story, but in certain situations you stop at the suggestions and let the listener's mind take over and build on those images into what fears they have. If they're scared of spiders, for instance, there are certain spiders for different people that they're scared of if they're scared of spiders. Instead of me saying exactly, 'This, it's a tarantula,' I don't, because other people are more scared of a black widow. So, if I don't say what kind of spider it is, it becomes a different spider in a different person's imagination."

His aim quickly became to create that rush of fear, but then again, says King, "I think it's the release afterwards that really counts. If it's a theatre, you can walk out and say it's just a movie. But while it's going on, you get sucked in if it's done right. But those thrills, those shocks, a lot of people put themselves through a roller coaster ride. Not that it's a pleasant feel but it's a thrill. People jumping off bridges with parachutes on their back. People do a lot of crazy stuff that you'd think they have a death wish or something, and it's the same kind of thrill when you see a movie; it's just safer. You see through the character's eyes standing on a building swaying about, about to fall off. Or someone is kicking your hands as you hold onto the railing and you're going to fall down fifteen stories. When you see it done the right way with a camera, you can get sucked into that feel with the camera. Like, oh my God, this is up so high, but deep down there's going to be that relief of walking out of there."

As King alluded to, the makeup had started with that important second band Black Rose, who, really, despite having no other future Mercyful Fate members, sound like a proto-Mercyful Fate band. It's a little more straight-forward, a little more Deep Purple, but still, the chill is there.

"There were several things with the makeup that really work well," explains Diamond. "Of course, I saw it with my own eyes in '75, how it came across. Alice's facial features came across further out into the hall. It was not just these blank faces you couldn't see. I was up front, but if you were twenty rows into the hall, it might have been harder to see the facial expressions, but that helped magnify all that stuff."

"Even from... maybe not Brainstorm, but as soon as we started Black Rose where I started singing, we had these crazy things on stage. The wheelchair was there already back in that time, '78,

A DANGEROUS MEETING: IN THE SHADOWS WITH MERCYFUL FATE

'79. I used to work in a lab—I'm a trained lab assistant; I have an international diploma for that—and I would borrow, with nice words, chemicals and make our own home-made bombs that we used on stage. In the beginning it was insane. We had created this little metal cylinder that would stand on a plate and had filters on, and then I actually had a torch that I would stick in there. And when I did that we caused this explosion with this nice cloud."

"One of my friends was working at a big butcher factory where he would steal pig's heads and pig's blood. We'd fill a plastic bag with pig's blood and open up a doll in the front, cut it open and stick it in there so when I stabbed it blood would come out. We threw it into the audience and it was nasty. I would chop the pig's head in half and throw that into the audience. I remember it was so sticky, this pig's blood, on the microphone afterwards. We didn't have the money so we used whatever we could come up with."

"So already it went together with having a show on stage, and it really became a challenge as well. When the makeup became part of that show, it gave the people something extra to bring home. Back then we didn't have albums out, but people certainly remembered us better than the supporter who played before us. But it wasn't just a personal thing. It wasn't done just for image. That's always been a part of me and that's one thing that I guess is different from a lot of people. So many people say, 'Are you happy today that you started that image of yours back then?' It was not an image. It never felt like an image or what we had to do—I *wanted* to do it. It was part of me. That's what it has always been since."

King figures his stint working in a lab helped inoculate him from being shocked by blood and guts. "We are being bombarded by so much stuff these days; on TV you are getting everything. You don't have to watch a war movie to get war in your living room—just turn on the news. You can see all the dead bodies you want. It's horrifying, but that's a fact, and you get numb to a lot of that stuff. It's amazing how human beings get numb to a lot of things."

"Like I said, I was a lab assistant. I worked at a lab in Denmark that was developing medicine. I was in charge of testing certain medicine that would enhance the blood flow to the kidneys of human beings. But we were testing it on rats. I had these big white rats with tails that were probably this big. They never felt anything except for when they were sedated. But doing these tiny operations on getting everything out and opening them up, their veins and little things to give them shots, hooked up to things, beep, beep, to see how everything was working on them. Dig in to find their vein, a little magnet around to measure their blood flow and all this. Then you give it a shot to give it a heart attack, and it never felt anything."

"But still, I stood there... it took about a couple of weeks and it didn't affect me. In the beginning I'm like, 'You're kidding; you want me to do this?!' 'You'll get used to it.' 'Really? I don't think so.' Then you get numb to it. It's so weird. But that has a lot to do with... you get so much of it in the door to the point where what does it take today to shock? People almost have to get naked in front of a camera to have shock. How can you shock with horror today? There's so much horror in this world coming right into your living room every single day. So, I think it's much more a matter of creating moods and feelings so you can put people in an uneasy mood."

With Black Rose, King says that "There was no white in the makeup, just black at that point. It always developed. It was never like this is the one makeup it must be. It was what would fit. So, it changed over time as well to fit certain albums and storylines."

Then there was King's legendary falsetto, the shrill siren up top that everybody remembers and hotly debates, but a technique that is only one part of his prodigious vocal prowess.

"My style developed early on with that Black Rose band, listening to the fans," divulges Diamond. "It was a fan who came up to me after a show and said, 'Man, you should use that falsetto more. It really sounds good.' I didn't even know what the word meant. I said, 'What does that mean?' 'Oh, the high note.' Then I started working on it. I started developing how you control the flow with your stomach muscles and suddenly the vibrato came out and holding longer notes and holding them in key and all those things."

Backtracking to the very origins of his vocalist role, King explains that "I was thrown into that special way of singing, you can say, by doing covers of Deep Purple right off the bat. The first night I ever sang, I snuck into a band as a vocalist/guitarist even though I'd never sung before. So, I just stood there; I had never sung in my life. I had no voice when I came home because I was just screaming. You can just imagine them saying, 'Okay, let's play "Space Truckin'" by Deep Purple.' Okay, I knew the song, but how on earth was I going to sing it?"

"So yes, to explain further, I was thrown into being a singer actually, because the band I played guitar in had quit. Then I was looking for another band to play guitar in and I saw this ad in a supermarket. This band is looking for a singer, Deep Purple style.

A DANGEROUS MEETING: IN THE SHADOWS WITH MERCYFUL FATE

Okay, maybe I can sneak in with my guitar in my back pocket and say I'm a singer/guitarist. Like I say, I had never sung in my life. Lead singer? All right, I'm a lead singer. I had my Marshall stack and my Gibson guitar just sitting at home for no use. But they had a killer guitarist already. So, I got in there, and they said, 'Can you sing "Space Truckin'?"' Sure—never sung before. So, I was just screaming. After a few hours rehearsal I went home and had no voice, because I could not sing. I was just screaming trying to hit these notes by screaming and not being a singer."

"Eventually something happened, although I don't know what happened. I think I started learning how to breathe on my own because I never had a lesson. Same with guitar. I know what an E and an A string is but that's where it stops. I write 75% of King Diamond's music but I don't know... what chord is that? Looks like this or that. I don't know, but that's probably what it looks like. It helps you a little because you go outside the norms. There are certain things I have done several times that I would never have done if I could read music, where Andy (Larocque) would tell me, 'Don't do that.' 'But it sounds great, doesn't it?' 'Yeah, it's weird. It shouldn't, but it does.' So, you get into those things. Vocals, I learned how to use stomach muscles to hold notes a little longer and start to actually be able to use vibration, vibrato."

"Then by practice, it developed, and I learned to sing that way but not from... I would say I was inspired by singers from that era, specifically David Byron who still today—he's not here today—but he's my favourite singer. No doubt. The range he had and the feel he had, unbelievable. Alice Cooper is probably my favourite for the moodier, raw horror stuff because it's absolutely mind-blowing how he can put himself... he can make it sound like he is there in the middle of what he is singing about and that's what I admire about him."

"But David Byron stood out as the best singer ever," continues King. "It was his range and his emotion. It still gives me goose bumps today listening to *Look at Yourself*. That song 'Shadows of Grief' on *Look at Yourself*, unbelievable. The vocal work there, amazing, done on an eight-track. I saw him live five times at least, maybe six times, with Uriah Heep, back in Copenhagen and he blew me away every time. I couldn't understand how he could sing that way live when he was downing two bottles of wine during a set. Unreal. It would kill my voice. But it was the mood and feeling and range that he had that just blew me away."

THE EARLY YEARS

"There were lots of other great singers," adds King. "I was very influenced by Ozzy, Rob Halford, Robert Plant but again, Alice, specifically for the way he could put himself into the situation of what he was singing. Hearing it was like he must have been there when he sang it. 'I'll put pennies on your eyes;' all these feelings he has in the way he presented his lyrics—unbelievable. But with the others it's range of singing that influenced me a lot without me trying to sound like anyone. I don't think I sound like any of them. I don't think that would be my goal, to sound like any of them."

To underscore, all the theatrics and thespian delivery, the multiple characters, not to mention the makeup and the darkness—that's all right there wrapped up in Alice Cooper. But King's love for the dearly departed Uriah Heep front man is telling as well—David Byron and King shared not only two singing gears, the high and the tenor, but they also shared use of falsetto. The only things Byron didn't do that are part of King's repertoire is the speaking voice and the growl, with King inviting in more of a sense of vocal fry than Byron ever did. But the main point there is the falsetto—your ears pricked up when Byron did it (and your nose wrinkled a bit), which is the same reaction most listeners had to King Diamond as the Mercyful Fate albums started denting metalheads.

Disagreeing that his vocals are in and of themselves shocking, King rather calls them, "unique. I've learned to use my voice. I had the opportunity. I didn't know from the beginning. It was when we started doing the concept albums that my voice developed into all those different voices I can do and trying to portray all the different characters. That was a big development for the voice. If you play a song of ours for our fans and I don't care who it is, they can hear if it's me or not. It's distinctive; it's the same thing with Ozzy. You can always hear if it's Ozzy, and there's where it becomes tough to accept a replacement for a band where a vocalist has such a unique-sounding voice. Same with Halford. Ripper Owens, amazing singer, but when I saw them live with him it was just not that same Judas Priest. Halford's charisma I was used to. Dio is a mind-blowing singer, but him singing the old Sabbath that Ozzy... for me, it's just like, I want to hear an Ozzy-sounding voice for that. It's not saying the singers are less or anything like that. Same with Robert Plant. Zeppelin with another singer? You don't do that ever. That would crush it."

You might be getting the impression King is a huge music fan and that impression would be correct. This musicologist-level obsession would prove instrumental in make Mercyful Fate so good so fast. In tandem, future Mercyful Fate guitarist Michael Denner would turn out to be just as taken with a vast selection of hard rock from the '70s, to the point where he would jump at the chance to run a record store later in life.

"My first concert ever was Grand Funk Railroad in 1970 with Mott the Hoople as support in Copenhagen," continues King, expounding on the training he got on the ramp-up toward Mercyful. "I'll never forget that show ever. That was the time, '71, I got my first turntable and I had albums. I had the first Black Sabbath on cassette tape, but now it was time to go out and buy the vinyl. I was out every weekend in a new record store in the city buying new ones that would come out. Every Saturday I was in there and the first three vinyl albums I ever bought—and like I said, I knew music before that—but now suddenly I had the turntable. What are you going to buy? There were three albums that had come out. There was *Fireball*, Deep Purple, *Black Sabbath* and *Aqualung*, Jethro Tull. Those three were the first vinyl records I bought, although I already had *Paranoid* (laughs)."

"I remember seeing Purple, I think it was '72, which was Lars Ulrich's first concert ever in Copenhagen. I remember standing in the rain outside waiting for autographs. Geezer Butler, Dick Wagner from Alice Cooper, I got his too, and Peter Gabriel, I think I got from that '74 concert. It meant so much going into the centre of Copenhagen to this big record store that would get all the imports. Every weekend I would be in there spending my allowance. Every weekend, all my money went to buying vinyl and discovering new bands. They knew my style, the people in the shops. 'You gotta check this one out!' I remember my arms would seize up from standing, because you stood like this (mimicking holding turntable tone arm) for so long listening to the albums in the store. I couldn't hold it anymore. I could barely move my arm. I couldn't wait to get home and hear it on my own stereo."

"When I got that first turntable, I didn't have speakers. I was playing that turntable through a reel-to-reel tape recorder that had speakers hidden on each side of it, and it was sitting... I remember my bed. At the end there was a little end table and I would lie with my head close up so I actually got something out of the stereo listening to 'Whole Lotta Love,' the things flying back and forth, and 'What Is and What Should Never Be,' and hearing that stereo. I remember lying there. My dad felt sorry for me and he built me a couple of speakers to hang on the wall and then I really got into the stereo feature of music."

THE EARLY YEARS

No surprise, at the same time, it was all about heaviness. "I remember there were certain albums I wouldn't buy if they had trumpets on them or horns. I simply wouldn't buy them because it was not heavy for me. Or if an album had more than one quiet song, I wouldn't buy it. Today, some of those songs I like, but back then I simply refused to buy if there was that kind of stuff on it. In those days so many bands came from England and they came by Copenhagen, all of them. I was supposed to see Queen in '73 but the show was cancelled because they only sold 100 tickets. The next time they came around they had a hit and they sold out. I saw so many bands, obscure bands, like Geordie, and a lot of them I discovered. Heart, they were supporting Nazareth. I saw these two girls on stage with amazing vocals and thought, 'What is this?!' Roger Fisher, the guitarist, total Jimmy Page freak, was doing his solo with the violin bow. There was Silverhead with Michael Des Barres. I saw them as a support act with somebody—might have been Uriah Heep—or Deep Purple and Tucky Buzzard, a band that did one good album."

"We did Purple songs with Black Rose that no one else did," remembers King. "We played 'Fools,' for instance, and 'Living Wreck.' Everybody plays 'Smoke on the Water' and it's like why?! But our original recordings, you can really hear the influence of Purple and Uriah Heep, with the organ and stuff. The guitarist wanted to look like Blackmore on stage. He had the white guitar and the black outfit, but also he played it... if Blackmore suddenly had not been able to play they could hire him. He could do it. He had that feel and the touch. Unbelievable guitarist who never did anything after we stopped Black Rose. Gillan, big influence learning and trying to sing—like I say, he's a big part of why my voice started developing and how I found out I could sing high."

Black Rose also covered Golden Earring's "Radar Love" and paid tribute to Scorpions. "'Dark Lady,' I think we played," recalls King, proving his metal mettle by picking what is arguably the heaviest Scorpions song ever, tied maybe with "Virgin Killer." "That was the late '70s. And UFO with Michael Schenker of course; I saw them in '74 or '75. They were just about to release *No Heavy Petting*. Those guys are so good live. But I never saw his face. He stood bent over his arrow guitar and I just saw that hair. I never saw his face the whole show, but man what a guitar player."

Which brings up a point. Michael Schenker infuses classical into what he does, to create his richly Teutonic heavy metal. So did Sabbath and Heep and especially Deep Purple, specifically in the ranks, Jon Lord and Ritchie Blackmore. The soaking in of all this would resonate back through Mercyful Fate. Taking that next step, King was not averse to prog rock, which had even more classical up its arsenal.

"There were the heavy classical influences on Jethro Tull," explains King. "They would do a lot of classical music in there, and they certainly had some heavy songs. Of course, 'Aqualung' and the 'Minstrel in the Gallery' song, extremely heavy and extremely complex. It's like listening to Rush and Kansas, extremely complex stuff where you have five guys playing five different melodies but they all tie in together and fit perfect. You had Yes in the early days, very inspired there. Genesis, I saw before when they did *Broadway*. They did the whole album back-to-back, all the songs. Then in the end there was forty minutes extra where they did 'Watcher of the Skies' and all those. An incredible show there."

King took theatrics from Genesis as well. "Yes, they were very visual with Peter Gabriel in the early days. I remember with a lot of my friends, it had to be all heavy. Later on, you got to appreciate ballads here and there but that was the way with a lot of my friends. They didn't want to go see Genesis back then. Are you going to miss out on this?! So, I went alone and it was amazing; I still remember it today. They certainly had some heavier songs, too, 'Musical Box' and quite a few really cool Genesis songs that are heavier."

"But very impressive show," continues Diamond. "Seeing Peter Gabriel hanging up in thin air. That was the first time you saw them onstage; they lit it up and he was in the air on wires, but you couldn't see them. He was walking on thin air down onto the stage with his wings up on his head and he looked amazing, plus he changed costumes all the time. So, the theatrical thing can give people something more they can bring home. When they listen to your stuff at home, they can associate with it all these visual things that they remember from the show."

But despite accepting Genesis into his life, amusingly, there was no patience for the likes of Black Sabbath in a light mood. "No, well, *Never Say Die* has some great songs on it too. But when it came out, it was a little hard for me to accept the ones that had the big orchestral things on them. I never got the sad mood of 'Changes,' for instance, when it came out. *Vol 4*, this slow song—why?! They would do a jam in the studio and put that in because they felt things were getting too heavy and so they had to slow it down. Why? Don't do that. It's not cool. One of the heaviest Uriah Heep albums and suddenly...

what is that song called? That one I still skip today; I'm not too happy about it. On *Look at Yourself*, this piano... it's not even... still today I don't see the great thing about it."

When I remark to King that "Shadows of Grief" on that album is my favourite Heep song of all time, he exclaims, "That's my favourite song of Uriah Heep too! I always set up my stereo... if I get a new stereo, for that album. When he goes, 'North, south, east and west!'—magic. That aggression when that riff comes in, and the vocal middle passage—oh my."

Oh my, indeed.

We don't have to imagine what King Diamond sounded like in the early days because in 2001, King's long-time record label, Metal Blade, put together a CD called *King Diamond and Black Rose – 20 Years Ago: A Night of Rehearsal*. The band playing on that night in Copenhagen, September 30th, 1980, consisted of Jorn Bittcher on guitars, Ib Enemark on keyboards and synthesizer, Jesper Weber on bass, Kurt Jurgens on drums and of course, King on vocals.

Two months later, Diamond would leave Black Rose and join a punk band, one that would introduce him to musicians who would join him in the bold experiment called Mercyful Fate.

"Originally, Michael Denner and myself were playing in a Danish outfit called Brats," begins guitarist Hank Shermann, speaking with Bernard Doe of *Metal Forces* back in 1983. "We recorded a track for a compilation LP entitled *Pære Punk* which was released in 1979. It seems a little strange now that there should have been this punk/heavy metal crossover, yet at that time there was only a fine dividing line between the raw power of punk and the heavy energy of metal. People are quick to forget, but Iron Maiden originally came from the punk circuit. Paul Di'Anno was sporting a skinhead haircut back in those days! Then within a few months the emphasis had changed to heavy metal, with all the leather and studs and Di'Anno grew his hair long. Anyhow, the guys at CBS liked what we were doing and offered us an album deal."

In Brats, Hank Shermann, born René Krolmark on July 11th, 1958, was known as Hank de Wank, in accordance with punk parlance! With regard to adopting the moniker Hank Shermann, he says, "It's an artist name, something that came up when we started the band in '78. We thought that we should have some cool names like everyone else in the music business and the theatre business. Everybody had an artist name, so we just found some names that sounded cool. Michael Denner, that's his real name. Timi Hansen was also his real name, but Kim Ruzz was not—his real name was Kim something else, and King Diamond is Kim Petersen. It's just silly to give out my real name, I think, because then there is no use in having an artist name. Hank Shermann... it just sounded cool. That was more an '80s or '70s thing."

"So yes, I started to play guitar in 1977 and I formed this punk band called Brats. We did one single; we did an LP and then King Diamond joined and was part of Brats and sang those songs. Then when we were about to do the second record with Brats, on CBS. They fired us, and that was when the first band was split up. There was only King and I who stayed together and then we started to compose some songs. We played about four to seven concerts with King Diamond as the singer; that was basically in Denmark, in 1980, 1981."

Adds Michael Denner (born November 5th, 1958), also to become a Mercyful Fate guitarist, "Along with Hank and I—we played lead guitar and did some vocals—were a couple of other guys: Yenz (Leonhardt) was the bass guitarist and lead vocalist, and the other guy Monroe (first name, Lars) played drums and piano. We spent the early part of 1980 in the studio in Copenhagen and laid down 12 songs which were later put out by CBS on the continent, on an album titled *1980*. Basically, it was a heavy metal album tinged—or tainted some might say—with a punk feel. Eight numbers were metal songs, three were punk and the other was a Russian folk song, sung in Russian by myself. That album was very useful to us in a number of respects. It gave us some very important studio experience, a good deal of exposure on TV and radio throughout Europe and through a quirk of fate brought us together with our current English manager and publicist, John Kibble."

"Without talking specific figures," continued Denner, "we were selling thousands, especially in France. So much so that we were in the process of setting up a French tour, when out of the blue CBS dropped us. At the time it seemed catastrophic, yet with hindsight Mercyful Fate would probably never have come together, but for that decision. The CBS thing caused Brats to go their separate ways; I started a new band called Danger Zone with Timi Grabber, while Hank joined forces with an already notorious singer named King Diamond, who had been working with a band called Black Rose. Danger Zone wrote five numbers for a demo, and we decided to ask Hank and King to come along and work with us on the recording. The demo complete, we realised that the four of us clicked; we set about writing new material and looking for a new name. Our ex-manager's girlfriend came up with the name Mercyful Fate and it stuck."

The *1980* album is a professional affair, befitting of its major label status. If it's to be faulted, it is indeed a little all over the place, convincing metal mostly, marbled with not so convincing punk, with varied production values to boot. In the main however, it's chock full of riffs and solos and topped with a vocalist charmingly youthful, like a punky NWOBHM punter.

On the occasion of the release of the Black Rose rehearsal tapes, Tony Oliver from *Demonzine* spoke to King about the CD and this transition period from Black Rose to Brats to King Diamond.

"Actually, the idea to release the material came last year. A good friend of mine was visiting me and he brought up some of his friends who were King Diamond fans. We were just sitting there listening to music when I remembered an old tape I had in my car and I said, 'Hey, I got something you've never heard.' They really freaked out, man; they wanted a copy. But I was like, 'No, no, no, can't do that.' Then they were like, 'You gotta release that. You can't just sit on it; it's part of your career.' They are actually right about that."

"It's the first band I sang in, and you can really hear that it's me. You can also tell it's before my falsetto was fully developed. One specific song that's on there called 'Road Life' is the song that after seeing us live, a guy came up to me and was like, 'You should do that falsetto you used in that song more.' That's what made me concentrate on developing that falsetto in a way where I could control it better, and develop my voice, actually. I was more conscious about what I was doing because at that point I didn't think a whole lot about what I was actually doing with my voice while I was singing."

Further on putting the tapes out for public consumption, King remarked that, "It became like, well yeah, maybe they're right. You start thinking like it was yourself. If I had a chance to get an old 'Black Sabbath before they were called Black Sabbath' rehearsal where they are talking and making mistakes and stuff, I'd love to hear it. Suddenly you can picture that, yeah, well, a lot of our fans would probably like to hear that. It's a different sounding band, of course, than King Diamond; it's built around one guitar and the organs, so it gets more of a Deep Purple feel than Mercyful Fate would. If those same songs were played with two guitarists, it would probably be leaning more towards Mercyful Fate: not being as heavy, but still quite complex. What really amazes me today when I listen to it is that those musicians were that skilful at that time. We were all good musicians. Then the fact that it was 11 original songs that was recorded that night... we recorded our own songs on purpose and not all the covers that we normally did, so we would be able to go home and listen to it, maybe even improve on it."

"So, it was quite an interesting evening. We'd probably already warmed up by playing several Deep Purple covers before actually turning on the tape recorder to record. It was never meant for release, but it was specifically those people's idea that made me think about it. Then I asked the record label what they thought of it, and they were like, 'Wow,' and I was there. It doesn't mean the band will reunite or go in to record or anything. It's just what it is, a good piece of my career's history."

"It was really a band effort," continues King, asked about Black Rose's songwriting. "Everything about that was very much a band effort. Today I couldn't write with someone else. I really couldn't, because I go into such detail that it could be two notes that I wouldn't know how to get them right, and I have to stay calm to get the right beat out of it. That's just how I work."

As for the dissolution of Black Rose... "It was actually a very ridiculous reason: the keyboardist showed up to rehearsal one day and told us he'd sold his keyboard. We asked him why he did that and he explained that him and his girlfriend just got a new apartment and needed the money to afford it. So that was the end of that. At that time Hank was playing in Brats. They released an album, and Mike Denner also played on the album. Hank and their manager called me up because they knew of Black Rose and saw us live as well, and they were looking for a vocalist, so they approached me. We agreed on dropping the punk songs and playing only the heavier songs they had, then start writing extremely heavy metal songs. We all agreed on that and I was in."

"Then we started writing some of the songs, recorded some rehearsals, and presented the material to the Brats' record company, saying this is material for the next album and they freaked out. Man, they hated it. They said, 'You can't do that; it's too heavy and needs to be more melodic.' That's where Hank and I said, 'Okay, bye—we aren't going to change it.' But the three other guys in the band, at the time, they were all worried about not having a record, so they tried to accommodate the label's needs. But nothing ever came from it. We went through a couple different musicians before Mike Denner called. He called Hank up 'cause he was about to go into the studio and record a five-song demo with his three-piece band, and he needed Hank to come help him out with guitars—and he told him to bring that vocalist with him. So, we did that and it worked so well that we decided to become a band—that's when we became Mercyful Fate."

Notes Hank on the origins of the name, "Actually, at the time it was the tour manager, the guy who helped us. His girlfriend came up with the name. I came up with some names and some other guys came up with some names but then that girlfriend came up with Mercyful Fate, and we thought, wow, that's a cool name. It sounded cool to me; that was in 1981."

Notching their first gig in Taastrup, Denmark, September 6th of 1981, Mercyful Fate then got down to the business of putting out some product. The band in fact debuted on a NWOBHM compilation, *Metallic Storm* issued by Ebony Records, ran by producer and businessman of dubious ethics Daryl Johnston.

As Hank Shermann told Bernard Doe, "Basically, up to that point we had been fairly frustrated. Although we had done support spots to Gillan and Girlschool back home, we were having some difficulty interesting the major record labels. It was by this time early 1982, and Mercyful Fate had already recorded two four-track demos. John Kibble had been knocking on all the major label doors, but nobody was willing to take that big chance, although a lot of the A&R people liked what we were doing. Then, Daryl Johnston asked us to record a couple of numbers for the compilation. We did 'Black Funeral' and 'Walking Back to Hell,' the first of which appeared on the LP, while the latter, though scheduled to appear on the follow-up Ebony release, was at our request omitted due to a lineup change."

These original couple of tracks featured Benny Petersen on guitar, now replaced by Michael Denner. "Black Funeral" would get the coveted track number one position on *Metallic Storm*, although the accolade is minimal, given that none of the other 11 bands on the record were ever heard from again. The song is up to snuff compared to the music on the ensuing EP, but once it would get redone for the debut album, there'd be a tightness and urgency added commensurate with how ruthlessly professional the band had become by the summer of 1983.

Mercyful Fate's first record (bearing only their own name) would come out on a new joint called Rave-On Records. Recalls "Metal" Mike van Rijswyck, from *Aardschok* magazine and Roadrunner Records (he joined in '86), and signer of the band quickly after the indie days, "The story starts long before, when we got the Brats demos on cassette sent by a guy who owned a record store in Copenhagen, Ken Anthony, and then demos when they started a band together with King Diamond. One of the writers of my magazine, Stefan Rooyackers, he started a record label with Jac Hustinx. The first record that came out was a compilation record with Dutch bands and one Belgium band, put together by *Aardschok* magazine. It was called *Metal Clogs* and the second one was an EP with four songs recorded in Roosendaal in The Netherlands by a band called Mercyful Fate."

"So that's how we got in touch with the band. During the recording, they had a show on a Tuesday afternoon in September 1982 at the Dynamo, which is still on film—we still have the video. Then in '83, I had them playing on the Aardschok Festival where Venom didn't play, but they were booked as headliner. But then I booked Venom a year later, on a tour with Metallica, with Metallica opening up. But that year I had Accept as a replacement because Venom's gear was still in Canada at the border and we had Vandenberg and Raven as well, and Trance from Germany. So Mercyful Fate played their first big festival in June of '83."

"After the Ebony release we began to receive some good publicity in Holland through *Aardschok* magazine and Radio Hilversum," King told Bernard Doe. "Rave-On, being located in the same town (Eindhoven) as *Aardschok* meant they soon caught wind of us and offered us the deal. We recorded during September '82 and also played our first Dutch gigs. The reception of both was so strong there, that we were able to return again in March and June of '83 for more concerts. There's really no doubt that the Dutch headbangers are among the finest and most knowledgeable in Europe, if not the world. Just after the release of the EP, *Aardschok* held their annual readers' poll and Fate were voted 'Best New Group' and to my great pleasure I was voted 'Best New Singer!'"

The *Mercyful Fate* EP, otherwise known as *Nuns Have No Fun*, was recorded at Stone Studio in September with Jac Hustinx producing and mixing, and with Willem Steetjes serving as engineer. It was issued by Rave-On on November 8th, 1982, with catalogue number RMLP-002. It consisted of four substantially professional tracks, namely "A Corpse Without Soul," "Nuns Have No Fun," "Doomed by the Living Dead" and "Devil Eyes." It was issued as a 45 RPM 12-inch with roughly 11 minutes of music a side, giving it rich bass and an overall earthy yet vibrant sound. Every song bar one is credited to

THE EARLY YEARS

Hank Shermann and King Diamond, with Michael Denner getting a lone co-credit on "Nuns Have No Fun." The band was rounded out by Timi Grabber on bass and Kim Ruzz on drums. There would be three pressings, fist with white border, second with black border, third also with black border but a note designating distribution by Bertus Holland.

Opening track "A Corpse Without Soul" is a speedy rocker with a note-dense riff. King is relentless with the falsetto, although he gears down just as the music does, to a grinding half-time break that exposes the band's creativity, its easy profusion with—and of—ideas. The band is tight but there's also enough raucous rock 'n' roll to what they are doing, with much credit going to drummer Kim Ruzz. All told, there's a steepness of band chemistry that evokes thoughts of *The Number of the Beast*, a chemistry that wells up from Clive Burr on that record and Kim Ruzz on this one.

Closing side one of the original vinyl is "Nuns Have No Fun," which starts groovy but then collapses into a half-time grind like Sabbath but with obscure melody that again evokes Maiden. Once more it's the rhythm section of Ruzz and Grabber that propels this one forward, pints clinking at the pub.

"It was done to provoke the priests," said King, speaking with John Ricard. "They always see themselves as being people who are better than others, as if they are so pure. But that's impossible. Nobody can live without sin. When you start reading to find out what they have done, you see how they have started wars, extorted money, tortured young girls. The priests who couldn't get girls would say, 'Hah! She's possessed.'"

As for the upside-down crosses on the front cover of the EP... "It was simply what I believe in. An upside-down cross means adversary turned upside-down. That's what Satanism is all about. Since Christianity is so dominating in the world, it is the one that you measure other religions up against."

"Doomed by the Living Dead" is a sophisticated, speedy rocker with King using his natural singing voice punctuated by falsetto stabs. Yet again, the band make groovy use of cutting their timing in half, here for an extended break that includes the bed for the guitar solo.

Closing the EP is "Devil Eyes," where Ruzz plays hi-hat with both hands, again something Clive Burr often did. But he's opening and closing it artfully, while doing four-on-the-floor with the bass drum. The bass riff from Grabber is artful as well, and there's even some twin guitar soloing. This one moves at a constant hypnotic speed, exhibiting a discipline of songwriting away from the prog tendencies of the band. At the melodic end, it's almost post-punk, evoking one of those dance type songs dominated by bass guitar and drums.

"When we rehearsed it, everyone went wow, this is great," recalls Hank. "It felt really good to play and we were sure this was even going to get played in discotheques because it had this nice groove to it. So, everyone was like wow, this is really going to be a hit in the rock discotheques and clubs."

Reminisced King, in conversation with Tim Henderson a dozen years later, "The *Mercyful Fate* mini-album was done on a really small budget and recorded/mixed in two days in a studio in Holland. A lot of the stuff you hear is first takes and you'll hear the development from that one to the *Melissa* album where we were given more time and a better budget after we'd been picked up by Roadrunner. We still did the *Melissa* album in 12, 14 days. On *Melissa*, we were able to use the ideas we had, whereas on the EP, time was really a constraint and we were forced to hold back. On *Melissa*, you'll find songs that we still play today. There are some songs we can't get away from and these will be in our set indefinitely. I still find great pleasure in playing this older material. That album opened up a lot of doors for us and many people were becoming aware of us. When I put those albums on today, it puts me in a weird mood. I recapture that same mood from the exact time we did that album. That goes with all the albums, including King Diamond as well. You suddenly get a lot of those feelings and emotions back that you were going through. It's a little treasure chest that you can open up at any time."

"Like I say, those four songs on that mini-LP were recorded and mixed in two days. Clearly, there was no time for anything. I had backing vocals prepared for those four songs, like you hear my vocals on *Melissa*. I remember clearly the solo on 'A Corpse Without Soul;' Hank was forced to do it on the first take. The producer said, 'We don't have the time. Whatever you do now, just do the solo and that's what goes on the album.' Shit, talk about pressure."

Miles less sophisticated than the pricey-sounding music enclosed, the front cover art of the EP, drawn by Ole Poulsen, features a crude black and white illustration of a naked woman being crucified while evil-looking hooded figures congregate. The band's logo is registered with a gothic font similar to Fate heroes Judas Priest back on *Sad Wings of Destiny* and *Sin After Sin*.

As well, there are two stylised upside-down crosses on the cover which bear a similarity to the Judas Priest cross iconography adopted years later. A lyric sheet, typed simply in courier font, was provided for added shock value. On the back cover, King is resplendent in his simple "raccoon" "corpsepaint" flanked to the left and right with the band's two guitarists, each of which wields a Flying V.

"Of course, to buy a Gibson Flying V was very expensive in those days," chuckles Michael. "So, we had cheap copies, and we painted them, and even tried to put a fake sign that said Gibson (laughs). They cost ten times as much as the copies we played on. We tried to adjust to make better microphones in them to get a beefier sound, but it was just copies. I do believe I had five or six copies of the Gibson Flying V before I could afford the real deal."

"Now I have a whole army of them," laughs Denner. "I still play them. It's like an extension of my arm. It's a light guitar to play live on stage. Especially when you get older, with small back problems and stuff. The V is very light and easy to work with on stage. I also play the Gibson Les Paul if I need a more beefy, earthy sound. But live, they're very heavy to play, especially the Custom. I have a collection of guitars, but nine out of ten times, I do the leads with the Flying V; that is true."

Thinking back to the days of the EP, Denner rolls his eyes at the memory. "We got a lot of bad press in Denmark. Because they translated it into Danish, what we sang about and all that shit. Also, the cover with the woman... in those days heavy metal was very unpopular here. Danish radio only played folk music with political stuff and only sung in Danish. It was like a mafia in Denmark at that point, with music, on the Danish radio. So, in the beginning, to get a decent radio program, you had to go to Swedish radio. You had to go to Sweden to buy some of the records. If there was a new Judas Priest album, I had to go to Malmö to get it, two weeks before it was in Denmark."

"So, it was very tough when we started out. Even with The Brats before that, everything we did got so much bad press. Once we got the success and recognition from all over the world, then the journalists said, 'Oh, I always liked Mercyful Fate. I always supported them. I always thought they were great.' That made me sick to my stomach. The same people who slagged us and gave us bad reviews, they turned because then it was popular to like Mercyful Fate, in the '90s anyway."

"They were just young kids," muses Metal Mike, who already at that early date and in that isolated environment, had a sophisticated ear for heavy metal. "But really serious how they were recording this stuff. They were well prepared because the songs I think, had already been demoed for a year or so. Live, they already had the *Melissa* skull and they had the candles on stage and stuff. The makeup was a little bit different, a bit less professional. The first show outside of Copenhagen I think they ever did as Mercyful Fate was September of '82, so they were just kids. Andre (Verhuysen) had them play the Dynamo club a lot of times. I booked them at some other little clubs in the area. I remember most of the shows were on little tours that ended on a Sunday and then straight after the show, they would drive in to Copenhagen for whatever, 12 hours or something, to just start whatever work they had the next day."

Already, this early in the band's touring and recording life, spooky things were beginning to happen. "Yes, I mean, you'll hear all the stories," laughs van Rijswyck. "You think it's bullshit or, to gather interest in the band. But as I did shows with the band, there was always some weird stuff happening. Then eventually we said, 'Well, Mercyful Fate is around.' I know when they had that festival... around the festival we did some club shows and I know driving back from a show, going back to the Eindhoven, I think from Hengelo in the Northeast of our country (early April, 1983), three in the morning on an empty road there was a woman in a white gown standing in the middle of the road. It was a two-lane highway, one lane each direction, she's in the middle of the road and she was stepping in front of the car as we were approaching and I just could swerve around her not hitting her. So, we had that coming back from a Mercyful Fate show. I had a bird diving on my car at night. We stopped once and there was a huge puddle of blood in the middle of the road. We always had that kind of stuff when we had shows with Mercyful Fate around. So, by a certain point we would just say, 'Well, Mercyful Fate is in town again.'"

Then there was the time in Copenhagen when Kim McAuliffe from Girlschool got electrocuted. As King told Malcolm Dome, "We'd done our set, with me using the same microphone that was later to give Kim such a shock. At one point, I'd said something like, 'We're gonna bring Satan into the house tonight.' Anyway, we did our stint and went back to the dressing room. But when Girlschool started to play, I could distinctly hear some strange noises coming from the PA. I've still got a tape of it at home—it was very strange. One of our roadies came in to tell us about the noises, and for some reason I still don't understand, I turned to him and said, 'I know, and the band will have to stop playing in a few minutes—and they won't play another note tonight!' Just why that came into my head, I can't explain. A few minutes later, Kim was electrocuted."

"What was even crazier was that the police called in some expert electricians to go over all the gear, and they could find nothing wrong. The promoter of the gig actually went on the radio and said that he'd felt a very strange atmosphere surrounding the hall on the night in question, the likes of which he'd never before come across. He told the DJ it was almost as if something had to happen, because it had been decreed by forces beyond human comprehension!"

A DANGEROUS MEETING: IN THE SHADOWS WITH MERCYFUL FATE

2.

MELISSA
"PLEASE USE YOUR FAME FOR THE GOOD OF THE YOUTH."

Much more than a classic, *Melissa* is a record that could make you a Christian believer. For within its incendiary grooves, one found an advancement of brainy metal might that was illogical to the point of diabolical, conjuring visions of the King and his charges making a pact like Paganini's, Robert Johnson's and Jimmy Page's. *Melissa* is a record of unholy precision, and (as was alluded to in our introduction) this was from a band of rookies—from Denmark, no less.

Metal milestones from the past such as Deep Purple's *In Rock* and Judas Priest's *Sad Wings of Destiny* had now been joined by new tremors—and I very deliberately left out anything from the New Wave of British Heavy Metal. This music we love had been reborn with Satanic skill, Mercyful Fate forming a triumvirate (in this writer's positioning of all this) with Metallica's *Kill 'Em All* and Savatage's *Sirens* as records creating a new renaissance for the art form.

Even if the last rush of records, those from the NWOBHM, included treasures like *Iron Maiden*, *Killers*, *Angel Witch* and *Stand Up and Fight*, there's really nothing there that felt like these three from '83, from Florida, from San Francisco, from Denmark.

"The main thing was Judas Priest," says Michael Denner emphatically. "Judas Priest were like our gods at that point. But it was with Les Binks—*Killing Machine*, *Stained Class*, these records—plus *Sin After Sin* which was Simon Phillips, who did a fantastic job of the drums on that. But of course, we liked bands like Accept and Overdrive from Sweden. We knew these guys, some of these Swedish bands and so on. We grew some kind of relationship."

"After that it was bands like Evil from Denmark, with *Evil's Message*. We were close to these guys; they lived just in the next neighbourhood. Also, bands like Pretty Maids, even though they were from Jutland, from the other side, the west side of Denmark. We connected with these guys because there were so few people who were into this kind of music. Yeah, there was close friendship, and even to this day Artillery are friends of ours. We stay in touch with the guys from the old days."

Credit to Rave-On, that would be the label of choice for the five-track *Evil's Message* EP in 1984, catalogue number RMLP-010. And credit to Michael for calling attention to it. The professionalism of that release is nearly as uncommonly impressive as that of Mercyful Fate circa *Melissa*, even if the songs are a little more heads-down speed metal. Also, RRMLP-003 (the first release being *Metal Clogs*, followed by Mercyful) would be represented by the fine French band Sortilège, and their self-titled debut EP.

"But yes, Judas Priest for us were like our gods," continues Denner. "They were so far ahead of anything else at that point. The closest you would get was maybe the Scorpions with Uli Roth at that point; they also did some excellent records. But Priest, from *Sad Wings of Destiny* upwards, up until *British Steel*, they made some brilliant albums. They were far ahead of the rest of us."

Mercyful Fate's debut album would see these great Danes—okay, allow that once, please—signing on with feisty heavy metal mid-level label Roadrunner Records. Says Metal Mike, "Around that time they had a whole record done and Jac Hustinx... well, I asked Roadrunner to sign them. I made sure bands got signed to

Roadrunner, because there were a lot of good bands, and so many were just available as imports. So, I arranged for some bands to get a deal with Roadrunner. Then a few later years later, in '85, '86, somebody told me, 'Well it's called A&R manager, you could make a job out of it.'"

"The ground floor of the second location of Roadrunner in Amsterdam was their office and the second floor was *Aardschok* magazine. So, we shared the building where I did the Roadrunner work and also did the magazine, because I always had been doing the magazine since 1980. But I booked shows on the side, including a lot for Mercyful Fate in Belgium, the Netherlands and Germany mainly. Then I said to Cees Wessels, who was the owner of the label to get in touch with Jac Hustinx to sign Mercyful Fate. I didn't know how the rights were and how that stuff works. I just wanted to see them out on a good label."

As King told Bernard Doe in '83, "Quickly one thing led to another; we came over to England during March '83 to record our session for the BBC *Friday Rock Show* and had a really memorable day with Tony Wilson (producer) putting 'Satan's Fall,' 'Evil' and 'Curse of the Pharaohs' down on tape. The BBC session was a big success for us and ultimately led us into our current deal with Roadrunner Records."

Explaining the recording of the album as well as the new label deal to Malcolm Dome at the time, King said that "There are two really good studios in Copenhagen, this one and Sweet Silence, where Rainbow did *Bent Out of Shape*. Personally, I think Easy Sound is the better of the two. We are all delighted with the way *Melissa* turned out. Part of the reason for our satisfaction is the production work of Henrik Lund. As far as heavy metal goes, he's a complete unknown. Henrik has never done a heavy album before, but he's into early Zeppelin and Sabbath so was in tune with what we were after. He came up with lots of ideas, some great in practice and others which didn't come off. But at least he gave us an extra dimension. Our mini-album last year was very poorly recorded. The difference in quality is astounding."

"Originally, Gregg Parker was going to do the album, at Trident Studios in London," continues Diamond. "He suggested doing it for practically nothing because he was into our music and promised to get the studio for a knock-down price. But when it came to the crunch, he wanted an astronomical fee, way beyond our means, so we had to say no. I think Gregg talks in a very big way but hasn't what it takes to deliver. It was a pity that the partnership came to nothing, but we are very happy with Henrik and hope to work with him again."

Dome helpfully explained that *Melissa* was just hitting the shops on Music for Nations in the UK, whereas it had been licensed by Jonny Zazula's fledgling metal outfit, Megaforce Records in the US, out of New Jersey. These were both licensing deals with Roadrunner. Jon and his wife Marsha would of course be the first to sign Metallica and Anthrax, using their good taste to do further various licensing deals as well.

"We were going to do the LP at first with Rave-On," continues King. "The problem was that they said there was no money to fly us from Denmark to Holland for the recording sessions. The only way the finance could be raised was through reducing our studio time from about ten days to a mere five! We weren't interested and felt that if this was the way the company acted at such an early stage, how much backing would they give us for promotional purposes? So, we elected to throw them over."

"In fact, it caused quite some hassle. You see, when the idea for us to do a full album for Rave-On came up, the company also arranged a series of gigs in Holland to tie in. So, when we blew them out, the label had to cancel all planned shows, and tried to save face by claiming the cancellations were due to me breaking a leg. Unfortunately for them, Metal Mike took over the promotion for the dates and we eventually *did* play them. Everyone therefore saw that I had not, in fact, broken my leg at all. Rave-On were made to feel stupid."

"We made no money from *Corpse Without Soul* (King repeatedly called the EP this at the time, which caught on with the press). True, it did sell out completely. But only 5000 were ever pressed up and studio costs took up most of the royalty payments. Doubtless, if *Melissa* sells well, then Rave-On will reissue it to cash in. As for Roadrunner, they came to us. Originally, the plan was for us to sign for a period of five years. That's a long time to be committed to one label. So, we compromised by offering them five LPs in a three-year slot. I mean, we'll be kept very busy indeed, but that's the way we want it. We've already got two complete songs ready for the next LP ('Come to the Sabbath' and 'The Oath') plus three other half-finished numbers. I'm thinking ahead to our third album right now. I want this to contain a one-sided concept, a heavy opera, if you want to put a term to it. It would be a real challenge to conceive a proper cohesive musical piece like an opera, lots of different voices, all interpreted by me."

King would eventually get more involved on the writing of the Mercyful Fate (and King Diamond) records, but at this early juncture, it was Hank Shermann who was the primary music composer.

"Singers always tend to compose for the songs," explains Shermann, "for the melody lines, whereas I'm a composer as a guitar player, i.e. I don't think too much about that. I'm a little rawer, certainly, in my composing, whereas singers normally tend to be a little too soft, a little too much after the vocals. In a good way, all these melodic sing-along structures with Iron Maiden and stuff, that's perfect, but for my writing it's too boring. I want to have a little more edge on it. But that always worked with Mercyful Fate and King, because he would just sing on top of it. But it's clear... you can hear when a singer has composed the songs; it's very clear, and sometimes a little boring."

Of course, as discussed, King isn't your average singer. The man's patented falsetto either has you scrambling for the exits or captivated at the unearthly sound. Then there's his sorrowful regular singing voice, and his poisonous, vengeful growl. It's like an army of demonic phonics emerging from his slashed throat. Top that off with the legendary corpsepaint and outspoken Satanic beliefs to go with the frightening look, and Mercyful Fate was fast becoming much more than just the most progressive and professional new metal band in years.

"At first it was just a mistake," muses King, asked about that alien and polarising falsetto of his. "Or at least that I was unaware I was singing these high notes. Then, as I said, that fan came up to me and said, 'You should use your falsetto more than you do. And I didn't even know what the word meant, and he explained it to me. So, I started to work on the upper register a lot more. It really took off with *Melissa*, because on the first mini-LP, we had two days to record and mix. We had just as many backing vocals and harmony guitars planned as you hear on the *Melissa* album. But we were told, 'No, no, there's no time. Do it now. You can have one backing vocal.' On some of it, it was hard. It was like, 'Aw man, all this stuff we planned out for nothing.' Then we finally signed with Roadrunner and got twelve days in the studio to do the *Melissa* album, and we could suddenly start experimenting with these harmonies and stuff. And then it starts developing."

The band, recording at Easy Sound Studios in Copenhagen, commencing July 18th, 1983 and concluding on the 29th, got for themselves a superlative result, even if the guys oddly don't think fondly of the record's production. Dialling in sounds was producer Henrik Lund, who with his brother co-owned the studio.

One interesting wrinkle, Roadrunner was pushing for the band to cover Led Zeppelin's "Immigrant Song" on the record, no doubt seeing in King the perfect character to re-visit Robert Plant's signature high parts on the song. Indeed, the band worked it up but found the idea of the song too foreign to the oppressive Satanic vibe of their original material. They never actually got to the stage of putting a vocal on it however, as the band also had trouble with its challenging rhythm.

But first there's the album cover and immediately one is greeted with class. In an age when ridiculous illustrations on metal jackets were mounting, Mercyful kept it simple with a Thomas Holm painting of a devil in muted blacks and reds. On the back, the band is the band while King is pictured away from any rock 'n' roll stage, performing a ritual, framed in an upside-down cross very much like the one in the gatefold to *Black Sabbath*. A professional inner sleeve has lyrics on one side and on the other, a band shot rendered consistent and classy, with King appearing sans makeup.

The epic cover art almost didn't happen. The first proposal was an amateurish painting depicting the band staring at a big skull in the sky, with only King looking back at the camera as if to say, "What the hell is this all about?"

As King told David Perri, "The *Melissa* cover actually wasn't the cover that we meant to have at all. It was picked out of a lineup. We were shown 25 covers and then we picked what ended up being the *Melissa* cover. Someone had tried to do a cover for us. I remember one night we had this meeting and we looked at the cover. You might have actually seen this cover; it came out on some bootleg. The cover is of a skull swaying up in the air and the band is standing underneath it. It looked like a child had drawn it with crayons (laughs)—it looked horrible. It was the biggest disappointment up to that point. I remember we all just looked at that cover and we didn't know what to do because it was horrifying (laughs). So, then someone put us in touch with a Swedish artist who came down to Copenhagen and had this stack of art that he had done, and that's when we picked the *Melissa* cover."

So yes, unlike Led Zeppelin *III*, *Melissa* opens not with "Immigrant Song" but with "Evil," possibly the band's most recognisable track of all time. It's no surprise the song has become an anthem. Its groove is legion, and King's opening "I was born in the cemetery" salvo is instantly impressionable. Plus, it was short and logical. This was high-minded metal that was also effortlessly headbang-able, not always the case with the band's often circuitous constructions.

Muses King, "You might have heard some of the early Mercy demos where bits and pieces from three different songs turn into a song later on. On *Melissa*, there's so many songs that suddenly turn into things, where we chop and take this from that. Suddenly we had more time to live out the harmony guitar pieces and the vocal parts in the harmonies. We were rehearsing four times a week back then. We wrote the tracks in the rehearsal room and some of them we didn't even have a version on tape to go by and remember them."

"Everybody was very much involved in the production side of things too, reasonably early on. With *Melissa*, during the mix, the guy knew what he was doing but he was not sure of our taste, and it was almost like being at the dentist in a waiting room. We were not allowed in, which was bothering, and then suddenly we were just called in, all of us. 'Okay, listen to this version of "Evil"' or something like that. We're sitting there like, 'Where's the guitar? There's no rhythm guitar.' 'No, you gotta be louder than that. I did backing vocals at this part; where are they? I can't hear any of them. No, we don't treat backing vocals as backing here. They have as featured a role as the lead because they are mood-creators.' We'd go back outside and wait and then we'd come back in again. We wasted so much time."

Recalls Hank, "I really don't have any bad memories from the *Melissa* recording, except for one experience that I have in a diary somewhere here. I don't know what specific day it was, but there was a thief inside the studio, stealing King's jacket."

"Hank wrote that song," notes Michael Denner, on "Evil." "At that point we were rehearsing six days a week and it was only for a funeral or a birthday that you could get off rehearsing. We were so serious. I mean, somebody could wake me up at night and say, 'You play "Satan's Fall" without any mistakes' and I could do it. It was so tight at that point. It was very much like a family thing. We spent all our time in the rehearsing room. Hank came out with these riffs and I remember it so clearly. He would say, 'Okay, now I have something for you guys,' and he came with some of the riffs for 'Evil.' I said wow! I knew this would be a strong song. It came so easily, all those solo parts, like, 'This is mine, this is yours, this is mine,' and it was such a pleasure starting that song off."

Adds Shermann, "'Evil' of course is pretty hard-hitting, a pretty simple song. But especially with those lyrics, it's a classic. 'I was born in the cemetery'—that's a classic starting line."

"'Evil' is definitely trademark Mercyful Fate," reflects King. "It was the first song you ever heard if you bought something from us, the regular stuff anyway, the first album, *Melissa*. The first song on the album, right in your face. It's a great sing-along song, and that has always meant a lot to both us as a band and the fans. You can see it in the response when you're playing it."

Like the listener, both Hank and King seem to have fallen prey to the trickster. In fact, the song's best part, that opening "verse," never returns, with the song stacking speedy and even thrashy part upon part, with Ruzz utilising double bass drums. A nice touch is the opening twin lead, which echoes the dramatic start of "Victim of Changes" on *Sad Wings of Destiny*. But yes, then "Evil" becomes that which it is not remembered for, as King's cemetery-born character descends into necrophilia and finally cannibalism—*Piece of Mind* indeed.

You just gave the answer to your own question," laughs Denner, confronted with this idea that no metal record quite impressed like *Melissa* did, pretty much since classic Priest, say *Sad Wings* and *Sin After Sin*. "Those two records, for Hank and I, they were like the *Bible* (laughs). Of course, also, I have a very big record collection and I'll always have; I started collecting in '69. So I knew King Crimson and Emerson, Lake & Palmer, all the technical, difficult bands. *Force It* by UFO was the album that inspired me the most as a lead guitarist. The early Rush records were inspiring. The same with King. It was so funny, when I met King the first time, we would be like, 'Oh, do you have this one? Oh, do you have that one? This one, that one...' It was so funny. King came to me and said, 'Do you know Budgie?' 'Oh, give me a break—of course!' We could just go on forever. Of course, we've always been inspired by these unknown small bands who wrote differently and could play so well."

Underscoring why the band sounded so confident and accomplished, Michael says, "We rehearsed six days a week, every week, so we were very sharp and very determined with what we wanted to do. It was a very, very close friendship in the band at that point. We stayed in each other's apartments and we lived together. I had a day job and so did Timmy, and we had girlfriends. Still to this day, I cannot understand how we could find time to live a normal life, because Mercyful Fate was everything. You couldn't miss rehearsing unless you had to attend a funeral or a wedding. You had to be there. If you had a cold, you were going to the rehearsal room. That was a not enough to say no to rehearsing (laughs). So, we were very sharp at that point, and we were very eager to go to prove that we were the heaviest band in the world. Somehow we achieved that: to be one of the heaviest bands ever at that point."

Next, "Curse of the Pharaohs" is another Mercyful classic, Fate's guitar team coming up with a sinister doom-laden plod to lay waste to the multi-disciplinary tale from King. After its militaristic verse riff is put through its paces, the song grinds into a hooky, double speed, almost rock 'n' roll chorus that again, galvanises this idea that Mercyful Fate's songwriting prowess is simply not of this realm. Twin leads and beautifully composed single leads also elevate the song toward a regal authority. The construct is much more conventional than "Evil," with the verse/pre-chorus/chorus pattern showing itself three times.

"'Curse of the Pharaohs' was already made," notes Shermann, "but it was with another vocal line done by another singer. So that was later adopted into being 'Curse of the Pharaohs.'" Adds Michael, "It's actually the oldest Mercyful Fate tune ever. It's from the Brats days. We even played that song before King was ever considered to be a member of the band. It was with a guy called Jens on vocals, and it was called 'Night Spiders' in the beginning and then it became 'Night Riders' and then it became 'Curse of the Pharaohs.'"

For his part, King remembers it this way. "I had joined the band, Brats—that was an early version of Mercyful Fate. It wasn't really Mercyful Fate, but I joined the band that Hank was writing a lot for at that time. But he was not there when I joined. They had a deal with CBS and had released one album, that silver album, where half the songs were heavy rock and the other half was punk. When I joined, I was like, 'You've got to only be heavy; otherwise, I can't really relate to it myself. It's got to be just the heavy stuff.' They all agreed on it and those songs were written at that time. They were there, where the bass player who used to be the lead vocalist, now just played bass. He was the one who was writing lyrics for them. So, I was singing completely different lyrics. From my memory, I think that 'Curse of the Pharaohs' used to be called 'Night Riders,' way back then. It was not 'Night Riders' in an occult sense, because none of those songs were really occult."

At the lyric end, King delivers in a cool and headbanging plain-speak manner the story of how archaeologists in Egypt are said to have fallen under various curses by desecrating the tombs they found. It is of note that despite King intimating that he wasn't confident with his English this early on, even the most astute headbanger saw nothing wrong. Even as the band's elders like Scorpions and Accept stumbled through laughable wordings, Mercyful demonstrated an eerie acumen for perfect English, as if King was possessed by a foreign entity!

As King relates, not knowing English well yet proved more of a problem in interviews. "Yes, we did an early tour of Mercy in '84 in the US, and I was starting to do interviews. It was difficult because I had to sit and actually try and translate the question into Danish and then think of an answer and then translate that to English. It was not second nature for me. I was still dreaming in Danish. I don't do that anymore. So, it was a lot more difficult doing interviews, but it was still very important when people came and said, 'Why do you write something like that? Do you really stand behind that stuff?' Absolutely we stand behind it. You gotta realise what it's about. It talks about not what I *want* to do but it talks about that there are people like that. There is evil in this world, whether you like it or not."

Next up is "Into the Coven," introduced with elegiac minstrel music that would make Blackmore's Night proud. Or a more relevant comparison, given the precedent—Queen. At first the two-guitar arrangement is delivered 4/4 but then switches over to 3/4 waltz time as if dropping a beat would get us to the metal faster. Once the song proper kicks in, there's a synergy and solidity with the track before it, given its measured pace and resolute craft. Also, the band is proving themselves masters of modulations as they wander through keys at will. For extra window dressing, one solo is played over a sombre, Sabbath-like mellow section and then the other, over metal of various persuasions.

"'Into the Coven' was another song that had a different title," recalls King, adding the tale of the band defying the brass and becoming the evil force they became. "It might not have had the intro as well; I'm not quite sure. I rewrote some of the lyrics to fit me better. We approach CBS and said, 'Well, here is the next album' and as I said, they basically freaked out, man. That's when Hank and I said, 'Fuck you; we're not going to do that' and we said, 'Those of you who want to continue just to have an album deal, go for it, but we're going to do our own thing.' So, we did that and we started finding new members and started what was then called Mercyful

Fate, but used some of those songs, because Hank wrote the music, and then with new lyrics. So that's how that came about. That song went through several titles, including 'Walking Back to Hell,' and a lot of changes."

Another title from an earlier incarnation was "Love Criminals." In its final naming, "Into the Coven," the song almost became the record's title track. At the lyric end, this one is all-in Satanic, featuring the stripping-down of some nubile maiden, who then must don a white coat and crush a cross. Amusing however is the opening line, "Howl like a wolf and a witch will open the door."

"'Into the Coven' was the very first Mercyful Fate song that King and I did together," adds Shermann. "I had the riff in the rehearsal room while the others were down the gas station to buy Coca-Cola and stuff like that. Then King and I stayed at the rehearsal room and I presented the opening riff to 'Into the Coven' and we tried some ideas and approaches. So that has a historical thing to it."

"I had heard a version of that with another guitarist," recalls Michael, addressing the same track. "I was kicked out of Brats at one point and he replaced me with a guy named Carsten. He's actually the guy who co-produced our *Force of Evil* album (laughs). He's an excellent guitarist; he played for Michael Schenker and Uli Roth. He could've easily been the replacement. He was a small part of the early Mercyful Fate. He plays on some of the early demos and he played the beginning of that similar to what I played. It was very easy for me to transform his stuff and just make a few changes and do it my way. He's partly responsible for some of the melodic parts of that intro."

"Into the Coven" was included in the PMRC's "Filthy Fifteen." Led by Tipper Gore, wife of then senator Al Gore, the Parents Music Resource Centre led a successful effort to have parental advisory stickers added to albums considered to be profane. The songs picked as examples were cited as bad news due to sexual content and violence, as well as the use of bad language and glorification of drug use. Mercyful Fate was joined by Venom as bands championing occult themes.

Commented an exasperated King, speaking with Sam Dunn, "That's a thing that makes as little sense as a priest once in New York who wrote me this long letter—I still have it somewhere— that was almost begging me, 'Please use your fame for the good of the youth instead of now you're corrupting them in songs like "No Presents for Christmas,"' was the example he gave me. I'm like, are you kidding me? Have you ever read the lyric? It's more like making fun of Disney than anything else. There's Donald Duck in there and it's nothing to do with any of the other. Such a different lyric, but he hadn't read it. Like in the background research, 'Oh you have... ooh,' without hearing anything. There are still people today, of course, and it's understandable. You see that: 'Ooh, devil worship or this and that—he's a Satanist; he said so himself.' What's a Satanist? You tell me first what you mean by a Satanist; then I'll tell you if I'm one of those. Sacrificing animals and babies... no. I wouldn't be sitting talking to you if I did that. Come on, seriously."

"But there's a philosophy from (Anton) LaVey that I totally stand behind, and there are earlier experiences with the occult which I couldn't explain when other people were present with the glass floating in thin air. When we had done the first demo with Mercyful Fate, we had just come back with the demo and it was Kim Ruzz, the drummer, and my brother was there. We were sitting there just listening to music. We bought a ton of beers and we were waiting for the other guys, but we just opened one beer each. My brother's glass suddenly rose up in thin air and came back slowly, about two yards up in the air. It was pretty substantial."

"I don't care if people believe it or not—those that were there saw it," continues Diamond. "It was so weird. We didn't get scared or anything. We didn't say anything for a few minutes, actually, and then I said, 'I know you both saw that.' We just nodded our heads and then we didn't talk about it until three or four days later."

"And that apartment where it happened, it was a very haunted apartment in Denmark for eight or nine years. It was almost every day things would happen. Things would be moved around, people would be tossed, pulled by the hair. All kinds of stuff. Malcolm Dome and his photographer, Ray Palmer... Ray experienced the thing that was in my bathroom that would growl at people. There was a girl that had once been growled at there who was staying with me for a short while. It was crazy stuff."

"Lars and James were there from Metallica, and we had a nice drinking session, and they were recording either *Ride the Lightning* or *Master of Puppets*, one of those two. They recorded both of those in Denmark. So, they spent a night actually in my bedroom where I had a foosball table. We were playing that to give my friend Jimmy and the girl a little space in the living room, and suddenly it sounded like Jimmy had fallen over my coffee table and all the bottles had just fallen over. I opened the door, 'Jimmy, what are you doing?'

He was white as a sheet. 'Kim, what's going on here?' Then I saw, I had an altar in my living room and everything from the altar was just spread all over the floor. They couldn't have touched it. So, 'It's all right, don't worry, it's just them.' I picked my things up and put them back."

"Those things, they of course affected me. But I got a very respectful relationship with these powers and I felt they were there specifically because these things happened when we had just done our first demo with Mercy. I took that as congratulations and we're here to help if you need something. You can't say what's right and wrong because it's different opinions. If you ask a Christian what Satanism is, it's all evil and bad. That's not how I see it at all. Because for me, Satanism is not a religion. It's a life philosophy, and that's exactly what Anton LaVey put in his *Satanic Bible*. Should have been called something else, maybe. Satanic philosophy. As soon as it's called a bible people start associating it with a religion and it's not a religion."

"I had that same life philosophy before I ever read his book. One day I saw it, I said I want to read this. See if this is the way it really is. So, I read it, and this is a life philosophy. This is how I live my life already. Then later when I got invited to visit the church and him in San Francisco in 1988, '89, and to meet him face to face and get confirmed that he was dead serious about his philosophy... nothing was done for anything else, and I spent the whole night at the church there."

"It was amazing spending two hours in the ritual chamber. We were talking and I told him that I would like to give him my view on Satanism instead of him talking first and me nodding like a puppy. I would like to tell him mine and then he could tell me if he felt that was right or wrong or whatever. I spoke for about an hour, maybe 45 minutes, and then he took his symbol off his jacket and pressed it into my hand and it was an unreal feeling. There was an understanding. That was amazing, and what we talked about in there, I'll never tell anyone, but the whole experience was great, being there that whole night and meeting Blanche Barton too and seeing the house."

Barton began a relationship with LaVey in 1984 and eventually, in 1997, served as co-High Priestess with Karla LaVey, an arrangement that crashed almost immediately over disputes about Anton's will, following his death on October 29, 1997. She's currently Magistra Templi Rex with the Church of Satan, which she won control of through a probate settlement.

"He played keyboards for me," continues Diamond. "Big black cat lying on a velvet pillow. He had all these different keyboards and his kind of humour. He would start going into this, 'Wonderful, wonderful Copenhagen,' and then with his bald head, it was almost like watching Lurch from The Addams Family—it was so sinister. He looked over his shoulder with this smile and it was like, that's where I'm from. So, it was a very cool experience. Then I talked to him. I got the red line, phone line, so I could call him night or day. I have a handwritten letter of his, which is very unique. I was told by his daughter, Karla, because I usually try to hook up with her when we're playing in San Francisco. I used to know the other daughter as well, very well, and her son, Stan. But I told her that I had this handwritten letter, and she said, 'I don't believe you; I'm sorry.' After we had dinner, I showed it to her. She saw it and saw what he had written to me and she started crying. It was a pretty intense letter."

Back on the subject of the PMRC and its effect, Diamond says, "I honestly don't know if it helped or hindered us. I guess certain things would give you some publicity. There might be other places that would say, 'Oh we're not going to play that on the radio.' I think it went both ways. I don't think it's made a big difference either way. You're always going to hear people who might now know what we're about. There's been many of those things, of course. Tipper Gore, when she was in charge of the PMRC, they were trying to have bands banned because they were singing about certain things and they didn't even do their research. They didn't even know what people were singing about. Putting Mercyful Fate on the Filthy Fifteen list, suddenly we were in *USA Today* and all kinds of stuff, which we would have never been. So, thanks! It makes no sense a lot of the time and if they did a little more research before they start their things, then they would realise that, whoa, we shouldn't torch that because it's really not what we were thinking."

Not sure what King's point is. In this context, he's known to bring up Dee Snider and how "Under the Blade" is about going to the dentist (adding, amusingly, that he was "in the dentist business") but it's hard to defend against Tipper Gore and the like that he wasn't some form of "Satanist."

As the above association with Anton LaVey would convey, Mercyful Fate is in a very different place from Iron Maiden or Ozzy Osbourne, let alone Twisted Sister. There's a coyness to putting it down to "not doing their research." Very likely "they" didn't, but then again, they didn't have to—King's lyrics hit you right between the eyes, with little ambiguity, little veiling.

"I guess we were serious about what we were doing," admits Diamond. "It was not just an image. It's never been just an image. I always had a lot of candles back then. Playing, writing music was just by candlelight. I used to have it in the studio, too. Only candlelight. Of course, they needed electricity and very low lights in the control room, but I used to have just two candles so I would just see the lyric. It's always been part of me. King Diamond and Kim Petersen are absolutely one in the same. I would never try and do what Alice did, which I think was genius. I think it's awesome when he talks about Alice in the third person. I think it's so cool, but it would be so lame if I did it. Again, with the makeup, I never wanted to look like him or anyone else. What would be the point in that? You want to try and be original in what you're doing."

"A lot of people had makeup before Alice had, as well. He wasn't the first, but it was the combination of what he did that created that one thing. Other people wore it before but in different contexts. So, it's always been that. We can thank the record labels for a lot of the stuff, too, because with us specifically, both Mercyful Fate and King Diamond, we were always given complete artistic freedom, and that means so much. That you can still play from the heart, even today. Brian Slagel sometimes will not have heard one note of a new album because he gets it from us. Here it is, finished. That's a lot of trust going both ways, and that gives you a lot of originality because it all comes from the heart. When we think about what things we want to have in the show for production for the next tour, it depends on how we can do things best and what certain songs would fit better than others to do."

Besides the likes of Madonna, Sheena Easton, Cyndi Lauper, Prince, Def Leppard and Judas Priest, as mentioned, also on the PMRC's Filthy Fifteen list was Venom, with a little something called "Possessed."

An important band in the history of heavy metal, Venom might be considered the first thrash metal band, the first death metal band, but, crossing into Mercyful's wheelhouse, also the first black metal band, notching two blatantly Satanic albums before *Melissa* would emerge.

Noted King back in '83, "To be perfectly honest, it wasn't until relatively recently that we first heard of Venom. We've said many times; they are just one big publicity stunt! A sort of Sex Pistols '83. In fact, that appears to be their main musical equivalent. Metal has built its good reputation on the enormous skill of the likes of Blackmore, Schenker, Van Halen etc. We feel that we can contribute as much to the progress of metal as they have, because we are doing something fresh, vital and original. Sadly, Venom, through poor musicianship and a string of concert fiascos, have disillusioned a great many heavy rockers and generally give metal a bad name."

Of course, therein lies the major difference between the two, with Mercyful Fate and Venom being polar opposites musically. Mercyful was all about bettering *Sad Wings of Destiny* with musicianship, complexity and recording finesse, and Venom were unhealthy Kiss fans (granted, Priest fans too) with a predilection for wanting to blow up everything, from the music industry through to their own recordings and their own live shows.

Years later, King's perspective had somewhat shifted, with Diamond seeing the point of Cronos, Mantas and Abaddon.

"What's a black metal band?" asked King, rhetorically. "We were one of the earliest, with Venom. Well, what is black metal? What do you have to do to get a certain sticker? If you start explaining, I think you find all those brands you can put on us because especially with King Diamond there are so many styles of music in that. We even have a few ballads; you could call them. They have that quiet sad mood in them but that's because of the story line. That's not written for, 'Hey, let's write a ballad.' No, normally I would not write a ballad. But if something fits in the storyline and we have to get to it afterwards, then it's a matter of mood-creating. If it gets a stamp of being a ballad in the album, then I don't care. For me it's not a special thing; it's part of the whole."

"Venom shocked people because of what they sang about," continues King. "We have very different opinions. People started talking about Satanism at the time, 'Ooh, it's a Satanic band.' I didn't write about any specific thing just to shock someone. It's all being honest and part of me and what I've done. There's nothing where I'm faking it. I saw so many occult things in that haunted apartment in Denmark and that's what brought me into that side of things. Seeing firsthand and being able to actually not go crazy but talk to my parents because they had seen them too, but they didn't know that until I brought it up one day. I thought they're going to think I'm losing it and they're going to send me to a hospital."

"But they were like, 'Really? Have you ever...?' 'Yeah, absolutely.' Then both my mum and dad start telling me these stories that they had these encounters, and I thought it was cool. I went to the library, borrowed tons of books about the occult, and found out later most of them are written from a strict Christian viewpoint. One day I saw *The Satanic Bible* in a bookstore. I wanted to know. I've always been extremely open-minded; I am an open-minded person. I'm always willing to hear both sides of a story and I almost demand myself to make an opinion. Otherwise, I'm just going by hearsay."

"If someone says, 'Don't ever buy a Ferrari; it's a shit car,' well I haven't driven a Ferrari. So, I say to that person, 'I'll get back to you if I ever get the opportunity one day.' I always get the facts before I spit out an opinion. That goes right back to all the stuff here. I bought *The Satanic Bible* and I read it. It's not a bible; it has nothing to do with religion. Like I say, to me, Satanism is a life philosophy. According to Anton Szandor LaVey, I got something confirmed for myself that what was written in that book was how I always lived my life. It's not like I got the book and went, 'Now I'm going to live my life by this philosophy.' It was like I was reading about myself and how I felt about the world. I'm not a religious person, I never was, I have never seen the proof that I need to be a religious person. Then you get into some other issues, which, I respect people having their different religions and gods, because who am I to say there are no gods? I can't prove that. But no one else can prove that they believe in the only right God. Because if anyone could do that and had the proof, we'd all believe in that. It's never been proved, which is why we have so many different religions."

Which is a little confusing, because King swears up and down, he's seen paranormal things. When you're sure you've seen paranormal things, you sensibly believe in paranormal beings. Yet, one supposes, that doesn't lead to a belief in gods, maybe only poltergeists.

"That's true," answers King, "and I can't shape it into some kind of religion. It doesn't create a belief system. It's way too little. There is no proof. I can't prove that to others. Those who were around when those things happened, sure, we can talk about it, but to say it must have been a god like this and if you do this then you go there... that was not enough for me to believe in it. I know there's more between Heaven and Earth, to me, and I don't expect others to believe it. Some people might say he's crazy and invented those stories, some of those things he's experienced: 'Oh he must be making it up.' I don't care. It doesn't matter to me. I talked to my parents about it and people that are very close to me and who have experienced these things too, and some of them with me—that's all that matters."

"It doesn't matter if... and that's the same with some other people that I respect. They might have had other experiences that they feel they can't shape into some religion that's described in some book. But the majority of people are narrow-minded and will only see their own little way. If other people don't believe in the same thing as they do, they are thrown to Hell, and I think that is completely wrong because I think you have to step back and look at the facts. You can't prove to others that you are right because then everyone would believe in the same thing. So, you really don't know. It's fine if you believe and that's what it is. 'I believe it might be this way.' But you can't prove it. But again, I'll be the last to say there are no gods because who am I to prove that? I don't know if there are any, how many there are or if there are none. I have no clue and I admit that I don't know that."

"Can I just say one thing about Venom?" continues King, bringing himself back to the boys. "I met them and I became, not good friends because you had to know each other for longer but became... met Cronos and the guys and we had a great time together. We actually went too far one time as to try and say, 'Hey, can we slag each other because then we will get more press? Is that cool?' We did that for a while. It was in *Kerrang!* for a while. He was saying, 'Ah, King Billy,' and I would say, 'Ah, CronAIDS.' At that point AIDS was not the thing it is today where you don't joke about it. It was so new; practically no one knew what it was. So, we called each other these names."

"After a while I guess the press caught on and said they were full of it. But we had a great time. Cronos and I got thrown out of a hotel in Holland three times in one night, and they called the promoters to get us back inside. They were supposed to play a festival that we played but their gear was stuck somewhere so they just showed up in person. That night we were howling like wolves outside because we got so drunk together. I have a lot of respect for them because they certainly created some unique things."

One of those unique things with Venom, again antithetical to the Mercyful way of thinking, was recording lo-fi on purpose.

"That's true; that's how it felt," shrugs King. "I guess it was part of their trademark, part of their overall sound. It got so raw. Then with those lyrics you could barely understand what he was saying. That's the case with many bands. You had to sit over the lyrics with some of our stuff, too, or had to wonder what the hell he said there because you're so in the feeling and mood of things. Then you go in there and suddenly you can hear, yeah, he's doing that. They were singing all that stuff but I'm not sure they believed what they were singing, that that was their actual philosophy."

"I know it was ours, what we did. Again, you don't always know the thought behind what's written in a lyric. I remember the early times when we first came to the US and started doing interviews, I was not good at English at that point. It was a slow process; it was not natural. I would get these… 'The song "Evil;" is that really what you stand behind?' The song was written for a specific purpose. You're bringing it up now and we're talking about it. Do you realise that the phrase 'necessary evil' is valid? Because without evil you don't have human beings. A human being only appears because you are having feelings. You're having input usually through your ears and eyes and nose and mouth and your nervous system, that enables you to describe things on these different scales—sweet and sour, dark and light, all these things—so that you can say I like this, or I don't like that."

"But if you only had one of the two, only good or only evil, you stop being a human being because you can't put anything on a slider any more. There is no scale. So, everything good, how would you appreciate that good? You can't appreciate a good day if you never had a bad day. How would you know? So that's what 'Evil' was about; it had the purpose of bringing up the talk of evil being necessary."

"Maybe this world is 50/50. I would like it to be 90/10 or maybe better, but you have to feel a bad thing to appreciate the good. A lot of those songs were written so that the first impression was not exactly what I wanted, because maybe some of the lyrics were written a little clumsy. I was not great at English back then, but in the end the purpose of the songs came out. Discussions were made about things and people started to understand that there's more to this than let's try and be evil. We're not that shallow; there's more behind it."

"Strange thing when you think, comparing Mercyful Fate to King Diamond, most people think Mercy is this Satanic band and King Diamond is more a horror band. In my eyes, King Diamond is much more a Satanic band than Mercy will ever be for the simple reason that King Diamond is so full of that life philosophy that is stated in *The Satanic Bible* that I've always believed in. There's a horror element in there because I love horror and I've had those experiences, but the majority, the underlying thing of how they treat each other, all Satanic life philosophy. Mercy is more myths, legends, the legend of the headless rider, talking about religion sometimes, saying, 'Are you sure it's this way or that way?' and 'Why can't it be this way?' Asking some questions about things. For me, Mercy is not Satanic in that way. The word Satan is used more there, but not in a Satanic philosophical way. There are things that when you look deeper into it, you get a surprise because it's deeper than you might think."

As alluded to, at the music end, there's a fierce level of almost statesmanship, with the guys striving to be the very best. The riffs are smart and they are played tight. The drumming is perfect and catchy, with enough complexity but never too much. At the vocal end, King utilises his three gears but also layers in harmonies or obvious backing vocals, voices that are definitely him, indicating that this is a studio experience that cannot be duplicated on stage and damn the torpedoes.

"I have never felt we were in competition with anybody," counters King. "We were not thinking of ourselves as being better because of the unique style we had. That's the reason why we're here today, I think. We've always discussed things together. Some people have said, 'Ah, King Diamond is a tyrant and people have to do what he says.' No, with the lineups we had, we had discussions about things. But what you need in that discussion, for all of us it has to be for the best of the music. It's not a fight to show what I can do on this album and then I'm going to be all over the place with my drums or solos, or I'm going to turn this riff into being played half lead. Hey, there's plenty of space for showing what you can do in our music. There's lots of places. Because of the style, probably, too, we're able to keep that factor totally in the background and write and record for the best of the music."

King was blessed to be accompanied by an embarrassment of wealth when it came to the four musicians backing his experiments in vocal terrorism.

"We're similar because we have the same inspirations," says Hank, on being half of such an imposing guitar team this band had, bookended with Michael Denner. "Especially the early Michael Schenker stuff; I've always been into Uli Roth, but he's na little special. He's on another planet, I guess. But the early Michael Schenker stuff from the '70s... Michael and I basically originated from there. And the difference is probably Michael's natural born musicality. He has a nice feeling, a nice singing, musical way whereas my style is a little more aggressive, harder on the notes. Even back then, 25 years back, it was exactly the same. I was more aggressive. No matter what Michael is doing, he always gets a melody in there, some nice musical guitar solos, where I'm a little more hard-hitting."

Michael adds his take on the contrast between his style and Hank's. "I started playing with Hank in the late '70s. That's one of our secrets, because Hank is a very fast picker. He picks very fast on the strings and I tend to play more legato. I don't pick that much with my right hand but the left goes fast. I have this feeling, an old blues type of feeling, where Hank is more like a fast and modern metal guitarist; that's the difference. Technically he's much better than me (laughs), but I have this old-style feeling; that's my strong point. That's why I feel we have something. There's never any discussion who plays whose solos when we start recording and writing songs. We always know exactly, from the first note, who's going to play what solo. There's never been any jealousy between Hank and I. It's like two brothers, on guitar (laughs)."

Back to the track sequence upon *Melissa*, "At the Sound of the Demon Bell" begins on an amusing melodic note but then once again, the band cuts the speed in half for the verse, King shrieking "Halloween!" while the guys slash away obtusely and progressively. Come chorus time, the band again expertly balances the melodic against the creepy and claustrophobic. There are a lot of parts to this one, and the result is a track that doesn't quite stick to the memory banks like each and all of the opening three.

"That's a very strange song, actually," reflects Michael. "I didn't like that song for a long time, because I thought it was odd and strange, the arrangements, also some of the riffs. I thought it didn't work. But actually when we recorded it, it came out good. Now I like the song (laughs)."

Lyrical, all manner of evil deed is unleashed on the Hallows Eve depicted, including most horrifically, Christ burning on a cross. Another graphic image has some entity in the cemetery swinging a "sword of hate" between the graves. Apparently a saint will be uncovered—"see for yourself."

"Black Funeral" is the original vinyl's side two opener and the band is back to the searingly memorable, housing a phalanx of great riffs in a very short song, well composed but still slyly progressive. This one contains the signature and anthemic favourite concert line "All hail Satan, yes hail Satan," the first part delivered with malevolent growl, the second in falsetto.

In December of '83, "Black Funeral" was issued in the UK on Metal for Nations as a 12" picture sleeve single, backed with completely pro non-LP track "Black Masses" which, across from its various musical sections, evokes images of a Diamond Head epic, sounding very much like a rhythmic rejigging of "Am I Evil?" The track, credited to King and Hank, was the first thing the band recorded on the sessions. It was slated to be on the album, but the band felt a vague dissatisfaction about it and left it off. "How it came about, I'm not 100% sure," muses King. "Hank, at that time, presented the music and we would work on it and learn it and maybe we would say, 'Maybe the chorus could be this part instead.' We were all part of the arrangement of it. Especially me, because I had to do vocals on it; I would write the lyrics."

But yes, you can't get much more Satanic than "Black Funeral," given King's consciousness-shocking instruction delivered to his minions. Says Michael, "That was a bit more commercial in my opinion compared to some of the other songs, but it's always been, right from when we started writing and arranging it, it was very nice to play, especially live. When you play this song live, I can't help smiling. This song always leaves me smiling. The funny thing is, when Snowy (Shaw) was in the band, he had the same feeling. Sometimes when we were on tour, Snowy and I, when we started playing 'Black Funeral,' I would turn around at Snowy and we'd start laughing. It's very... nice."

Denner goes on to say that King's beliefs in Satanism were never a problem in the band. "Definitely not. We were all close friends. When he started up with his interest in the occult stuff, actually it was in my apartment. We were sitting at night in a thunderstorm (laughs), listening to Black Sabbath talking about magic and witches and then he got more and more into it. He was very deep into the occult. But he's always been a gentleman and he's always managed to separate things. He told me, 'I have this belief, but it doesn't mean that you have to feel the same way.' I don't. I'm not Christian or a devil worshiper; I've never been. I'm just... what you call it, atheist."

"It started with Anton LaVey's books and also the things he had at home, all these rituals," furthers Michael, on King's path to blasphemy. "He started experiencing things. All I said was, 'I don't care (laughs). I don't want to know which ghost does what.' I said, 'I don't care about this and I don't want to know about it.' He always respected that. I like the person I am. As a child, I had a lot of bad experiences about spirits. My mother and father were very much into it and that made me a very scared child when I was small. I told King that and I said I don't want to know about what you saw and what you did and he respected that. He said, 'Okay, Michael, no problem.' He was my roommate on the tours and stuff and he always respected that, so that's great."

That represents an eerie sense of destiny, that Denner's parents were involved. "Oh yeah. Very much. They saw all kinds of things (laughs). Ghosts and sounds and things moving, ghost-writing through my mother's hand—the pen would move on its own. So, I was a very scared child. I have my own son now and he asks me about ghosts and stuff and I say, 'There are no ghosts. If there ever came one, I would take it and throw it out the window, no problem.' That's the way, because I don't want him to be so scared like I was when I was a kid."

Michael's parents are still around, but they're quite tight-lipped about the issue. "I know my mother and father these days are very embarrassed that they put us through all this. I have a brother and sister and they had the same problem. They're very sad about it, that they made us so scared when we were children."

Asked if anybody else in the band was into the occult, Michael says, "Let me see. Yes, Timi at one point was a bit into it, and also Kim Ruzz. I also know that Snowy and Sharlee were a bit interested in it, but it was more the horror side of it, old horror movies, vampires and stuff."

As for King, there's no connection between his hobby in occultism and that of Michael's parents.

"Michael's? No, not at all. That goes all the way back to my own parents. My parents had had occult experiences, and at the time, when I had my first experiences like that, I could talk to my parents about it, completely open, without feeling like I was some lunatic or liar or whatever. Because they can tell me a lot of stories too, and it was nice to have someone to bounce these things off of. It did happen to me, and it doesn't matter if other people believe it or not. But it's nice to have someone to talk to about these things. Because there were some heavy things that I experienced quite a few times. The interest in horror overall also comes back to my parents allowing me to watch it when I was a kid, *Frankenstein* and *Dracula*, old black-and-white versions. I remember clearly lying in bed thinking or being almost scared that they would come out when I fell asleep from under the bed and grab me into this other world or whatever. Waking up was this huge, great relief—oh man, it didn't happen!"

But King knew about Michael's parents... "Oh yeah, absolutely. That's why he could relate to a lot of this stuff I was writing about.

Because he had that... not fed to him but he was able to bounce whatever experiences he would have had off of his parents. So, it is not something strange or out of this world, these ideas I came up with."

Says King on the subject of Timi's and Kim's level of interest in the occult, "I don't know if they were into it, or how much personal experience they had with that kind of stuff. They were probably more like fascinated, I would say. Hank was more like, he thought it was cool. He has later on gotten to really appreciate it in a different way, because he had some personal experiences himself where he came to me and said, 'Man, I saw some things and I totally didn't understand it.' He did know how to handle it. I couldn't really relate to it other than to say, 'Oh, different.' But Mike Denner was the one I could really bounce lyrics off of. He would say, 'Oh man, I really feel this one; that happened to me.' Timi was a big soccer fan, and Kim Ruzz, he was probably the guy I got to know the least, personality-wise. Because I was hanging out more with the other guys. Maybe because Kim Ruzz was living twenty minutes or half an hour out of the city. Normally when we hung out, we would go into the city and usually meet at Michael's apartment, and Kim wouldn't come because it was too far of a trip. So, the four of us were hanging together the most. Not for any specific reasons, other than he lived a little too far outside of the city."

I asked King if the intellectualising of religion takes the emotion out of it for him, whether this all becomes science to him in the end.

"Yes and no. That's a hard question to answer because it's both. You can see some of it in my lyrics, where I'm just stating the conclusion I came to have at a certain point, probably years ago. But finely stating it, you could say, to myself, that I believe that there is something because of the experiences I had. I had no chance... I can't theorise about it and make up all these theories, but in the end, I came to the conclusion that I can't waste my time, because I know I will not know in this lifetime, how everything is put together and why we're here and where we're going, all this stuff."

"No one will know that. If any single person knew that or was given that information, they might go insane. It never happens that anyone, no matter what faith they belong to, has been able to prove to the rest of mankind that what they believe in is the right thing. Because if it was proven, we would all believe that, of course. So, it is what you call faith, what people believe, that it could be this way. I do not have the proof. I can theorise about all kinds of things. I think

I might have lived before because I only dream about this and this time period and I'm so fascinated by this time period. I have seen these powers, not just me, but with other people present too, seeing exactly the same weird occult things happen in front of our eyes. But I can't explain them. There is no logical or scientific explanation to it. But to me, I have seen those things and I have felt them. So therefore, there must be something."

"But I can theorise for years and never hit it right on and I'd never know if I hit it," chuckles King. "So, it becomes a waste of time. People say, 'Well, then are you an atheist?' 'Well, not quite.' 'Then what are you? What do you believe in?' 'Well, it doesn't really matter what I believe in, because I can't prove any of it.' Not even to myself can I prove if I make a theory about this. Therefore, I leave it alone. It's fascinating, it's interesting; when these things happen, I suck it in. Because it does totally fascinate me. It actually gives me a few things that are comforting. I believe 1000% that I'm going to be able to recognise my dad who's not here anymore, once it's my time. The cat I lost that was my best friend ever. I know that I will meet those entities again; in what form, I have no idea. But I know I will meet them and when it's my time to go to some other place, I will definitely recognise them and I'm looking forward to that part of that bad experience. That's one thing I've been convinced inside of."

"But that doesn't give you or me any religious directive or belief or something like that. That's the reason that I do respect all kinds of religions. People have different religions, different beliefs. If they help people through life, that's great. But once anyone starts this thing where they want to push their religion onto other people, man, I back off so hard. I can't stand that. I can stand even less when they look at other people who believe different than they are as if they are inferior to them. I think that is sick. They have no right to do that. They can't prove that what they believe in is the right thing. So, keep it to themselves, you know? I don't judge people by what they believe in but keep it to themselves and don't judge other people because of it. You should judge people by their personalities. If the person is a decent person and they treat you with respect, you are to treat them back with the same respect."

"And then I've come to other things too, where I realise that every individual on this earth, we're all the centre of our own universe. We all are, we have to be. Every day when you wake up, whatever your schedule is, whether you get out and get into a certain car, you say hi or goodbye to certain people, certain faces you see, you drive by certain parks and certain trees. All these things come into your eyes and eventually turn into some feelings inside of you. All of that stuff is probably a big basis of how you make up opinions about different things in life."

"And I have different inputs. I don't see the same things you do. Therefore, I can understand that people have different opinions about certain subjects. I may not agree with them sometimes, but it doesn't mean that the other person is wrong. They might be totally right in their environment and their universe, because well, if you live next to a nuclear plant, I'm sure you will be hardcore pro-safety in nuclear plants, where another person can't relate to that. 'Oh God, of course it's safe. People work there all the time.' You can come up with all these different arguments but people usually... the interesting thing is meeting people with different opinions, but if you want to get a little deeper, find out where these people come from. Then you often get an explanation for why you might be getting a different opinion from yours. I'm talking about ordinary, normal people, not lunatics or something like that, where you're thinking, why did they suddenly kill this or that person?"

Asked about other specific paranormal experiences he's had, Diamond says, "I can't mention one single thing because there has been a combination of many things. The apartment I lived in in Copenhagen was really haunted. Several people have seen things up there, felt things up there, been touched by things, things moving in thin air, swaying in the air. That's where some of these things come from in the lyrics. I couldn't pinpoint one specific event that would be the most striking because there were so many. There was even one that was just... where I felt like it was evil. That's the only time I felt being really evil. I felt this being mocking someone else who was there because they were mocking the fact that they could be there."

"One night I came home, and it certainly was not the most impressive thing I felt. It was something more like a sensation of smell. Coming into my living room, pitch-dark, but I felt this horrible smell. I mean, it was 100 times worse than if it had been a mix of puke and shit lying on the floor. But the room was divided in half. One side of the room was that smell. Going to the other... it was like an invisible wall and I could sway from one side to the other and it was totally normal, nothing. You could stand and bend back and forth and get the smell and get nothing. I told this thing to get the hell out of my house, and it did. But the feeling it gave, it was not that smell from a sink or a bathroom or anything like that. I simply can't explain it other than it was for sure evil."

Speaking of evil, back to the record, *Melissa*'s next track is a huge epic to the horned one called "Satan's Fall." Riff after superlative riff cascades down upon the listener and comparisons to hallowed era Priest are again in order.

"That one is really fun playing live," notes King, "because you just get thrown all over the place. Of course, it's so long that you have to get around, but you certainly do in that one. There's all kinds of music in that one song. It's so great, but at the same time so heavy. It's got everything that you know Mercyful Fate for."

"'Satan's Fall' is a favourite because of the complex structure," adds Hank. "I don't know if it's complex; it's basically just adding another riff every two minutes (laughs). But that was composed at home in my living room. Even at night, I went up and took my guitar and composed without any restrictions, just whatever came to mind I put together. That's also very popular when we play live. But I never had to write that all down; it's up in my head somewhere. Everything is just memorised."

"When we started early on with that song, we had a discussion, can we do this?" recalls Denner. "Because this is way too much. I was nearly desperate in the beginning, saying, I cannot play this one. When Hank came in with all these riffs, he just played all these things together, and he told me, 'This is a number that will go well over ten minutes and there won't be the same riff twice. If we do this, people will just say, wow.' Like I said, we practiced so hard that somebody could wake me up and I could just play that without any mistakes." Michael chuckles then corrects himself: "There's one repeating riff, the first one—that one returns at the very end!"

Hank has been cited saying that there are 16 or so riffs in "Satan's Fall." At 11:23, it would be the band's longest song until the title track of *Dead Again*, 15 years later.

In the realm of what was then called black metal—essentially Mercyful Fate and Venom and on one else!—this is the type of track above all others that makes the statement that one of these band's was wanting to be classy and clean with their blackness.

"Yes, exactly," says Michael. "Because, with all respect to Venom, I felt that we were much better musicians. I mean, it was a very different style. The way we played it, it was more technical, there were different paces and changes in the rhythms, up-tempo, down-tempo. I didn't feel that Venom were a heavier band. That's not the way I see what is heavy and what is not (laughs)."

A DANGEROUS MEETING: IN THE SHADOWS WITH MERCYFUL FATE

Offering further opinions on Venom, King states, "I've always been against labels, because it's so hard to label bands. Would we be black metal? I think of growly voices, then there's speed and thrash. That certainly doesn't cover us at all. I just know that we're a band that plays heavy, and that there's not a whole lot of other bands that sound like us. That has a lot to do with the artistic freedom we've been given by the record labels. That's a very positive thing, that we've been able to carry on writing and performing. I think that has to do with why we're still around. The fans are still definitely out there for heavy metal. It's a mutual respect between the fans and us. They know that we aren't pretending to be something other than what we are. So, it's total honesty. We have a lot of respect for the fans. It's not like we show up to gigs stoned, drunk or can't perform. We do whatever we can to perform as best we can under whatever circumstances. Every night. Because we know that it is those people that make it possible for us to do what we love the most. So, you owe them a lot of respect, to not just blow them off."

Melissa ends with the album's title track, a black metal power ballad as it were, quite progressive and dark, but truly in the realm of dynamics, with mellow passages balanced against the riff-framed architecture. Like Metallica in the early days, the band just left all their electrics on, plus had Ruzz drum along, making it a casual ballad arrangement. The heavy bit in this one is somewhat awkward, sounding like Budgie or something off of *Rocka Rolla*.

"'Melissa' is a song we always considered a bit odd," says King. "We tried playing it back in the early days live and we couldn't pull it off very well. We decided it wasn't a good song to play live. So, we didn't play it live until not that long ago. It was five years ago that we tried it for the first time and we thought wow, this is pretty cool! We figured, why don't we do it as a total surprise to the audience on this next tour? We never even played it on a tour before. It was just one little gig in a bar back in Copenhagen that we had tried it out and said, 'Oops, not good.' But it worked so well and people were so surprised because they'd never heard this played before."

Denner simply calls the song "a ballad" adding that "in the beginning, that song was very hard to understand because of course it was so different from everything else we had done. Our aim was to be the heaviest band ever, in the world. We said this is the way we will be the heaviest band ever. So, when we started writing and arranging the song 'Melissa,' it was like oh, can we do this? But as we went more and more into it, it felt so natural. King had this skull, a cranium, which he called Melissa. He liked the name, so he gave the skull the name Melissa. We were going through some artwork; the guy showed us this cover with the skull, and King just said 'Melissa' (laughs)."

Noted bassist Timi Grabber back in '83, "Melissa was a medieval witch who lived in Denmark. She's always been a source of inspiration to us, so we 'obtained' her skull and she now joins us onstage for every gig, resplendent upon the altar!" Not entirely true of course—Diamond obtained the skull from a local hospital and called it Melissa because that was a common name for witches.

The lyric to this light one finds King at his altar, mourning the death of his Melissa. Ominously, late in the track, he mentions that there is nothing left at the stake. He vows revenge on some priest, the tacit message being that Melissa met her end burned at the stake (after all, there's nothing left) at the instruction of the clergy.

All told, *Melissa* remains arguably *the* fan-favourite Mercyful Fate album, with Hank in agreement. "I think my favourite is probably *Melissa*, not because I wrote all the music, but I think it's a little raw. Also, it's the first full-length album that we did and it's got some classic lyrics."

What was the competition at the time, really? Let's not forget, there was no thrash scene yet. The standard-bearers were *The Number of the Beast*, *Piece of Mind*, *Screaming for Vengeance*, *Blackout*, the Ozzy albums, and maybe the two Black Sabbaths with Ronnie. *Melissa* could hang with those no problem, the positive being its professionalism, but the negative being that King's vocals left a sizeable chunk of the potential fan base passing.

The very first issue of *Metal Forces* magazine included reviews of Metallica's *Kill 'Em All*, Savatage's *Sirens* and Mercyful Fate's *Melissa*, each being landmark albums of heavy metal achievement not heard in a generation.

Wrote Dave Constable of the latter, "Well, here it is. At long last the eagerly awaited debut album by possibly the greatest Satanic metal band of all time, and what a superb first outing it turns out to be. This is what Black Metal is all about. I'm sorry Venom and Co. but for sheer talented overkill and evil I doubt if this will ever be beaten. Those of you who bought Fate's debut EP last year on Rave-On Records got a taste of the awesome power this band could unleash, but nothing could have foretold what was in store."

After analysing each track, Constable concludes, "The overall strength of this as an LP surpasses the sum of its individual tracks.

A DANGEROUS MEETING: IN THE SHADOWS WITH MERCYFUL FATE

Be warned, Fate are here to stay—they have arrived with one of the best heavy metal albums of all time. You may not like this if you're a disco freak or dead or both, but if you're a true 100% metal fan you cannot ignore this. Satan will surely get you if you do!"

Concerts in support of *Melissa* were few and far between, the band playing a few shows in the Netherlands and Italy. Fortunately, the limited exposure happened while the show was still evolving.

Recalls Shermann, reaching way back, "In early '81, we did a couple of concerts in Copenhagen and Sweden and King was in these really high-heeled, kind of Kiss boots with stars on them and stuff; he was inspired by Kiss and Alice Cooper of course. The rest of the band, we thought it was a little too much. So, we had this band meeting, I recall (laughs), in Michael Denner's home, discussing King's outfit, which we thought was a little too Kiss-like (laughs). Then he dropped the Kiss boots and put on some others. But looking back now, it's funny to think about it."

"Actually, when we'd just started, he was just dressing up in leather pants and all that and he had these lyrics, but it was not until we were getting into the recording of the mini-album, which we recorded in Holland in '82 or something, that we ... because at our live shows we had these upside-down crosses and these nuns that exploded on the stage. But to me, it was basically entertainment. To our advantage, there weren't too many bands that dealt with that stuff; we had a lot of attention going on because we were Satanic preachers and all that (laughs), and King was always in interviews with Christian people on radio and on TV, so that brought a lot of attention. But the only thing was that that overshadowed the music. The rest of the band, of course, was into the music and not too much into the image and the lyrics side. So, we were a little pissed, 'Hey, what about the music?' But all in all, it certainly helped us a lot. King says, even today, this is entertainment. You might as well go in to see a scary movie. But personally, he's into the occult, whatever that is."

The only show the band performed in their home country in 1983 after *Melissa* had already been released was a December headline date in Copenhagen, after a show supporting Ozzy had been cancelled due to Ozzy being ill.

Into January of 1984, the band performed a date in Hilversum that was broadcast on Dutch radio, followed by a show in Amsterdam where the band's "Melissa" skull got stolen. Italy was next followed by a single show in England in March, supporting Manowar, who treated the band poorly, cancelling sound checks and shortening their set to a paltry 25 minutes. Appeals from Roadrunner to Manowar to improve their level of hospitality were spurned. The band subsequently pulled out of the ten more shows planned on the English tour. April had the band back home for a couple dates featuring an elaborate new stage set before it was time to get back in the studio and craft a follow-up to *Melissa*.

Recalls Hank, "We had an Italian tour for a week. That was a huge success but being to Italy was weird for us. Of course, we had playing in Holland—even before *Melissa* and the mini-album. We went touring down there for five shows because that's where we started it all, actually. I think it was only Holland and Italy we did. Then of course we did the usual couple of shows in Copenhagen."

Even though King missed his chance to support Ozzy, that didn't stop him from being a hellion fan of the Oz man.

"I don't think I ever told anyone this in public," begins Diamond, "but there was an incident going to an Ozzy concert. You have to hear this because it's just way overboard. I had this great bootleg, and I think it was just around the time of *Bark at the Moon*, and we were sitting up there partying at my old, haunted apartment, my friends and I. We were getting so drunk that we started smashing bottles up against the wall. There were so many bottles that the next day when I came home, I couldn't believe what had happened. I just saw all this glass everywhere."

"We went on this bus ride and the bus driver was about to throw us off on the way to the concert. Eventually we got off the bus, but we were pretty mad, so we threw some bottles at the bus and then he stopped it. We ran over to the concert hall and tried to get in. They were still holding people outside, and then suddenly the police came. Like, are you kidding me, man?! Not now, I have to see Ozzy, not this stuff. Sure enough I got arrested. Some cab driver with this big beard was pulling me out, saying like, 'He's this guy who did it!' I got taken to the police station. They shone a big light in my face, 'So now tell us you did it.' I'm like, 'I'm not Al Capone. Can you get the light out of my eyes?' 'Okay, back in the cell.' 'Ugh, come on, I've got to go see this.' 'Well, if you admit that you did it, then we can write you a ticket for disorderly conduct and that'll be it.' 'Okay, where do I sign? Even though I didn't do it.' I kept refusing to have done it. So, I signed the paper and then I ran all the way from the police station down to the show and I missed Whitesnake—they were the support act. But I came in right when Ozzy came on. Okay, still a perfect day."

A DANGEROUS MEETING: IN THE SHADOWS WITH MERCYFUL FATE

As King explained to Bernard Doe back in '83, the highlight of the band's scant tour experience thus far would have been the Aardschok festival, in June just before *Melissa* was birthed.

"We opened the proceedings mid-afternoon in bright sunlight and yet we were the only band which really got the fans involved in the show. There were still 2,000 people outside when we came onstage, and when they heard us start-up they began rioting because it was taking so long to get in. The local police ordered that they all be allowed in free, to defuse a potentially explosive situation! The response from the audience to the show was magnificent. We burned the cross and exploded the nun, despite the fact that we were on a tiny budget. Many much wealthier bands do nothing for their fans. It's all one-way traffic; they rake in the money and give little or nothing in return."

Kerrang! was not impressed with the band's set, added Timi Grabber. "Nobody likes to be described in the terms *Kerrang!* used. They send somebody like Neil Jeffries to review a metal festival when he'd be far happier at a Men at Work gig! We just felt sorry that all the Fate fans in Europe and North America who weren't present were told nothing of interest. Quite honestly, it's just a case of journalists forgetting their responsibility to their readers."

"Of course, we have a great many ideas which we hope to put into practice when the finance and technology become available to us," continued King. "Without giving too much away, we are at present working with one of Europe's leading pyrotechnic experts on many different forms of special effects. Furthermore, we aim to be the first band to combine our lyrical imagery with onstage magic and illusion. We want people to go home thinking, 'Well I saw it and heard it, but I don't know how they did it!'"

Also, in '83, speaking with Malcolm Dome about the band's plans for the live show, King said that "We really want to get people into a certain mood at our gigs, rather than just nodding their heads to the music. On stage, I always wear the same type of makeup, because it represents death and makes me feel rather maniacal. We also use quite a few props. One of my favourite tricks was a thing the band did in Eindhoven once. One of our roadies gave us a small volume of his own blood, which I put into a glass vial. We had two crossed goose feathers on our altar that night and were gonna perform a Satanic ritual whereby human blood is sprinkled on the feathers and they come to life. When we did it, I smashed the vials onto the altar and then smeared my face in the blood. The fans obviously thought it was theatrical blood and reached out to touch my hands. It was only then that they realise this was real blood and some of them turned visibly ill. Unfortunately, we had to drop this part of the act because although it had a great effect on the kids in the first two rows, anyone further back in the hall wasn't aware of anything happening."

Speaking with Sam Dunn years later, King recalled the notorious exploding nun effect. "Malcolm Dome from England used to call it that. We had a long stick and it had hanger wires and it was made to look like a body. Especially when you put a long… it looks like a monk suit with a hood on, and then a mask, and behind this mask was this bomb we created and this long fuse would go down to the bottom. What we would do with Mercy in those days, when we finished the main set, I would light with a torch that fuse and we would run. Then boom! This thing would just be blown to pieces. We actually blew two our security guys off stage once from the concussion of it, the shockwave. Then it became like, 'It's too much, guys; we really need to find some other things to do.'"

A DANGEROUS MEETING: IN THE SHADOWS WITH MERCYFUL FATE

3.
DON'T BREAK THE OATH
"WHEN I SAW THE OTHER GUYS' FACES, I KNEW IT WAS REAL."

One more classic era Mercyful Fate album would emerge before the band would crack apart, truly due to musical differences, mainly between chief songwriters King Diamond and Hank Shermann. *Don't Break the Oath* would be every bit as classy and artful and evil as *Melissa*, establishing for all time Mercyful Fate as an enigma, a complex band to categorise, surely icons of progressive and power metal, but also definitely fathers of black metal, even though the quality craftsmanship of this band couldn't be more diametrically opposed to what the church-burning Norwegians would conjure more than a decade after King Diamond's rise to devilish distinction.

"The good thing is, we had something going with *Melissa*," Michael told Jimmy Kay. "The fan base increased. There were more and more fans. We started to tour around Europe, Germany, the

Netherlands and Belgium and so on, and we got a following. In the US, we got on the Filthy Fifteen list, some Congress thing or something. So, when they put us on this list, then suddenly there was a lot of interest for us to go to the US. When we did *Don't Break the Oath*, we were quite sure now, that this is gonna be the big one. We hoped for the best with *Melissa*, but we were quite certain that this album would bring us up into the big league, as one of the bigger metal bands."

But there were cracks showing. King felt like he was doing too much in terms of the live show, yet he wanted to contribute even more to the band, at the writing end. So far it was mostly Hank providing music, with a bit from Michael and nothing from Kim or Timi.

"Well, usually Michael would write songs alone," muses King. "He would write a few songs with Hank, and a few more with me, I guess, but he barely wrote on *Don't Break the Oath*. He had some stuff; it was more like a riff here and a riff there. It was more on King Diamond *Abigail*, where he started writing a bit more, and *Fatal Portrait* he was in on some of the songs. But there was never a song just by him. It was always a song that he and I collaborated on. I wrote alone, or he and I collaborated because he had some ideas. But they never were really full songs."

Into the studio on April 30th, 1984, the band was still rushed but not as badly. They would also wrest some of the power away from producer Henrik Lund. "When it came time to record *Don't Break the Oath*, we had a better budget and about 18 days in the studio," explains King. "I think you can hear the extra attention on that album, too. I would say it's a better album songwriting-wise, but it was a development, staying within the Mercyful Fate frame. We used different instruments to create a heavy mood and my voice developed more so. We were able to go even more in-depth, adding extra stuff to it and turning it more into a studio recording than we had ever done before."

"On *Don't Break the Oath*, there were a couple of songs that were... not funny, but different," reflects Hank. "But both are very close to me because we started that when we were very young, our early 20s. Recording-wise, for *Melissa* we had two weeks altogether, the mix and everything. With *Don't Break the Oath*, we had three weeks to record and mix. The difference is probably that Mr. Diamond stepped in on the scene as a composer for the second one, meaning that he contributed two or three—four songs maybe; I can't recall—

and that changed the direction a little bit. Especially with the newer releases, we divided that. I did about 50% and he does as well, and that makes a big difference. He has a completely different style than me, which also accounts for the big difference between the '80s recordings and the '90s recordings."

It was during the mix that the guys laid it on the line with Lund. "Like the first one, while he was mixing he wanted us out of there," explains King. "You know, 'You sit outside and you'll get your turn.' I understand; he had a bunch of young guys who didn't really know about this stuff. He didn't want all these thinkers over his shoulders—I understand that part of it. But on the other hand, we didn't learn much."

"So, it started the same way with the mix and then I said, 'That's enough. We're not going to take this shit anymore. We're going to sit in there. It's going to be much easier if we point out from the beginning, 'Hey, could you lift the rhythm guitars?' 'Yeah, that's fine.' That's the way we did it. We started getting involved. Then when Mercy stopped and Diamond started, we were full-time part of mixing *Fatal Portrait* and *Abigail*."

"But it was the same feeling we had on the *Melissa* album. You're outside, and then you come in and say, 'More guitars, more guitars in the middle,' 'Okay, go outside, we'll do a new mix; Okay, come in now.' During *Don't Break the Oath* I said, 'You know what? I don't fucking care. I'm going to stay here whatever you say. I want to hear you make the changes. This is a waste of time going out, coming back, and I still don't hear the right thing. I'm going to sit here and you jerk the levels this way and that and we'll go, 'There, that sounds really good. How about that? That will save some time.' 'Well, okay, just don't sit here.' 'No, no, we'll sit back there.' 'Okay.' Then we finally got an idea of what goes on in the mixing process. The same thing, it was hard to hear the keyboards. We had this keyboard player coming in who played for us, and there we sat and directed, 'Oh, okay, can you make it a little darker? It's got to be darker,' this and that. But to be part of the levels at least, that was a very important difference between *Don't Break the Oath* and *Melissa*."

Michael isn't too sure all the problems were rectified, figuring that, "The only thing we did by mistake, is when we did *Don't Break the Oath*, we did it with this guy who was used to doing pop music, and he was a big name in Denmark at that time and it didn't work out the way we hoped it would. But even to this day, even with the weak guitar sound and shit, they still stand strong, these albums.

But on the second one there are too many effects on the guitar sound. It's a bit thin in places. I would sure love to go in and remix it, to give more beef to the rhythm guitar sound and remove some of the effects, which are outdated in my book. But then again, like I say, they stand strong to this day, these albums. So, I just prefer to be happy with what we did and not concentrate too much on the small errors here and there."

No real problems with the actual recording though. "No, we knew what we wanted," explains Diamond. "He was just going to make sure that what we put down sounded good. That we didn't make something that was totally horrible. 'Oh, you're not quite pitching.' 'What does that mean?' 'Oh, you're not in tune with the music.' 'Oh, okay, well, I'll try it again.' Sometimes it's hard when the headphones are blasting away. Or there's a part with single harmonies. Then it's very hard to put yourself in the right spot. Especially in those days when we didn't have that experience. Now it's a natural thing where the pitch just comes naturally."

"I noticed that, that at one point, we did some shows with Metallica, and one night in Italy, they did the Mercyful Fate medley that they did on *Garage Inc.* They did the whole medley. We rehearsed with them a couple times, backstage, Hank and I, to do that with them. But they de-tuned a little bit and I'm thinking, 'Oh my God, how am I going to get my voice to fit that?' When they played it, I found out it's a natural instinct and I just sung it. It was actually easier to sing those parts because they weren't as high (laughs)."

"But it's totally natural. You just adjust on the spot. I didn't know I had that ability back then. But it was mainly that issue about wanting to be in the control room when the mix goes on. We don't want to go outside and we don't want you to trick us and we come back in and you say, 'Do you hear it louder now?' 'No, it's not going to be like that, because they're still not loud enough.' He goes in increments of half a decibel each time. Who knows when we're going to start hearing the difference? It's a waste of time. Let sit here and be a part of it. We finally got a bit of insight into how to do this."

Once the record was completed but well before its emergence in the shops, the band played the Heavy Sounds festival in Belgium. Taking place June 10th of '84, the show included the likes of Lita Ford, Baron Rojo, Faithful Breath, H-Bomb, Metallica, Twisted Sister and Motörhead. It was very international, and more so given the inclusion of our metal ambassadors from Copenhagen.

Issued September 7th, 1984, *Don't Break the Oath* arrived

wrapped in a lurid yellow album cover, devilish to be sure, but bright to the point of blinding.

Asked where the original painting is (executed once more by Thomas Holm), King says, "Not sure. None of them are on my walls. Usually with the artwork, I guess the artist owns the original, and we get to buy the license in some way, or the label does, to reproduce them. I think that's how it works. These days, it's not like that many artists are sitting with an airbrush anymore. A lot of it is done on computer, right? So, they're using special paint programs where they can insert and add to. But in the old days, I've seen the actual painting of *Don't Break the Oath*. There is a real oil painting. That's the one that was brought up. He had a stack. He had about 20 paintings with him, this Swedish painter. He showed them to us, 'Here they are, here are the choices,' blah blah blah. But that was for the *Melissa* album. *Don't Break the Oath* he did specifically for us. But when we chose *Melissa*, that was one out of a stack of stuff he had. Those are there for real. But I don't even know. Maybe the painting got sold. Or if he didn't sell it, maybe he still has the original somewhere."

Elaborating in conversation with David Perri, King said that, "It's so perfect, and the credit goes to the artist. We knew what cover we needed because the cover had to do with the story that takes place on the album. So, he came down to Copenhagen another time and he showed us some new things he had done. One of them was the *Don't Break the Oath* cover. When we saw that, we were like, 'We're going to take that one for sure.' The cover is like that old World War I poster where Uncle Sam is saying, 'I want you.' It really comes at you in a very unique way (laughs). It's one of my favourites; I think it's very striking."

Past the wrapper, Mercyful Fate's second album opens with "A Dangerous Meeting," instantly giving notice that the guys are still on message lyrically and musically, but that there are to be improvements when it comes to songwriting. Riffs are kept to a minimum and most of them are more effortlessly memorable than those across the expanse of *Melissa*.

Explains King, "There was the band Brats, which turned into Mercyful Fate, and some of those songs were integrated and changed in the rehearsal room. 'A Dangerous Meeting' was called 'Walking Back to Hell' before that and had a few riffs that were different in it. That goes for quite a few of them, that they had different titles."

Diamond displays his full arsenal here, including harmonies

A DANGEROUS MEETING: IN THE SHADOWS WITH MERCYFUL FATE

with himself. "When I do backing vocals," explains King, "I do several sets of backing vocals to create choirs and stuff. I might hold notes different from the lead and then they start vibrating. When I sing the second one, that has to match the first one. I get so close; it's a natural feel. I don't have to think about, okay, I did five quick ones and then I went into the slower ones three times. I just do it and the same thing comes out. It's a natural feel. Actually once—it only happened once—I cancelled it out, my two vocals. Singing a full line, first with one backing vocal and then on the other track, the other one, and playing back, there was nothing because they cancelled each other out. They were identical. But that's only happened once. We had to re-do a perfect take just so we could hear the parts."

Concerning "dangerous meetings," King goes back to the subject of the New York priest who wrote to him. "A lot of the time I think it's for their own self-promoting; that's what I think it comes to. They want to get up in the limelight and be recognised. Because there was a priest in Denmark too, that was after us right in the beginning when we'd only done our demos. The Danish radio wanted to play our demos and it was a great opportunity. The national paper wanted to write about us and they wanted to get us banned, and of course we got mad about that. So that's the reason why the cover on the mini-LP shows a nun getting burned by a coffin. The opposite of what took place during the Inquisition."

"Of course, this priest said fine, let's have a discussion. We got on the radio and we talked and he left in the middle of the whole thing, because we said, 'Well, let's talk about the Inquisition. This is a drawing of what you guys did, or what you guys believe in, for real, to thousands and thousands of people. Don't come here and give me that stuff.' So, he got up and left because there was no defence of his side."

"He brought up 'A Dangerous Meeting.' I said, 'Do you really know what it's about?' It's about a dangerous meeting of young people who at that time I was fixated with doing the Ouija board. I said that can be dangerous because it is real. It can certainly happen. Some of these kids went crazy because they would sit there, ask their little questions, and if there was a power present, could feel that there was lack of respect and would give a couple of right answers and then it would slam a bad one in there. 'You're going to die before you're 20.' You got confirmation of other things and you'd sit with that answer. You're pretty much sure that it's the real thing, and it could just be toying with you. Dangerous stuff to fool around with.

That's what that was: a warning against that."

"So, again, he didn't get his facts. I have to say also, some of the blame is certainly mine for not being that great with the English language in the beginning. Hell, the same subjects in some of the early Mercyful Fate songs, today I would have written them different and smarter, with smarter choice of words and stuff like that. It's almost like you get this cardboard thing and it's right in your face because it's so blatant. But you could write it in a much better way where it could get more of the answers in there that should have been in there. It was black-and-white instead of being what it should have been."

Notes Hank on "A Dangerous Meeting," speaking with Jimmy Kay, "We had to decide which songs should be on side A and on side B, but it was very democratic. So, everyone wrote down on a piece of paper and then we would look at them and combine and see what songs to start side A and side B. I know King really wanted to have 'The Oath' starting on side A, and the rest of the band chose 'A Dangerous Meeting.' So King was a little upset about that, but because since we are a democratic band, he had to give in (laughs)."

Shermann is the writer of this one, and as he says, once he's done, he hands it off for careful handling. "I myself, as the main composer of the songs, as a guitar player, all the rest of the guys were really focusing on performing the songs well and making the musical foundation as good as possible."

An early version of this song exists under the title "Death Kiss." The guys figure it's the first thing they ever recorded. It can be found on the 1992 compilation *Return of the Vampire* as well as the 1997 reissue of *Don't Break the Oath*. The main difference between the two is King's vocal and the lyrics. King is just much more conventional a singer on the early versions, more Glenn Danzig-like on the *Return of the Vampire* take and more punk rock and new wave on the take used as a *Don't Break the Oath* bonus track. What's quite remarkable is how tight the band is, and how the parts are all there—it was perfect to begin with.

An amusing element to "Death Kiss" is how busy drummer Kim Ruzz gets. "The thing is that Kim was all over the place," chuckles Michael. "Sometimes we had to control him a bit and say, 'Hey, don't overdo this,' because he had so much passion and power and energy in him. It was like a Mustang, like a wild horse (laughs). But he played a major part, really; to this day, when I hear the records, I go, 'Wow, what a great drummer he was.' He was a very heavy hitter;

he hit his drums very hard. Kim was a very varied drummer. He could start playing a tango over a very heavy riff. He did whatever he felt like and it worked. He was a brilliant drummer and a very important part of the Mercyful Fate sound, more than people will ever know. There was always a lot of focus, obviously, on King's way of singing and the Satanic lyrics and shit, but then again with me and Hank's signature guitar, the twin leads, and the Kim Ruzz drumming on these albums, that's all very, very important. It's a big reason why the classic albums sounded the way they did."

The falsetto-heavy—or falsetto-light, as it were—"Nightmare" demonstrates the band's ability to swing despite switching up tempos. Notes Kings, "That was a great high point to be able to do more technical things like we did on 'Nightmare,' the fade-down, and the feedback and all this crazy stuff. Things were being done technologically that we never dreamt of doing before. It definitely felt like a step up from *Melissa* production-wise."

"Also, for 'Nightmare,' it was really difficult to write the lyrics in the beginning simply for the fact that the riff is a little bit close for comfort to an old Deep Purple song called 'Flight of the Rat.' It goes along, but then a difference happens. It might be just to the point where you're allowed to do so many segments of this and that, but it could be just a coincidence. You go whoa, that's close. You play it for someone and they go, 'Oh my God, it is! I never heard that thing or paid attention to it.' But that was hard when you have that in your head. Once I knew how Ian Gillan sings that... it was very hard for me to write something different. The end part of the riff was a little different, but I remember that it was hard to write the lyrics for it."

Diamond is being too gratuitous to Blackmore here, because the riff in question is set to a totally different rhythm. As well, it's used merely as set-up or connective tissue to the verse, which, as he says, marks "a difference." But the point is well taken. A crucial piece of the puzzle that the singer has to provide, beyond (usually) lyrics, is a vocal melody, and if you get one stuck in your head courtesy of one of your singing heroes, it can be stumbling block.

At the music end, this one feels a bit like an assembly of parts. "Yes, old songs were split up into different songs, and one of them turned out to be 'Nightmare.' A lot of things happened that way. We were rehearsing four times a week and that's where we developed the whole thing."

Late in the conflagration of chaos, where music and mobs of voices devolve into anarchy, suddenly we hear a horrific admonition from King, who growls, "You're only living on borrowed time." There's an interesting story behind this, the significance of which, as King told Malcolm Dome in 1983, helped turn his soul dark.

"I'm not a member of the Satan coven. But I do pray a little to 'him' back in Denmark. I've got a black altar in my home with two black candles always burning. In the middle of it is a human skull and a gold inverted cross. One important event that got me into this was a dream I had a few years ago. It was rather nasty, actually. I dreamt I saw a big black book with a picture of a strange lady on the back. As I looked, she suddenly came to life! I tried screaming for help to my brother who shared a bedroom with me, but no sound came out. The mysterious lady beckoned me to follow her. I felt compelled to do so. I then found myself in the centre of a coven of 13 hooded, shadowy figures, all of whom are pointing at me saying, 'You're living on borrowed time.' I woke up in a real sweat, I can tell you. It was truly a terrifying nightmare. After that, I began to investigate more deeply into the mystical style of life."

"Desecration of Souls" is another Mercyful classic, built of an insistent and plodding riff placed upon half-time double bass drumming from Ruzz. The opening salvos to the song betray the band's fecund creativity. King, utilising yet another voice as if multiple demons inhabit him, says, "Stay away white magician, young lovers and mourning wife."

Instantly images are conjured and the storyline is set. Next is a variant of the verse riff that includes extra licks that throw off its time. Once the song kicks in, the band strips those out and falls into a rigid and resolute 4/4. As expected, there are eventual prog-minded movements, as well as, from 3:09 to 3:48, a gorgeous lead that sounds like top-shelf Michael Schenker. Then we're back into the crushing and hooky verse, in which King sticks with his sonorous baritone, adding a hint of vocal fry—perhaps this song subconsciously bubbles up in terms of fan rankings because there's less falsetto than usual.

In any event, Hank knew they had a winner on their hands. "I remember with King, we were going to the train station to take a train back to his apartment, and we were talking about 'Desecration of Souls' being really cool stuff, and that we were going to make it. So, we were really convinced we had something good going on. But of course, you never know where the music takes you and how people hear and receive it. Everybody making an album thinks this is the best they've ever heard and 'We are so good,' but you never know how people in the street are going to react to it."

There's an admirable belief there in the power of high-quality art, but it's also laced with naivety. Mercyful Fate's market was always going to be limited, and that's in two departments: lyrical content and vocals, before we even get to talking about the limitations of heavy metal in general. It's almost as if the guys are so amusingly metal that they've been desensitised as to how inaccessible their art was.

At the lyric end, we have to remind ourselves that back in the '80s, whether you were an angry, grave-upsetting, animal-mutilating metal monster or not, chances are there was some religion in your upbringing or at least you were aware at how woven into the societal fabric God was, beginning with reciting "The Lord's Prayer" at school.

If among the bands asking for your dollar, Mercyful Fate didn't at least creep you out, much less scare the bejesus out of you, you were in the minority. Especially if you were in the lower end of the target demographic, mid-teens. Being so oppressively and directly Satanic across most songs (and then still horror-themed on the rest of them) probably took 20% of the band's market away, lopped it right off with a blunt hacksaw.

Then—to reiterate again and again because it's so important—there were King's vocals, specifically and only the falsetto. Point-blank, this was a band with novelty vocals, like Pavlov's Dog, Family, the Bee Gees and Zebra for falsetto, and then a little bit like Motörhead and Venom for gruffness, and then somewhere in the middle, not as insignificant but not flagrant also, like Rush.

I'd say four out of ten prospective fans of Mercyful Fate simply opted out because of King Diamond's falsetto. Let's not forget, singing high was seen as a skill, an admirable trait, as proven by the heavy metal love showered upon Robert Plant, Rob Halford, Bruce Dickinson and Geoff Tate. But a falsetto was seen by many as just dumb. Hell, even the six out of ten metalheads that were on board... I'd venture to say most of those would prefer King not to sing in falsetto.

But Hank's hopes for the band were less rash than, say, if this was Cronos or Mantas anticipating fireplace mantles full of lined-up Grammys. A few steps to the rear of their wacky front man, Mercyful Fate were quietly and studiously crafting heavy metal music that was *objectively* first-rate, written complicated and creative yet still headbang-able, played confidently with chops, recorded with skill and plush production values. Venom, on the other hand, had three strikes against them—vocals and lyrics, yes, but also trashy music—where Mercyful had two, both of which emanated from King Diamond. Is there any surprise that both bands suffered in the marketplace?

Closing side one of the original vinyl is "Night of the Unborn," five minutes of dense progressive extreme metal with falsetto all over the place. At the lyric end, you gotta hand it to King: the guy can write some truly hair-whitening tales. This one celebrates an evening over which the ghosts *of the unborn* will dance and play, in some chapel no less. As bonus, choral accompaniment will be provided by dead boys—who probably sound very much like King Diamond in falsetto. At the close, King asks us to forgive them, for they did not die.

"That was a mix of a lot of riffs and it was a bit hectic," recalls Michael. "Hank would chip in with, 'Yeah, let's go with this one, and I got this one,' and it was just a mixed bag of a lot of riffing. In the end it became a song and it made the album and it worked out perfectly."

One can see why King argued for "The Oath" to open side one of the record. There's an atmospheric introduction of horror music followed by lightning and then... church bells and rain, just like the first song on the first Black Sabbath album so many years ago. Then there's a church organ playing a melody in the tritone, diabolus in musica, followed by a commencement speech, the oath itself, essentially a "Lord's Prayer" but to a different lord. Even the high-quality music, not kicking in until two minutes have passed possesses an air of pronouncement. Another 35 seconds pass before King starts singing, and then we are into another pounding prog metal epic with a dizzying array of parts. The entirety of Kings lyric across the song's 7:31 expanse is a flowery oath of allegiance to Satan point-blank. Again, it's not a warning against evil, it's not a scary story, it's not an allegory, it's straight-up Satanism—and even then, not of a philosophical Anton LaVey life skills sort, but classic aggression toward Christ.

Diamond is the sole composer of this one, lyrics and music, and the evidence mounts with respect to why it would be inevitable that King went solo. He also gets sole credit on "Come to the Sabbath" and shares the music credit on two others with Michael. Bottom line, King's personality and image and philosophy is dominating—not just dominating the band but dominating.

Next is "Gypsy," which shares the top anthemic spot on the

album with "A Dangerous Meeting." The song is three minutes of superlative metal riffing, set to what is almost a disco rhythm from Hansen and Ruzz, who plays eighth notes on the hi-hat, opening and closing it deftly. Half-way through, we are hit with a fresh and almost stadium-rocking riff, which recurs as a bed for the guitar solo, shared by Hank and Michael.

Notes King, "'Gypsy' was written together with Michael Denner, the music, but when a singer is able to write the music as well, usually there you get the most vocal-friendly stuff, where you feel like, 'Put this here, this riff there,' and it gives me more of a good chance to come up with something really special for the vocals."

"The thing is, with 'Gypsy,' King came with the basic riff," recalls Denner. "That was the only thing he had. So, I just took over from there somehow and finished the song, with the B pieces and the solo parts and shit. Then we had the song—boom, it was just there. Same as with 'Nuns Have No Fun.' He came in and he had the idea. I took the idea and we finished the song. We worked it out together. These things happen. Back then, the difference from the *Melissa* album was that Hank did all the songs for that. He did all the riffing, everything. We arranged the songs together, but he did the writing on all of it. *Don't Break the Oath* was a different story, because King had some songs and he was very eager to be able to bring in his own songs and some songs we did together. Plus, some songs were prepared in the rehearsing room, which was exactly the same thing we did with *Fatal Portrait*, the King Diamond album."

The slightly bluesy and psychedelic "Welcome Princes of Hell" comes next, with the band shifting rapidly between parts, King going with heavy reverb on his voice at times. If Sabbath is conjured during the slow bits, the reference is even more apparent when the guys modulate at the 1:45 mark, after transitioning into a mid-paced groove about thirty seconds earlier. This music is the norm for much of the rest of the song, Mercyful happily breaking all the rules of song construction.

Speaking with Jean Ricard of *Metal Forces* in 1988 about this song, King prefaces his comments with, "I am a Satanist. I have been for the past five years. One of the phrases of Satanism is, 'Do what thou wilt and that shall be the whole of the law,' but you can't go and take that the wrong way. That would be insane. You have to choose things that make sense. If I'm coming home from work and I'm in a hurry and I see a red light, I can't just pass because I want to get home. I might hurt someone or even myself. I'd rather be a little late than do that. The big difference between Satanism and religion is that you were not told what to do. There are nine Satanic statements saying what Satan stands for. But it doesn't say you have to do this or we have to do that. Satan is not a guy with pointy ears and a long tail. I don't even like to use 'he' when I speak of Satan. Satan simply stands for the powers of the unknown and that doesn't necessarily have to be evil. I know because I've experienced it. Doors opening and closing, people being touched. People in Mercyful Fate have felt it too. In the song, 'Welcome Princes of Hell,' I was giving respect to those powers, saying you are always welcome in my house."

Not that King had any choice. Re-stating an earlier story, he says, "We'd just come back from recording the very first Mercyful Fate demo, and we had bought lots of beer. We had just poured the first glass and we were discussing whether we should listen to it now or wait until the other guys came. At that point, my brother's glass just rose high into the air. A lot of people might call it mass psychosis, but it wasn't. We weren't even discussing the occult. I thought I was seeing things, but when I saw the other guys' faces, I knew it was real."

So, in the song, King says, "We raise our glasses; welcome to my house, Princes of Hell." Elsewhere, there's the memorable refrain, "I'm alone with my friends!"

"I have had situations where I don't know how I could've gotten out of it, hadn't it been for these powers," continues Diamond. "We almost crashed in our plane the very first time we came to the US as Mercyful Fate. We were supposed to change planes in St. Louis, but there was a big storm. The pilot couldn't go down, so we circled for half an hour. Finally, we had to go down, and we dropped to 150 yards above the ground. It was just like in the movies; everybody screamed and it was really scary. We were still approaching the landing strip when the wind grabbed the plane again and the left wing was only about ten feet off the ground. It was going down, down, down. If it wasn't for the powers making sure the thing stayed the way it was meant to be, I have no doubt that I would've died that night."

"There are some things in the *Bible* that I'll be the first to admit are good," reflects King. "But in my opinion, most of it is for the trashcan. To tell people they are born with sin and born with guilt is absurd. 'You were born a sinner!' That's what it says in the *Bible*. It says you have to fight your way back into the kingdom of Heaven. It's not like that at all. No matter what we do in this life, we all go to the same place, a place I call 'Beyond.'"

"They misprinted the title by the way, on the album. Maybe it's not in the lyrics but it's on the outside or vice versa. There's 'Welcome Princess of Hell.' Totally wrong (laughs). It sounds like a Disney thing. It's 'Welcome Princes of Hell.' That's the real title. That was a nightmare for me to see that."

In fact, it's wrong in the title, and it's even wrong once in the lyrics, but right elsewhere in the lyrics, which flags the error even more so. It's correct (Princes) on the original issue Dutch Roadrunner record label, but it's wrong (Princess) on the green Combat label used for the original US issue. It's also wrong on the Canadian Roadrunner issue.

"But yes, I saw a glass rise up in the air and my brother and our old drummer Kim Ruzz, was there, present," King reiterated to me years later. "That was one of the first things I actually saw with my own eyes with other people present. Which could not be explained whatsoever. We were not drunk and never did drugs. No earthly explanation for it. Many other things like that happened. Little kids' fingerprints high up on a mirror where no kid could ever reach, and no kids in the home whatsoever. Things have been moved the next morning."

"Other people have heard these growling noises in my bathroom. The photographer Ray Palmer who used to do photos for *Kerrang!* spent two nights at the house after we did a photo session. Him and the journalist Malcolm Dome. They both slept in the living room, and in the morning—this was in broad daylight—he came out from there and was white as a sheet. I'm like, 'Oh, you heard growling?' 'What is that?! I want to get out of here now! I'm sorry, I'm sorry, I'm leaving.' I'm like, 'Oh my God, man.' He was like, 'How do you know that?' 'Well, there was a girl once who experienced that thing. She couldn't open the door to my bathroom, even though I could open it from outside. She couldn't open it from inside and this growling was there in her face.' It was during a party, and I heard her in there crying like crazy. I was wondering why she had been in there for half an hour. God, is she sick or something? What's going on? So, I went up to my bathroom, and from outside the door I heard the crying and I said, 'Hey, what's wrong? Are you okay?' '(in a sobbing girl's voice) I can't open the door; he's growling at me!' She's completely out of herself. So, I grabbed the handle and opened the door and I said, 'What's wrong?'"

"And so, the glass swaying in thin air was put right into 'Welcome Princes of Hell,' where I'm singing to these powers in my house. In a choir voice, back to myself, I sing back to myself saying, 'We raise our glasses,' which is totally that. The teacups flying in thin air from King Diamond was also of course from having seen that glass flying in thin air. I was looking at something the other day, this voice that you hear, the steep growling voice on the intro to 'House of God,' it gave me goose bumps when we recorded it because hearing it in these headphones, it was a voice I recognised from my apartment, that I had heard there and then another person had heard too. It's a breathing that you're hearing there and it was like, oh my fucking God. But that was something we did and then it turned out that I suddenly recognised that sound."

Next is a mellow respite called "To One Far Away," which consists of King singing harmonies accompanied by acoustic guitar and gorgeous solo licks reminiscent of Michael Schenker, much of it also harmonic in nature.

"To One Far Away" sets up closing anthem "Come to the Sabbath," which is a raucous double bass drum-driven rocker with—of course—many jagged parts breaking the flow. At the lyric end, the circle remains unbroken, with an extra actionable event at the party featuring a curse upon the priest who murdered Melissa.

"Another classic," says King. "'Come to the Sabbath' was the first song that I wrote for the band. These were written already when we did the *Melissa* album. But at that time, there was also a certain immaturity because it was a struggle to get anything past Hank musically. Which isn't the case anymore. We all grew up and learned things and we have none of the stupid fights anymore in either of the bands. But back then it was, 'Yeah, well, that works pretty well, but I have this song here!' But the way it started was we would play those songs live and people would say, 'God, man, why is that song not out?!' 'Well, it was already written at the time of *Melissa*.' 'No way! You should have put that on the album!?' 'Yeah, well, we didn't.' Then it was like, it had to be there on *Don't Break the Oath*."

This one is another sole King credit, Diamond remarking that, "The ones I wrote were more vocal-friendly, which is natural. Because I wrote them, the music for 'Come to the Sabbath' and 'The Oath.' Because for example 'Night of the Unborn' is quite odd. It's one thing—and it's a negative thing and I shouldn't really say it—but the songs 'Come to the Sabbath' and 'The Oath' were finished and actually played live before we recorded the *Melissa* album. Those could have been taken into consideration at that time. But Hank was very forceful at that time, I remember, of wanting his songs on the album and no one else's (laughs). Simply there was much too good a response to songs like 'The Oath' and 'Come to the Sabbath' that for the second album, everybody in the band said, 'That's enough—the songs are going on the album whether you like it or not. They have been received so well.' So, they came into consideration then, but they were actually written before that."

As good as *Don't Break the Oath* was, it did not break Fate into the mainstream, not that it had much of a chance given how evil it was. Still, the album, issued on Combat in the US, got to "bubbling under" status at No.202, just off the official Billboard chart, which starts at 200.

Reflects Michael, "To me, *Don't Break the Oath* had a lot of good songs but the production… there was something in the sound that I didn't like very much. Personally, I was a better player by that point, but the sound of the album wasn't to my satisfaction. I prefer *Melissa*. That's my favourite album by Mercyful Fate, all the way. Because four or five of my favourite songs are on that one, including 'Satan's Fall,' 'Evil,' 'Black Funeral'… yeah. Some of the very best Mercyful Fate songs are on that album. It was a fantastic experience when it came out, a full-length album. We had a lot of good press on it, and people said this is something totally different. So, it was a great pleasure to be part of that album."

He's got a point. There was an effect not unlike the slight drop in excitement level many fans experienced between *Heaven and Hell* and *Mob Rules*, or between *Discipline* and *Beat*. Or mor precipitously, *Back in Black* and *For Those About to Rock*.

Says Hank with respect to the tour dates supporting the album, "We went to the United States in '84 after the release of *Don't Break the Oath* but we didn't actually have that long of a tour. For us, back then, we didn't tour, just concerts now and then, until that U.S. tour in '84. Up until then the longest is probably the Italian tour in '84."

The first show in the States took place in Portland, Oregon on October 20th, 1984, after which the band played fairly intensively through to a December 16th closing show in Providence, Rhode Island. Part of this was on their own in clubs, part of it in theatres with Motörhead.

"Yeah, exactly," says Hank. "That was when Wurzel and Phil Campbell were in the band, I think. Also, Philthy Animal and Lemmy of course. We did one month with them and then we continued ourselves, for about another month on our own. That was like, wow!

That was many weeks away from home. I remember I got a teddy bear in San Francisco (laughs). That was in a signing session. A girl said, 'Hey, have a teddy bear.' I got a couple of those on the tour. But yeah, people maybe give you an upside-down cross. Especially for King, King gets a lot of strange stuff on tour, with occult themes. The weirdest thing I probably remember is a stick, a cane, with a shrunken head as the handle. I think he got that from a person in Toronto or Montreal. He now uses that as part of the show, especially as King Diamond. It looked expensive. But I mostly get the teddy bears (laughs)."

"It was a great pleasure to play with Motörhead the first time, because we were green," laughs Michael. "We came from Denmark, one of the smallest countries in the world, and suddenly we were on a massive US tour with Motörhead, so that was really something. They were crazy, but cool. No problem whatsoever. Of course, we had to respect that they were headlining and we were nothing compared to them. But it was a great pleasure. If I must say, one special concert for me with another band, although this was years later, was when we played Copenhagen, a big rock festival for nearly 30,000 people, with Metallica as headliners. Because with these guys, it's family. Such close friends. We formed so close to the same time. Lars called me immediately when he heard about the tour. He said, 'We'll clear a spot for you guys. You must come out and play with us.' That nearly brought us to tears. They remembered that before they made *Ride the Lightning*, they used our rehearsing room, and they paid it back, just like that. That's serious friendship (laughs). Also, Lars played on the comeback album. He had been on a long tour and he needed a vacation and he spent his first vacation days going to Dallas and recording with us—that's friendship."

As King told me, "Motörhead was headlining, and Exciter was there. Motörhead with Mercyful Fate and Exciter opening up. Then also we did our own leg in the US after that tour finished. I can't remember if we had different support acts or one act travelling with us. That's possible."

There was pushback in the US, however, concerning the band's overt Satanism. As reported in the *Pittsburgh Post-Gazette*, December 5, 1984, "'Mercyful Fate has been taken off the show,' (promoter) DiCesare-Engler's Ed Traversari said yesterday morning. 'We discussed it yesterday with their booking agent (Agency Division of New York). We just don't think it's in our best interest to have them in for a concert. We really can't discuss why until we discuss it with our attorneys.'"

A DANGEROUS MEETING: IN THE SHADOWS WITH MERCYFUL FATE

The piece continues, explaining that, "According to Mercyful Fate representatives reached in Milwaukee, where the band played last night, the reason why was made quite clear to them. 'They told us we had Satanic content,' Mercyful Fate road manager Hans Castensmith said, 'That breaches freedom of religion, freedom of speech, you name it. We may have more graphic satanic content than some bands, but satanic content is satanic content.' 'I'm really surprised,' lead singer King Diamond said. 'I don't feel I've preached Satanism in our songs. I don't feel we're any different than, say, Iron Maiden. We're just entertainers there to have a good time and give a good time.'"

The following day, *The Evening Sun* reported on the same cancellation. "'My lyrics are pure fantasy and imagination,' said Diamond, who dresses in Satanic garb for most of the group's concerts. Mystery has always fascinated me, so that's what I write about. So does Black Sabbath. Because I'm so interested in the mysterious, it makes it easy to write lyrics about it.' Jane Wartoke of the Wartoke Agency, the group's New York publicity firm, said the cancellation is the first on Mercyful Fate's current 21-city tour. 'We're stunned, and we think it's funny that in this day and age that a rock 'n' roll group could be banned on philosophical grounds. We've had no trouble with Mercyful Fate in any other city.'"

With respect to what has to happen to bring the character of King Diamond to the stage, King qualifies that, "It's not really a ritual, but it's something that has turned into a necessary ritual (laughs). First of all, I've always had a horrible time trying to sleep on something that is moving, be it airplanes or buses or whatever. Because of that it's hard to get the amount of sleep I need on tour. We travel so much and it's hard to get that sleep. I seem to need at least five hours. Another thing is that I stay away from alcohol completely. I hate waking up in the morning and going, 'Bleeechhh!' (laughs)."

"You have to take care of yourself and try not to get sick. Usually somebody on the tour gets sick. If there's a party on the bus of 12 to 15 people, and they're in contact with so many other people throughout the tour, if one of them gets sick, then two or three others get sick and pretty soon half the bus is coughing and taking medicine and all that stuff. When you're in that confined area, usually you will get it—you're on the bus together for six or eight hours."

"But I'm usually one of the last to get it because I have a pretty strong immune system. But the result of that is that I spend most of my time on tour just conserving my strength. You get to the next city about two or three in the afternoon and I will usually go straight to bed until show time. Maybe I will get dinner, or maybe that will have to wait until after the show at two or three in the morning. But I put that makeup on and I do the show and after the show it's a matter of really taking care of yourself. You're sweating from all those lights and all that moving around. You step out of that club and even on a warm summer evening it's like standing in front of a fridge. So, I try to get back to that hotel quickly to try and not catch a stupid cold. It's a matter of getting that makeup off as quick as you can."

"But it's a strange phenomenon when that makeup goes on," muses King. "Because it does take an hour-and-a-half. That procedure is like... I just get so anxious to go do the show the more I put on. Because as you see, I don't have a lot of fun on tour. The other guys, they have a beer and have some fun, but I have to go back as quickly as I can and try to grab those couple hours of sleep. That's a matter of having respect for the fans, it really is. Sometimes it looks like it isn't because I don't hang around after the show. If there's five people, no problem. I will sign autographs because it is quick and I still have that time off before I get all sweated-down. But if there are more people, you feel like a real asshole because you have to go to that hotel now to stay healthy for tomorrow and the next day and the next day because there are other people coming to see you do your best."

"And if you stay out there, you can catch a cold so easily. I just can't change a vocal cord like others can change a string. That's why it becomes a matter of actually having respect for the fans and saying, well, if I want to go off drinking and all that shit, I can do it when I'm off tour. But I have to figure that the hour-and-a-half on stage makes up for all the other bullshit. It *is* bullshit, believe me. It's not fun to ride a bus for six or eight hours every day and wake up in a different bed every day.'

All eyes were on King during these 1984 dates, quite naturally, given the psychic storm he was whipping up, here to be witnessed for the very first time in the US, to shocked metalheads right across the country from west to east.

"King was the guy who was the front figure," says Hank, adamant in his understanding of what was happening. "With the painted face and all these props on stage, he was in charge of all that Satanic stuff, and also with the lyrics. We were young guys, 25 years old, we didn't think too deeply into it—it was entertainment. But apparently back in the days, '83, '84, they hadn't seen anything that graphic before. When we started to burn crosses with real fire on stage, that would never happen today. But back in the day, the first time the audience saw that, they were mesmerised. Oh, my goodness. That's part of going in to see a horror movie. You expect to be scared, so maybe, going to a concert and having that there, that fear and at the same time, here's some cool, rocking metal… that's a cool combination."

4.

"Satan's Fall"
KING DIAMOND GOES SOLO

Perhaps the writing was on the wall for Mercy to be no more when back in 1983 King told Malcolm Dome, "I do feel at the moment there are two separate camps in the band—myself and the other guys. To be frank, I'd very much like to see the rest of them taking a greater role. I've done my best to encourage this. On stage, for instance, when, say, Michael is doing a guitar solo, I move out of the way and beckon him forward to take the limelight. But he's not got the personality to carry it off. He really just stands there and plays rather than trying to project to the fans as a guitar hero. So, inevitably, the kids turn back to watching me."

"The same is true of Hank," continued Diamond, seemingly bent on sending a message. "They're great musicians, but don't have any aspirations towards becoming public stars. Don't get me wrong, they have ambition enough and all of us in the band dearly want to become recognised as the best around. I know that however good I might become as a vocalist, I'll never be satisfied, even if I become regarded as the best heavy metal singer in the world. The rest of the band feel the same way. But it must be very hard for them to prance around trying to pose alongside me. You see, because of my makeup, I can get away with a lot of things that the other guys can't. So maybe this holds them back a little bit. Before they seemed quite happy to have me as the front man. Hank even went so far as to suggest that my face alone should appear on the cover of *Melissa*. I had to talk him out of it. Still, at the present time, we've all got the same goal, making this band big."

Said Michael, seemingly relinquishing any hold he had on the reins, "I used to write songs in my old band, but King is so much better than I am when it comes to penning songs that I'm quite happy to leave it to him entirely. I think this goes for the rest of the band too. Of course, I would occasionally like to see a song not about Satan included in our set. But I enjoy the music we play, so I'm happy to keep going along with what we're doing."

"Everyone gets the idea that as I'm the only one in the band with an interest in the occult, I'm forcing the rest of them to accept it," continued Diamond. "But that's not quite the case. I know Kim and Hank have an interest in this side of things. Both Michael plus Timmy have had strange experiences in my flat which have convinced them there's more to life than meets the eye. I can only write about what grips me and that happens to be Satanism. I couldn't bring myself to do a song about love or the highway. It would be false. Of course, I know sooner or later we'll have to broaden our appeal and probably I'll start soon to write songs that don't mention Satan, although they'll still deal with the nastier side of life, such as nightmares."

Nightmares. Reminds me of the guy who got King into this predicament in the first place. Almost exactly ten years earlier, Alice Cooper broke with his band and went solo and got more theatrical and conceptual with a record called *Welcome to My Nightmare* plus the attendant wildly expensive tour in lavish presentation thereof.

Among the many cited reasons for the split with his band, who had been with him since high school, was the desire to get even more into the character fronting the whole thing than had occurred before. Somewhat unreliably, Alice said Dennis, Michael and Neal (and Glen when awake) wanted to just get on stage in jeans and play and maybe cut back on the show to save some scratch.

Alice and manager Shep Gordon wanted to hit the visuals even harder, according to Cooper. Unspoken was the fact that Alice would keep much more of the money by going solo. One member of the band once called Alice Cooper, namely Vincent Furnier, around this time quietly had his name legally changed to... Alice Cooper.

In Mercyful's case, there wasn't much money, but that didn't mean that everybody didn't think there wouldn't be soon. Here the extra dynamic was that King wanted to write more of the music, along with the above stated things he saw as issues. Something somewhat similar was that the press focus experienced by King and Alice far outweighed that of the rest of the band. Both of them slowly cottoned onto the fact that they were already solo artists anyway, so why not take that extra step?

There's more. As King told me in 2007, there arose a major issue with Hank's writing.

"Well, yes, that was the whole problem. *Don't Break the Oath* was out and we toured the US and everything was going really well. But it was during that time where I think it was more like in his personal life that things started changing, and that reflected onto the music. I'm sure Hank would be the first to admit that that's what happened there. 'I lost my way for a while.' That's the way he put it to me. Then he found his way again."

"But he started hanging out in the nightclubs in Denmark, and a lot of these nightclubs had this disco funk music playing all the time. The circle of friends he was in at that time listened to that style of music, so it became less listening to metal, and suddenly these influences were brought into his new writing. I remember it very clearly. We were sitting in my apartment at that time, we were bringing our tapes, our demo ideas, riffs, songs, and he brought something and he put it on. He was a prankster in many ways and we thought it was a prank. We literally thought it was a joke. There was nothing I would call heavy in it whatsoever. It was like funk, mainly funk, pub-ish funk, like, Mother's Finest. Not when they played any of the heavy stuff, but their funky stuff. There was guitar with a little distortion on it, but funk notes. That was the style. It was very party-oriented, very soft rock, maybe mixed with some funk stuff. It was shocking and had nothing to do with Mercyful Fate."

"We were like, you must be fucking joking! When we found out he was serious... okay, that's not going to happen. If that's the style, I'm gone. I ended up leaving the band. I went solo. But he was serious. His suggestion was that we would have one side of his writing and Denner and I would write for the other side. That's not the development of the band. It might as well be... you may as well ask the fans to come stand down in front of our balcony and piss down on us. It was the most disrespectful thing to do to the fans, I thought. If that's the style you want to play, go start your own thing, play that way, and at least then we were honest to ourselves and our fans. That's exactly what ended up happening. We decided to each go our way and do our own thing. Under different names."

"It came pretty naturally," reflects Hank. "I knew that he actually had these other plans. But when he called me and said, 'I'm leaving the band and we're splitting,' I said, 'Fine,' because at that time, I was fed up with it because we had been doing it for about four years, that style of songs. I said okay, cool, and then I think three days later I had new musicians to form this band called Fate. Then within those months we got a recording agreement with EMI in Europe. So, I just went on to a level and style that was influenced by Europe and Bon Jovi. But there's a little more to it. It's something with strategy. That was his strategy, to bypass certain persons. So that's the strategy behind it. But that's not something we go out and say in the press. He said a lot of things that I don't want to put other stupid words out on it. Basically, it was misunderstandings and musical differences."

With a few more years' reflection, speaking with Jimmy Kay in 2016, Hank framed it this way. "King had crafted a plan, he wanted to go off on his own, meaning that he could use all his own ideas in recording and his mission of maybe doing big concert albums and stuff. So, everything was planned. Apparently he didn't see that with me on board. So, the way to get around that is to leave Mercyful Fate and basically split up the band. Then invite Michael and Timi back into his new band. Then he could start from scratch and build it up around his musical ideas and his vision. I think he didn't feel that he could reach the goal with me on board for some reason. Some say it was something to do with the clothing. Someone said I had presented some more pop metal songs, which is certainly not true. I think it was a very brave move, because it could've failed drastically. They're a really cool band, Mercyful Fate, three successful albums done, and then suddenly comes the break."

Back when memories were still fresh, in 1986, King spilled the beans to Bernard Doe about the split, indeed starting with "the clothing." "The main reason was because of one of the guitarists, Hank Shermann. We toured the States in '84 for two months, and the way he was dressing up just wasn't fitting into the band. He was wearing pink jogging suits and short trousers. Also, he didn't want to do in-stores or interviews and we were just growing apart. He just did not have the right professional attitude."

Not the first time this type of thing caused friction in heavy metal: Ritchie Blackmore grinned and bared it while Graham Bonnet looked suave. More recently to our story, after 1983's *Another Perfect Day*, Lemmy had to take the bull by the horns and kick Brian Robertson out of Motörhead, making the exact same complaint King is bringing up here—right down to the shorts.

"He certainly wasn't improving as a heavy metal guitarist as he had no influence," groused Diamond. "You have to listen to other bands to be influenced. A lot of people say that they are original and not influenced by anybody, but everybody is influenced in some way by the music that they listen to. So, Hank was listening to funk and there was no way he could keep up his speed or techniques from the old days. It even showed up live onstage when he used to go into his guitar solos. I had to actually pull him to one side and tell him not to play those funky riffs during his solo, because I could see the faces of the audience who were wondering what the hell he was doing."

"So musical differences was the main reason. I can listen to the poppier stuff—I listen to all types of music—but I don't like to play it. Hank wanted the next Mercyful Fate album to have some more pop-orientated/commercial tracks and thought it would make a great mixture with the normal heavier Mercyful Fate material. But I said no way; it would have been ridiculous to release an album with two such contrasting styles of music."

"So eventually I could see no alternative but to leave. I left Mercyful Fate on the 11th of April 1985, the day after we had played at the Saga in Copenhagen. I rang the other guys up and told them of my decision, and that was the end of Mercyful Fate. Hank and I are still good friends. We see each other and there are no problems, and he's now playing the music he wants to play, so he's happy. He actually told us after the split that he'd been playing in Mercyful Fate for the last year only because he thought there would be some money in it; he didn't feel anything for the music anymore."

King then makes the point Michael would later cite concerning the band's recording deal.

"As a band we wanted a better record contract than Mercyful Fate had. I'm not saying before that we had a poor contract, but it was only average and we wanted something better. We basically changed the name so we could start new negotiations with Roadrunner Records and we now have a lot better deal; all the percentages and advances were raised, so we're pretty content now."

Asked by Doe about Hank calling his band Fate, King says, "It's stupid. I feel sorry for him. At first, he wanted to keep the complete name, Mercyful Fate, but we forbid that, because people would have thought that it was the old band and musically Hank's band is completely different. What's more, the new King Diamond will still be playing a lot of the old Mercyful Fate material when we go on tour. So, this would have resulted in a lot of confusion."

"But even calling the band Fate is stupid because on one side you will have old Mercyful Fate fans buying the album who are gonna be disappointed with the more commercial approach that Hank is taking, and on the other side there's the people who Hank is trying to reach with his new style, who will ignore the band because they know that it features the old guitarist from Mercyful Fate, who they didn't like before anyway. So, Hank is standing in the middle of nowhere really." As for Hank's contract... "It's not really a good deal because EMI Denmark have no power abroad whatsoever, and Hank's discovered that out very quickly."

"It was mainly between King and Hank," adds Michael, "I was stuck in the middle of these two guys. It was terrible for me, because Hank continued with Fate. He called me and said, 'Would you join?' I said, 'I have to think about this.' Maybe four hours later, King called and asked the same question, man. These were two of my closest friends! Can you imagine how hard a thing that was? Then I had to take the decision. I sat down and listened to the stuff King made and Hank made, and I said to myself, okay, like, I'm a melodic player, so for that, it could be nice playing with Hank because it's melodic stuff. But deep in my heart, my taste is heavy rock. So, I chose King. Hank was fed up with the heavy music. He was fed up with Satanism, studs and leather, all this—he was so tired of it. Because he had been playing that since '77 or something like that. He needed a change, to do something else."

"King was eager to get a better contract and have more control of the songwriting because Hank and I, we controlled quite a lot, especially the way we did the *Melissa* album. Hank wrote all the music for that album. I knew King had some songs that he would like to bring in. He was able to do that on *Don't Break the Oath*, and we also did something together—the song 'Gypsy' was one song I did with King. But he wanted more space as a writer, and the only thing that he could do was to form his own band, King Diamond, the King Diamond band. Hank was fed up. He was tired of playing heavy, so he did this more radio-orientated rock band called Fate and continued under that moniker."

Michael did in fact play some uncredited guitar on the 1985 record *Fate*. Hank quickly followed his debut up in the fall of 1986 with *A Matter of Attitude*, both records recorded at Mercyful haunt, Easy Sound. Both albums are solid hair metal affairs and were issued in North America, and on a major label to boot, which is a step up the ladder past both Mercyful and King Diamond as a solo act.

Cruisin' for a Bruisin' was issued in 1988 followed by *Scratch 'n' Sniff* in 1990, but neither in North America. After putting Fate aside for most of the '90s—because Hank was back in business with Mercyful Fate—he returned with three more Fate studio albums in the 2000s.

Of the set, *A Matter of Attitude* got the most exposure in North America, being well distributed by Capitol. Like the debut, Hank was joined by Jeff "Lox" Limbo on vocals, Bob Lance on drums and Pete Steiner on bass and keyboards, with Steiner writing most of the material. There were two singles, "Won't Stop" and "Summerlove," both written by Steiner.

As *M&M* magazine reported, as part of a spread on Scandinavian rock, "It is a very well-known fact that the Scandinavian market is open to hard rock; touring bands find easy audiences and hard rock albums are healthy sellers. Fate comes from Denmark and is fronted by former Mercyful Fate guitarist Hank Shermann. *M&M* is quite impressed by the band's sound and impact: although employing hard rock idioms, the band's melodic stance definitely pays off with a balanced package of strong pop hooks and blasting rhythms. If Europe can do the trick, Fate can even do it better!"

True to Michael's decision, Denner found himself in the King Diamond band, and, ironically, with a full slate of duties.

"King called me up and he said, 'Michael, I need you in my band. You will be part of the decisions and you'll help me to find players for the band.' I found Mikkey Dee for him. He's doing fine now, but way back then, Mikkey was a complete unknown, a Swedish guy who came to Copenhagen to try his luck. King let me decide guitarists and who's going to play drums, who's going to be in the band. Timi was the easiest part, just politics. 'Are you interested in joining King and I?' He said, 'Of course,' and he was the bass player. So, I was also part of the production of *Fatal Portrait*, and we wrote songs together and arranged songs together. Of course, King was the front man, but I was the guy behind him who conducted the orchestra, hiding behind the star (laughs)."

5.
IN THE SHADOWS
"GOD DAMN, THIS IS GENUINE MERCYFUL FATE, MAN."

Then just like that, Mercyful Fate was no more. Michael had moved on with King, being on board for 1986's *Fatal Portrait* and *Abigail* the following year, before re-entering obscurity along with the other Mercy musicians.

King on the other hand thrived, at least as what they call a working musician, a man with a career, just not a particular rock starry one, good for 50,000 records sold in the US each time out and, unsurprisingly, considerable notoriety. *"Them"* emerged in 1988, followed by *Conspiracy* the next year and *The Eye* the year after that. King Diamond was now a walking cartoon character—or at least some character, a brand—like Lemmy and Ozzy. Like the Ramones.

The big one was concept record *Abigail*, which has now sold over 175,000 copies in the US. Wrote Andy Secher from *Hit Parader*, in his review of the album, "King Diamond has always been one of the most bizarre figures on the heavy metal scene, and on his latest LP, *Abigail*, the King plays his dark, demonic brand of rock to the hilt. Such songs as 'Funeral,' 'A Mansion in Darkness' and 'Black Horsemen' drip with devilish imagery and haunted posturing. But instead of coming off as cheaply constructed ditties—like much of this brand of black metal does—King Diamond has constructed an album of power, passion, and conviction."

Explained King, in the following month's issue of the same magazine, "There is a dark side within all of us, and I want to explore that in my music. People have developed misconceptions about Satan and what anti-Christian beliefs are. There's nothing inherently right about God and wrong about Satan; they both exist in all of us. I have studied Satanic principles extensively and understand the good and bad points of that approach. It's not something to be dabbled with casually, for the dark forces can be very dangerous. But when understood and controlled, those forces can be used to create many mystical and wonderful things."

"I decided that if I ever wanted to get my music across to the rock masses, I'd have to change my approach a little," continued King. "The newer music, as reflected on *Portrait* and *Abigail*, is certainly just as powerful as anything I ever did with Mercyful Fate, but it's much more accessible. There's a much stronger emphasis on the occult and on horror with the religious references more heavily draped within the lyrics. They're still there, but you have to search for them a bit. My environment needs to coincide with the music I write. On *Abigail*, for instance, the idea for the album came to me late at night on an incredibly nasty evening with storms and thunder everywhere. The whole album came to me in half an hour; a truly amazing experience for me. It was as if some greater force was guiding me—and perhaps it was."

He closed by promising, "We're bringing over our full stage production this time. On our past US tours we were never able to do that because of the size of the places we were playing. But now we want no limitations. I believe so strongly in the material we are performing that I want to give the fans the full visual effect of the show as well. When they see what we're doing, they may not believe it. It truly goes to another dimension. I'm out to scare some people, turn on others. With this show there's something for everyone."

Up into 1990, King had to respond to a legal trouble from Gene Simmons. "I hope everyone is aware that he actually tried to sue me in an attempt to make me stop wearing my makeup," said King, speaking with Andy Secher. "Isn't that unbelievable? First off, he doesn't wear makeup anymore. Second, if the truth be known, if Simmons wanted to sue me, Alice Cooper should sue him! He wasn't the first rock 'n' roller to wear makeup. The makeup I wear puts me into the character I assume when I'm onstage. It's obviously an extension of my own personality."

"But I do admit that on *Conspiracy* l am playing a character, much like an actor would," continues King. "The music, the story and the persona I project are all very real. King Diamond is the one who understands the occult and brings many of those elements, but on *"Them"* and on *Conspiracy*, I've written albums that are complete dramas—a fact that truly comes to life when you see that stage production. In that capacity, I am playing a role."

On June 24th, 1987, Roadrunner issued an archival Mercyful Fate album called *The Beginning*. This consisted of the four tracks comprising the swell *Nuns Have No Fun* EP along with performances of "Curse of the Pharaohs," "Evil" and "Satan's Fall" from *The Friday Rock Show*, recorded at the BBC Studios on March 19th, 1983 and non-LP B-side "Black Masses," recorded July 19th, 1983, during the *Melissa* sessions. The early version of "Black Funeral" from Ebony's *Metallic Storm* compilation was added when the album was remastered and reissued in 1997.

Five years later, Roadrunner reminded us once again of King's old band with two further compilations. *A Dangerous Meeting* offered 79 minutes of music consisting of seven Mercyful Fate songs and nine King Diamond selections.

Return of the Vampire, issued May 12th, 1992, was a little more interesting, offering rare early-days recordings. From the summer of '81, from Brenner Studio in Copenhagen, we have "Leave My Soul Alone" and "M.D.A. (Mission: Destroy Aliens)," from Michael Denner's three-piece band previous to Mercyful.

As King explains, he and Hank were brought in to help out on the sessions, with King penning lyrics in a few hours and providing the vocal for "Leave My Soul Alone," and just singing Michael's lyrics on "M.D.A." So this is half Mercyful, half Michael and his band. Both are solid heavy metal rockers and both are recorded quite acceptably, with "M.D.A" evoking Iron Maiden, both with its mellow intro as well as its fast-paced eventuality—even though it's about the video game Space Invaders! King sings these more traditionally, not using his later developing arsenal of growls and falsettos, which just underscores what a killer natural singing voice he has.

Non-LP B-side "Black Masses" shows up in its original demo form called "You Asked for It." King says that the band didn't have Timi Hansen yet, so this features Hank on bass. The awkward-of-title "On a Night of Full Moon," recorded late 1981, is the original version of "Desecration of Souls," while "Death Kiss," recorded in Hull, England in the Spring of '82, is an early version of "A Dangerous Meeting." King says that the band found themselves inspired by the fact that they were staying in a "cold little hotel" that was across from a graveyard.

"There *was* a cemetery," recalls Hank. "The police really came around, though they didn't catch us. It was a very big cemetery, opposite our hotel in Hull and we just ran around, not doing anything criminal, mind you, but just getting inspiration. Then we saw the police and the police saw us because it was in the middle of the night; you're not supposed to walk around there, five long-haired guys. They tried to catch us and we ran away across the graves. We got safely back to the hotel."

"On a Night of Full Moon" is notable for the halting, busy drumming from Kim Ruzz as well as the extra melodic intrigue at the chorus. As well, there's just something more vital about Mercyful Fate in demo form. You can hear the excitement of these players live as it reveals itself, as they work through the track illuminated by just how creative and how knowledgeable about heavy metal they are.

Explains King in the liner notes about "A Corpse Without Soul," the song was supposed to be ten minutes long, and on one final attempt to get all the way through it without a mistake, the guys finally succeeded, only to find out that the engineer had run out of tape. Hence the song rings it at an abbreviated 8:11, still longer than the version on the self-titled EP, which clocks in at just under seven minutes.

Rounding out, there's "Burning the Cross," music by early days guitarist Benny Petersen, plus "Curse of the Pharaohs" and "Return of the Vampire," all from those late 1981 sessions at Kharma Studios in Copenhagen. "Burning the Cross" is the record's gem, being full-on swaggering Mercyful, speedy, many parts, huge guitar sound, killer accomplished vocals from King, who intimates that the song never made it onto a record due to Petersen's exit from the band. "Return of the Vampire" is somewhat amusing but not without charm—the vampire will return yet again in 1993, re-recorded by a reunited Mercyful Fate, with someone called Lars Ulrich sitting in on drums.

Mercyful Fate 2.0 would come at the behest of Metal Blade Records head honcho and buddy of Lars, Brian Slagel, a long-time fan of the band and all-round super knowledgeable dude about metal.

Notes Brian's right-hand man Mike Faley on King, "Ever since we've had him, he's always been the consummate professional. He goes out there and puts together a No.1 show, delivers great records—I can't say enough good about the man. There's never anything weird. The guy just knows his marketplace, he knows his fans, knows his music and how he wants to present it, has a vision and this deal allows him to realise those dreams. But I've never had one problem with him on any kind of level. I have nothing but respect for him. I remember Mercyful Fate headlined one time at the Dynamo in Holland and it was unbelievable. This was 70,000 people, and when he comes onstage, it was ironic, because at one part a storm broke out, and backstage it was raining, yet onstage and out front it was sunny. It was almost like it was split right where the stage was, and as soon as he had hit the stage. It was raining backstage but not an ounce of rain out on the audience."

Adds EJ Johantgen, also with Metal Blade at the time but now long-time head of Prosthetic Records, "For a Satanist, he's one of the nicest artists I've ever dealt with. Believe it or not, him and Cannibal Corpse were nothing but a pleasure to deal with. King is a professional, and you just want to do whatever you can for the guy. He's smart, professional, just cool as hell. The guy, he's a Satanist! But like, super kind and super cool. The Cannibal Corpse guys, they're legends; they have every right to have an ego and they don't. King has an ego, but you have to. But these people have every right to be a diva, so to speak, and he's not. That guy is unbelievable. I've dealt with bands on other labels that sell two records and they have the ego from hell and then you have King who is a mainstay and people worship the guy. He's a cult and he's truly amazing—fucking amazing."

Then there's Metal Blade exec Mike Rittberg, who recalls that, "The thing that struck me the most is that when we put out the first reunion record, when I got to spend time with him, all the time I ever spent with him was him without his makeup, sitting around playing Sega soccer or something. Anytime you were with him before he went onstage, he had his makeup on. After a while I was laughing with him, 'Can you just take the makeup off?' Because you got so used to seeing somebody as the person they were, in terms of a smart and intelligent person, and then you watched him in makeup. It was a very strange thing. Or when you sat down and had a conversation with him about his beliefs and you say the words 'Satanic' to people and they freak out. He was more operating on the system of trying to be a good person versus being right or wrong or burning someone at the stake or sacrificing a goat. But I remember being in the studio with him and between takes he was literally playing video games. You normally think about something like that with bands with 18- or 20-years-olds."

The lineup for the reunion record would be resoundingly valid. There'd be King, Hank and Michael and even a returning Timi Hansen on bass. Drums was another matter—a messy one—with Danish unknown Morten Nielsen playing all the drums on the album but being replaced shortly after his work on the record by Snowy Shaw for the tour and even the booklet pictures—the fine print acknowledges Nielsen but most of the art screams Snowy.

Speaking with Borivoj Krgin at the time about the drum slot, King explained that "We never hit it off right with Kim Ruzz personally. He was a great drummer and really worked out great musically, but God, we had so many fights over this and that, personal things. On tours, you don't want to fight over things like who's first in line at Burger King to get his chicken and shit like that. That's not an actual example, but it's those kinds of ridiculous things that you always had to fight with him about. 'I want this, I want that;' egotistical problems. I just didn't want to deal with that shit again, and nobody wanted that, so it was a very easy decision to make."

It's true that Nielsen wasn't a known entity, but he had played with Mercyful offshoot band Zoser Mez. Continued King, "Morten has the same approach as Kim Ruzz in that he has an old-fashioned drumming style, but with a lot of new technique in it. He's also a very nice person. In fact, he's one of these people that you say, 'God, this guy is a little too friendly, isn't he?' He's always in a good mood and he's very easy to approach, so we know that we won't have to deal with the same problems that we had when Kim was in the band. Plus, Hank and Michael have been playing with him for the longest time now, so that makes everything really perfect."

Explained Hank with respect to the reunion rhythm section, "Timi played on *In the Shadows* and *Time* but then left. We knew he'd leave; he has four or five children with different girls and he has a good job, so he's really tied up there, with family and job, and it's very unstable to be in the music business. That doesn't give you any money and he has to support his children and be there for them. So, we already knew he was not going to do any tours and stuff, though he did play the Dynamo Open Air reunion show. Kim Ruzz was never even invited for the reunion because we know we couldn't get along with him on a social level, so we just didn't invite him. He was a postman back then and he's still a postman, and sometimes we see him. He came to the concert we did in Copenhagen in 1984 or 1985 and just said hi—looked the same as always."

With *In the Shadows*, Mercyful Fate found themselves further along the trajectory that revealed itself during *Don't Break the Oath*, namely King being part of the writing of the music only more so.

"Yes, the really big difference is that King started to write a lot of songs," says Michael. "In the old days, there was only room for very few songs by his own hand, because Hank did the main parts of the Mercyful Fate songs. So, this time around we had to make room for King's writing. That changed the whole outcome of it; it became quite different compared to the old days."

Speaking with Vanessa Warwick from MTV at the time, Hank explained that the band had split, "due to musical differences, and then I have been playing in some other bands. I've been playing in Zoser Mez together with Michael, and then we just decided to compose more in a harder way, harder heavy metal. Since we had a one-year break with Zoser Mez, and King Diamond being inactive for three years, it felt very natural to just join the two together again. We have been very good friends and still are, we've had really good relationships with each other. It may be good timing for us, because I feel that the more classic heavy metal is coming back. People want to hear something more melodic, very classic heavy metal instead of just a bunch of energy loading up. But of course, we are loading up a lot of energy with what we do too (laughs). We took up where we left off—same composing style, same type of music—but we have been developing a little more in our technical side."

Further on the timing of the reunion, Shermann told Don Kaye, "It's the same as when we started the first time. Then Priest and Sabbath were struggling against punk. The metal scene was having a hard time. Then it came right back in the early '80s. I think that's exactly what's going to happen again. All the thrash stuff is on a downhill course, and I think we will see that good, classic, heavy rock bands are coming back again, because people want to hear better material. Fans will embrace the new album. It's very similar in songwriting to the feeling of *Don't Break the Oath*, so I think they

A DANGEROUS MEETING: IN THE SHADOWS WITH MERCYFUL FATE

will accept it okay. When we go on stage, we almost look like the same persons, of course! We'll play a lot of the old material. We're even using the amps we used in the '80s!"

A common concern at this time had been the death of traditional heavy metal. With the rise of grunge—most notably Nirvana, Pearl Jam, Soundgarden and Alice in Chains—hair metal had become, seemingly overnight, a source of ridicule, dragging other traditional forms of metal down with it—note that there had not been a King Diamond album since *The Eye*, issued in October of 1990. On a positive note, Metallica and Megadeth were at their commercial peaks and other thrash bands did well in their wake. Death metal was the little engine that could (kill) and black metal was just around the corner. The new "it" band was "a bunch of energy personified"—Pantera had just issued their landmark second major label release *Vulgar Display of Power* the previous year, en route to what would be a whole decade's worth of deserved notoriety.

If these particular musicians were going to stick steadfast to their values in these times and make any waves, they really did need to aim high. Any band called Zoser Mez didn't have a hope in hell, and King as a solo act... it's debatable, but it could be seen that he had flooded the market.

A Mercyful Fate reunion was at least heavy metal news, so it had a fighting chance. Plus, it didn't hurt that long-time fans Metallica, just two days before Warwick talked to the Mercyful guys at the Dynamo festival, had the band open up for them on a Danish date in front of 30,000 fans there to experience metal history in the making. This was an outdoor show, May 28th, 1993, with Mercyful playing in stark daylight. Dynamo, on the 30th, would be Timi Hansen's last show with the band. Despite having to play the all-important Metallica show in a sunny shed environment, the band made the best of it, playing the songs with energy and increased tempos, their all-black attire matching the black amps and various bits of Metallica gear covered in black tarps. Of note, this was Snowy Shaw's first show with the band, followed by Dynamo—quite the two-fisted debut.

Michael Denner agreed with Hank that the band would still be the Mercyful Fate we knew and loved, when we got to hear the new record. "Because we're all friends, it was very easy to get the guys together again, and it's very much the same where we left it with the *Don't Break the Oath* album. It's very much similar to that but with a newer sound and better playing, in my opinion." As for live, Denner told Vanessa, "It's a bit different to the King Diamond project, because that was more like theatre, with actors on stage and stuff. We try to make it more like a classic heavy rock band."

Added Hank on coming full circle, "We had this invitation from Metallica to play in Denmark, when they were playing in Gentofte, and course we said yeah, so that was a really great experience for us. It was the premiere of the comeback with Mercyful Fate, and now we're playing tonight. This was the first country we played in (The Netherlands) when we were playing ten years ago, so this is very much like home, the second home for us. It's great."

Asked by Warwick about coming back into the current radically different heavy metal climate, Hank remarked, "I don't feel like there's a competition. We're just playing our music because we like it. If other people like it, it's good. So, I don't feel any threat, any competing or whatever with bands. That's the more business side of the scene."

In the Shadows was recorded in early 1993 at Dallas Sound Labs in Dallas, Texas, King Diamond's hometown at this point. Metal Blade boss Brian Slagel would be credited as Executive Producer on the album, but as Michael says, "He was just executive, just listed: the executive producer. He had nothing to do with the process. Also, because we never allowed anyone to go in and say, 'I don't like this song or this part.' We had full control over these albums." In any event, Brian would have his hands full running the label on the West Coast. He was known, however, for checking in on the band, physically coming out for visits during the recording process over the years. *In the Shadows* would mark the start of a long relationship, with King recording all his solo albums for Metal Blade from now on as well.

Producing would be local Tim Kimsey, with Hank and King receiving co-credit. "Tim was the engineer on the record," says Michael. "He was a soft-spoken guy from Texas. When I came into the studio, I remember, this guy, he was so like... everything was so relaxed and he was a brilliant technician. What he could do behind the mixer, I would say, wow. He was a completely professional guy. Very soft-spoken, a very nice guy, a guy you would love to work with because he made you relaxed to do your best. 'No worries, Michael, the things you do will be fine.' He said he was like a psychiatrist. He had a very relaxed way. One of the first things he did, we recorded in Dallas Sound, and he said, 'Can you see the spot over there, Michael? This is where Stevie Ray Vaughan did some of his greatest guitar solos, when he recorded the albums here.' He said, 'Go over there and do your solos, man,' and that's what I did, to get some of the spirit from the old master. That was a cool thing to be part of."

"I fell into the whole metal thing back in the early '90s," begins Kimsey, explaining his role. "My wife works for a major label here in Texas, in Dallas, and the band was looking for somebody to help co-produce and certainly engineer the records and my name got brought up. My wife had mentioned to one of her colleagues there at the label, 'Well, my husband's a recording engineer' and the next thing I know I'm getting a phone call from Kim (Tim usually refers to King as Kim, his given first name). Kim is like, 'Hey man, so let's give it a whirl. Let's see how this works out.' We did our thing for about six, six-and-a-half years."

Modest about his official status, Tim says that "Kim, I would say was the producer over all of that and we certainly did things as a collective group. There were certainly discussions as to how the record was going to go, what the idea behind the record was. Lots of discussion about all of that. Then we would get into the technical aspects of it. 'This is how we would like to move forward, how we're going to record stuff, what we're going to start with.' Of course, it always started with the concept of what each record was going to be and I was usually the last one to hear how the album was going to be thought of or what the concept was behind each one of the albums. I was used mainly I think for my engineering skills and the ability to hang in there, because these records would take six to seven months to get recorded and finally mixed and ready for production."

For cover art, the band went with the same Torbjorn Jorgensen/ Studio Dzyan team that had done the first two records and had worked with King Diamond as a solo act as well. Referencing a number of the songs, a girl who we imagine to be Melissa—or possibly Betsy from "the Bell Witch"—ponders an elegantly framed painting called "The Old Oak." As part of the painting, demons swirl through the clouds while "in the shadows" a headless horseman looks on.

In the Shadows, issued June 6th, 1993, opens with a heart-racing double bass-barraged rocker called "Egypt." King makes us right at home by utilising all of his singing styles.

"Amazing, amazing vocalist," muses Kimsey, on his impressions upon hearing King for the first time. "When I first got involved with all of this, it was a little unusual compared to some of this other stuff I had done. I was a pop producer, a pop recording engineer. I had done lots of orchestral stuff prior to all of this. So, let's just say that it was an education for me. One of the things Kim always pointed out, he said, 'It's really easy to sit in a chair somewhere and sing these parts in your head. It's a whole different ball game when you're behind a microphone and having to produce these high, high-pitched vocals.' Not so easy to do it when you're behind a microphone and you need to be absolutely correct on all of that. I always considered myself the guy who could sing in the shower and sing falsetto, but his vocals are amazing, including just the simple fact that he was able to get behind a microphone and pull these high vocals off and come up with these different strategies of how that was going to be done."

"I would consider it a baritone," figures Tim, on King's natural singing voice. "Actually, Kim has got a fairly low voice when he speaks to you. Yeah, I wouldn't say his voice is high-pitched, nowhere close to what he's pulling off with the falsetto. Yeah, I would consider it probably a baritone. We don't do anything special. It's, 'That's the mic—go to it.'"

But there had to be atmosphere. "Yes, Kim was pretty much left alone, lights down low. As a matter of fact, most of the time, I would say lights *out* in the studio. Most of the time he'd like the lights turned down pretty low in the control room as well. I wouldn't say it was dark and eerie, but I would say definitely dark. There were lots of times where all I could see was maybe his eyes. So, it was very personal to him—let him do his thing. If I noticed something that needed to be fixed or something that we might need to address, I would just make mention of it, come up with a plan how we were going to get out and fix it if it needed to be fixed or if it was going to be replaced. You also have to remember that a lot of this was recorded on analogue tape. It's not like today where we can do multiple takes and take the best of all of those. It had to be made right there on the spot as to whether it was going to be the one or you'd have to have a second go at it."

"So yes, there had to be atmosphere, always. But I can definitely tell you this: in the six years that I was around him and around Michael and Hank and just the band in general, we loved to have fun. Although it was down to business every day. In most cases, we were gonna be in the studio 12 to 14 hours a day. But amongst all of that, there was a lot of fun that we had. Lots of back-and-forth with jokes and stuff like that. When it was time to perform, it was time to perform, but otherwise it was light-hearted. It was lots of fun to be around those guys."

Back to "Egypt," we also notice that Kimsey has gotten a killer guitar sound and that the band is brimming with ideas. There's a gorgeous, thoughtful guitar solo over a beat where the snare whacks are on one and three, plus a groovy, in-the-pocket passage where King memorably sings, "I'm burning inside to know." At the close, one hears keyboards and then, amusingly, yet another new musical passage. The Egyptian theme of the lyrics establishes what will be a pattern throughout, namely that the direct Christian Satanic approach of the first two records will not be reprised, replaced instead by a variety of horror tales across disciplines.

Notes Metal Blade's Jon Kornarens on King's widening net of intrigue, "I remember dealing with King and going to his house to talk about doing the video for 'Egypt.' I go into his house and there are black candles and Satanic bibles on his desk and upside-down crosses. That was a little interesting to be there, but he's extremely professional and cooperative and I have to respect him for his professionalism. He broke the story down for me and I went in and did some research. It's basically about him going to sleep and his soul gets taken by the Egyptian underworld. The end of the song basically doesn't tell you which way it went, whether it went up or down in other words. It's left open and we tried to reproduce that on a very low budget but I think we were able to tell the story. There are some hidden things in there for someone who is really watching to pick up on. We weren't able to tell the story so visually because of limited budget, but I didn't want to tell the story too literally either."

Indeed, a proper production video for "Egypt" got done, but unsurprisingly, the song did not become a hit. A promo CD got produced for the track but that's about as far as it went.

Next is "The Bell Witch," which indeed saw commercial release as a single, or at least head rack status on an EP issued fully a year after the album from whence it came, and four months before the band's next album. The EP consisted of this song plus the record's "Is That You, Melissa" (yes, without a question mark), as well as four live tracks recorded on October 3rd, 1993 in LA, namely "Curse of the Pharaohs," "Egypt," "Come to the Sabbath" and "Black Funeral."

The inclusion of "Egypt" can be seen as a second attempt to push this track as a single, third if one recognises its placement as the first song on *In the Shadows*.

"The Bell Witch" has King retelling a popular tale of a purported haunting that had beset a family in Robertson County, Tennessee in 1817, culminating in the death of the family patriarch, John Bell Sr., by poisoning. The music on this one is written by Hank, which is fine as far as Michael is concerned. "There's a big difference, because King did a lot of writing for the reunion albums. That made the change, but I've always been preferring the way Hank Shermann writes songs. It's more riff-oriented and there's more guitar, to my taste. So, *In the Shadows* was a good album."

Adds Hank on the band's approach at this juncture, "It's '70s-inspired heavy metal. We used to get our inspiration from Judas Priest, which you can hear on some of the tracks on the *Melissa* and *Don't Break the Oath* albums. Nowadays it just comes from whatever comes out on the guitar. There is no specific approach. I just keep on going until I'm satisfied. There is this inner barometer—when I feel something is good, then it's good. I never set out to write a song in a certain key. It's more abstract than that. Some riffs are major or minor but it's how you perceive it that's important. There is no serious thought behind it; when you think too much about musical theory, then some songs tend to become predictable. You know which notes will come. This way of writing is probably part of the thing that is Mercyful Fate. As long as we feel the quality is there and everyone is performing okay, we'll continue. Or we might get bored and do other bands, whatever. There is no telling what will happen."

"The Bell Witch" indeed houses many parts that evoke the mighty Judas Priest, including the mid-paced headbanging passages as well as Hank's atmospheric solo, the second to last on the song at around the three-minute mark, set to a mid-paced double bass drum rhythm. Amusingly, King comes in for a brief bit of story wrap-up and we're into yet another guitar solo, this time a more melodic one from Michael, culminating in a dramatic and geometric conclusion to the song.

Further on Priest, Hank says, "That's my favourite band. The songwriting is fantastic and Rob Halford is really great, especially on the albums from the '70s. I like them mostly for the rhythm guitar playing and the songwriting, not for the lead guitars—that's where I like Uli Roth and Michael Schenker more."

Differentiating between the two axemen, Tim says, "I would consider Hank the go-to when it comes to rhythm parts and also, amazing solos and stuff of that nature. Hank was, in my humble opinion, the guy who held down the fort guitar-wise. Michael was more melodic, and the one to say, 'We're going to figure out what the leads are going to be.' He would practice those leads and pretty much verbatim knew exactly which notes he was going to be going to, even if we had to do repeated recordings of the solo. But I'm not saying that Hank was shooting from the hip either; he was well planned out as well. Both of those guys pretty much knew exactly what they were reaching to get. But Michael was more the soloist that really studied the parts. Hank, well, to be blunt about it, he was always in the control room when he wasn't playing with Kim and myself, putting his thoughts into how things were gonna go. I don't speak Danish, but there was a lot of Danish going on between those guys."

"The Old Oak," at 8:53 and hopelessly complex, is this record's "Satan's Fall." A dizzying array of parts confront and confound the listener. Once again, third song in a row, there's double bass drums, but there's also eerie, dissonant acoustic guitar, accompanied by King using a haunting falsetto. It's a progressive metal feast, with 3/4 time signature passages set against 4/4 grooves and other bits where beats are dropped. Six minutes in, new fully developed musical movements arrive and then are dispensed with, replaced by yet more. All told, there's not a lot of falsetto on this one, as King relates the tale of an old hangman's tree where nothing else grows around its poisoned ground. Like the song before it, the end of the song is a maelstrom of heavy metal math.

Reiterating how Diamond had been conjuring material upon new topics, Hank says, "King has definitely changed his words a bit but the subjects are still the same. Maybe he's a little bit milder with his words now, writing in a little different way. But it's about the same subjects, about occult things. It's toned-down, all the Satan, because it gave him too many problems. Back in the '80s it was a good thing because it gave us a lot of attention because nobody knew what Satanism was all about, so it was a big challenge to the reporters. King, Christianity, Satan... all the focus was on King, more on the image than on the music. We care about the lyrics but I'm into the music."

The writing on this one comes from Hank (unsurprising, given how many note-dense riffs there are), with Shermann even quipping that he'd pick this song to be played at his funeral.

Explained King to Don Kaye, "Hank came over from Denmark just before last Christmas to arrange all the songs. I was really... I wouldn't say nervous, but anxious in a way, because you're not really sure what it's gonna be like, working with Hank again after seven years. It was such a big relief to find out that we work better together now than we have ever done in our lives. It was like we had just finished *Don't Break the Oath* a week earlier! 'The Old Oak,' for instance, refers to 'Come to the Sabbath;' this old tree contains tremendous power and has been used as a sacrificial place. It's dark."

"It's 100% Mercyful Fate, minus the word Satan," continued King remarking upon the wider album. "King Diamond and Mercyful Fate are not that far from each other, but there are definitely differences. For the vocals in Mercyful Fate, you might find that I sing a bit more in my normal voice and use the falsettos less. I wouldn't say Mercyful Fate is a heavier band, but it's more straight guitars and it's orchestrated in a different way. It's rawer."

The difference in writing styles between Shermann and Diamond is underscored from "The Old Oak" to the record's next happy selection. "Shadows" is written solely by King and it's about as straight-forward and hooky and groovy as anything on the record, offering essentially two solitudes, a verse and a chorus, all the way up to the minute-and-a-half mark.

A completely diverging break occurs, but then we're back into the song's crushing mid-paced riff and mournful and very melodic chorus. The mid-song soloing—there are a lot of guitar solos on this album—is also performed over a variant of the verse riff but then the guys can't resist: the close of the song features a fast rave of a passage, a blaze toward a punctuated finish.

Explains Michael of "A Gruesome Time," "That was a song I had that was planned for the Zoser Mez album. When King heard the second Zoser Mez album, we were at his apartment having a cup of coffee. We played parts of the second Zoser Mez album that was never released. He said, 'Wow, that sounds like old Mercyful Fate.' Lo and behold, a few months later we reformed Mercyful Fate. So that could've been inspiring him to bring back Mercyful Fate, after he heard the second Zoser Mez recording."

King corroborated this sequence of events, in conversation with Borivoj Krgin back in 1993, remarking that, "Zoser Mez had a lot of heavy ideas, which didn't seem to be possible to put into reality because of the vocalist they had. It's like, 'Hey man, it doesn't fit with that kind of vocals; there's no way.' Because the music was genuine Mercyful Fate stuff. They decided to go in and just to have it, record an instrumental demo of some of the songs without the vocalist. Shortly before I moved to the States in March (1992), I got to hear some of that at Michael Denner's apartment, and I was like, 'God damn, this is genuine Mercyful Fate, man.' It was piercing right through the heart, that old feeling straight back. I said, 'God, man, this is such good material; it would be terrible just to waste it,' you know?"

"Throughout this time, I kept in touch with all the Mercyful Fate members, because we kept seeing each other. We've always been good friends. You go out and you have a few beers and you go, 'Oh God, remember those days?' 'Yeah.' 'Wouldn't it be cool to like reform it?' 'Yeah, sure.' Nothing came of it. Then you suddenly hear this material, which was like, 'Fuck, man.' So, I started talking to all the fans here, when I went out, and I talked to our booking agent and I talked to some radio people. I said, 'What would you feel if we put Mercyful Fate back together and still went on with King Diamond?' People freaked. I only had positive responses regarding that. So finally, having all these positive responses, I decided to call Hank up and see what the hell the other guys might feel about it. I called him up, and he said, 'God, I wanted to call you the past four weeks to see if there might be a chance in your schedule to do both.' I said, 'Fuck, man, this is so cool.' He said, 'Everybody else, Michael Denner, Timi, they're for it; they really want to do it.' So that was the point when I started writing my stuff."

Back to "A Gruesome Time," like most tracks on the album, there are duelling Denner and Shermann solos. "Hank is a very powerful guitarist," comments Michael. "He uses a lot of power to play, and very fast picking on the guitar and very aggressive. I tend to do more melodic parts of more bluesy stuff. Because that's how I was brought up. My father was a blues guitarist, so I have a much longer background. Hank started playing electric guitar in 1977 and I started playing guitar way back in 1971 or something. So of course there's a difference. Also, I play quite soft with my right hand, the picking hand, but I do a lot of stuff with my left hand because I'm two-handed. I eat with my left hand and I write with my right hand (laughs). So that gives me... it's a challenge, but at the same time it gives me some advantages, to be able to do both."

"Thirteen Invitations" has King regaling his minions with an interesting tale concerning a mansion by the lake that no one has ever lived in but "the Devil himself." If that doesn't grab your attention, 13 invitations to the diabolical abode are sent out promising eternal life. Of course, it all goes pear-shaped, with Satan winning a night-long card game along with the souls of the participants. At the music end, there's a bit of everything, mid-paced doomy Sabbath, plus more mellow music than is usual, framed by galloping double bass drums.

It's an odd one, but odder still is "Room of Golden Air," a progressive metal full-band instrumental of complex arrangement and howling guitars. Notes Michael, credited as the penner of the music, "King couldn't find any vocal parts for it, and so they just left it there without any vocals. That surprised me a bit, because I returned to Copenhagen before they started to do the recording of the vocals. So, I was quite surprised that it turned out to be an instrumental."

Affirms Sterling Winfield, second engineer on the record and co-producer on *Dead Again*, "That was originally slated to have vocals on it, but it ended up being an instrumental because the vocals just weren't working out. The melody that King had written wasn't fitting after all. It was one of those things that just didn't translate, which happens sometimes. That was the only weird thing that happened on *In the Shadows* that I can recall."

"Legend of the Headless Rider" matches what came before for mathematical complexity—at 7:43 there are many events and many shifts in tempo. This one contains some of the record's best riffs but the song is so late in the sequence of a jam-packed claustrophobic record that it's rarely cited or fondly remembered.

Back in '93, in the same *Metal Maniacs* chat with Borivoj Krgin, King warned us that the album was going to be complicated, calling the record, "100% Mercyful Fate, but updated. You'll hear fresh production and you'll here us do riffs and things you've never heard us do before. There has to be a progression, and there is, but somebody who hasn't heard Mercyful Fate in eight years, if they played one of the songs that are coming out now on the radio, they wouldn't have the slightest doubt that it wasn't Mercyful Fate. They'd probably say if they never heard that we'd been reunited and stuff, 'God, I never heard that Mercyful Fate song! Where the hell did that come from?!' So, it's genuine Mercyful Fate, man. It could've been taken off *Don't Break the Oath*, but it's of course fresher sounding. We haven't gotten less heavy or less intricate. On the contrary. I just feel that we write those things better now. We understand how to arrange things better to make it flow even better. But my God, man, you're in for some complex shit when you get that album. The only way I can really describe it is to say that it's the 1993 version of Mercyful Fate. But it's God damn Mercyful Fate—there's no doubt."

In the Shadows ends with "Is That You, Melissa" in which King laments again the murder of Melissa by a priest, with Diamond staying faithful to the original tale, in fact not adding to it, rather just reminding the listener that he still thinks of her. There's much metal in this one but there's also a lot of melody and even soft passages, with John Marshall guesting on harpsichord.

As Hank told Vanessa Warwick outside at Dynamo, "It's a shame that King Diamond isn't here today, but I think he would have probably told you a very long story about that. He had some very good ideas for writing the lyrics with this Melissa girl he's had some experience with. King's writing about the same stuff, but he has toned down the voice that he used to use in '84. It's actually about the same spiritual things, with the same story going on and everything. Maybe for some people it's probably a little dark, but the lyrics are very positive. Positive for humankind and everything. It has something to do with past lives and all that. On *In the Shadows*, Melissa re-appears. I'm not too much into the meaning of the lyrics. He probably never told me. Sometimes he writes from something he has experienced himself; sometimes he might mean people he knows, but he never uses their names."

The album actually closes off with a bonus track of sorts, with Mercyful re-recording old chestnut "Return of the Vampire" with Metallica's Lars Ulrich guesting on drums. The song is rechristened on the record, "Return of the Vampire... 1993."

"You have to remember, this is right during the year when Metallica was just absolutely blowing up," begins Tim Kimsey, on how the track came to be. "They were on a world tour. Kim goes, 'I've got a good friend who wants to do a version of "Return of the Vampire."' The next thing I know, we've got Lars showing up at the studio. Lars comes in and we spent literally about... I want to say close to a full week. We had about three or four days of tracking 'Return of the Vampire' and it was full band. Typically, when we would do these records, we would focus in on drums and then we would focus in on bass parts and literally build everything from the ground up. But 'Return of the Vampire' was full band. It was several days of just recording the song."

"I guess he'd gotten a little break from the world tour," continues Tim. "Literally flew in from wherever they were at the time and came to Dallas. We literally did three to four days. We had approximately three days of tracking and at least a day or two where we were making selections of parts of the song. So, we had a couple of days where it was major editing going on where we were pulling... I want to say about four reels of two-inch tape. That probably equates out to about 12 takes on 'Return of the Vampire.' Then from there

I wound up editing—out of those 12 songs—editing it down into about a five-minute song. Then looking at the five-minute song, had another 23—I've got a picture of this—23 edits to tighten the groove. This was all with Lars there going, 'Let's do this, let's do this and let's do this.' I'm going, 'Lars, we need to make a backup copy of everything. We need to have a safety copy of everything.' He's like, 'You're gonna be fine, man. You're just... make the edits. Don't worry about it.' I was like, okay (laughs). That's what we did."

Sterling Winfield confirms just how much work went into this special baking of "Return of the Vampire." "Yes, well, I wasn't really as deep into the audio as Tim was, but I know that the three days that Lars Ulrich was there were really, really gruelling, a tough three days with no sleep when he was there. Literally three days with no sleep—72 hours without sleep just to get it done. Because he had a limited time. He was right in the middle of the black album tour. We had Tim splicing tape until his fingers bled. This is before Pro Tools and so if we wanted it done, we had to do it with a razor blade. But yeah, I remember those three days like it was yesterday."

There were no other songs worked on during the sessions, confirms Tim. "No, it was just 'Return of the Vampire.' Totally focused on that. If I'm being very honest about it, I pulled Kim to the wayside and I said, 'Man, do we have budget to do all this stuff?' Because when Lars first walked in, he said, 'Look, I don't want you to EQ the drums. I don't want you gating anything. I want you to just capture everything natural.' We didn't have the technology back then that we have now. It was literally recording on two-inch tape. The one thing that I was actually proud of myself, I go, 'Lars, I can get away with not gating anything on the drum kit, but as far as EQing the kit, I have to do that because we've got a whole album that 'Return of the Vampire' is gonna go on that has already had that stuff done to it. So, I need to try to get this as close as I possibly can.'"

"So, he walked away from all of that. Literally after everything had been finished up... and it's a super-long story, but we didn't have internet back then. We didn't have cell phones back then. So, after we had tracked all this stuff, it came time to mix and it was literally three weeks' worth of mixing of that one song. The biggest reason was because Lars was back out on tour. We weren't gonna let that song go until we got his approval, got his thumbs-up on everything, including the mixes. So, what this meant was that we would have to figure out what the itinerary was for Metallica, and send a DAT tape to the next place where he was gonna be three days from the time that we shipped it out. So, we literally would mix for a day and then ship mixes out on DAT tape to Lars and literally sit around for a couple of days until we heard from Lars as to what changes that he wanted made. Then eventually we finally got to the mix where he goes, 'I'm giving approval to this; everything's good to go.'"

"I remember very distinctly, we were about to wrap the whole record up and the phone rings at the studio. It was probably close to three o'clock in the morning. Kim was sitting right behind me on a stool and the phone rings and I didn't know who it was, but I answered the phone. No one else there except for Kim and myself. It was Lars. So I hand the phone to Kim and they talked for a little while, and after a little bit Kim handed me the phone back and he goes, 'Lars wants to talk to you.' So I go, 'Okay, great.'"

"Lars was just the epitome of a true gentlemen through all of it. He goes, 'Man, I just wanted to say to you that I appreciate your demeanour. You guys... you handled everything like a true pro. Most people would have folded underneath the pressure I put you under. I'm pretty sure I probably pissed you off a couple of times, but you handled it extremely well.' He goes, 'If I'm being super-honest about everything, I'm just a drummer. You know, I don't necessarily know exactly everything that's going on with everything. So, I just want to tell you thank you for being the man that you are.'"

It's a cool story, but in reality, this was the Mercyful Fate way as well anyway. You can hear it on the early records and you can hear it on *In the Shadows*. These are very expensive sounding albums, and you can tell that a ton of studio time was burned up in the making of them.

"Yeah, it was," agrees Tim. "Again, back then we had to make sure that whatever was being captured was exactly what we wanted. We didn't have the luxury of, 'Hey, you missed a punch' or 'We stepped on something.' That was devastating if something got recorded over, because there's not an undo button that you could go hit and no foul, no harm. Back then it was you made damn good and sure that you're on the right tracks and you're making sure that you're not stepping on these parts and that you're not gonna create more work for us to do. But yes, I would say everybody was absolutely perfectionists. But it becomes delightful when that perfection means that there's less work in the back end of things to have to do. We live in a society where—and I've certainly been exposed to all of this—to where it's like, 'We'll fix that later.' Well, with Mercyful Fate and the guys in that band, especially Kim, it's like there's no fixing it later. We've got to get this right and we've got to get it right *now*."

But *Kerrang!*'s Jason Arnopp was having none of it, writing in his two-out-of-five K review of the album, "*In the Shadows* is an all-new Fate release which makes scant concessions to the fact that we're halfway through 1993. The sole update on their sound is the clearer production job. This aside, it's the same story of quasi-heavy guitars knocking out those strongly European riffs and King Diamond doing his demented choirboy routine over the top of it all. The old Mercyful Fate material was good and quite influential, just like a fair portion of King's solo stuff held merit. But that was then and unfortunately for the King and Co., this is now. 'The Old Oak''s a nine-minute yawn, which might've been so much better had King only added the line, 'Tie a yellow ribbon...' Whereas Cannibal Corpse go about horrifying with tunes like 'Man with His Bollocks Sliced Off and Rammed Down His Throat,' King Diamond is the Hammer Horror man of metal, with the harmless 'Legend of the Headless Rider.' In fairness, this album doesn't exactly sound like it was just tossed off one afternoon. Mercyful Fate have obviously tried to build a comeback vehicle to be proud of. But unless you're a diehard nostalgia freak, you won't want to climb on board."

The Morning Call's Frank Pearn Jr.'s review of the album struck a similar tone: "Mercyful Fate's progressive metal sound, dark lyrics and spooky image influenced countless bands during the band's heyday, and since its breakup in 1985 vocalist King Diamond and crew have decided to reunite (perhaps the devil made them do it). But the problem is, it's not 1985 anymore. All the bands that Mercyful Fate influenced have taken things a few steps further, making the reconstituted Mercyful Fate seem a little ridiculous. King Diamond's face painting, which now includes an upside-down cross on his forehead (oh how scary!), pales in comparison to the extravagant outfits used by Gwar. His falsetto, which is used to give the band a haunting sound, is nowhere near as effective as the violent and gruesome growling of today's death metal frontmen. The band's image is bland and boring, compared to the likes of Slayer and Brujeria. *In the Shadows*' only saving grace is the musicianship. Tellingly, the ten-song disc's stand-out track is 'Room of Golden Air,' an instrumental. My advice, the band should split up again and find a new frontman."

Besides the Lars wrinkle, as alluded to, the other drama in the band at this juncture is that Morten Nielsen was to be a done deal even before he was done his parts. Relates Sterling Winfield, "I think the biggest deal with Morten, quite honestly, at least from what I could observe, was that he was probably very young and inexperienced. He's a great drummer—I don't want to take anything away from him there—but it was hard for him, with the gruelling hours and having to do things over again in the studio. This is back before Pro Tools really latched on and we were doing everything analogue, with two-inch tapes. It was a non-digital world back then, as far as that digital editing goes. So, there were some long hours in there of him doing many takes on things. That frustration and fatigue, it'd get to you after a while. So, it took a little longer than we expected; that was one of our hang-ups, for sure."

"That was fairly brutal for him," agrees Tim. "I think expectation were high, and don't get me wrong, I think he did a really good job, but I think he really beat up on himself a lot. There was a lot of pressure on him, pretty much to the point where there were conversations between he and I where it's like, 'Man, all you can do is do your very, very best. You're here for a reason. We're gonna hang in there. As a recording engineer, as a co-producer on this stuff, just know that I've got your back. I'm going to do everything within my power to make sure that we get your best performance.' At the time I definitely had a realisation that the brain can be a terrible thing sometimes. You can talk yourself out of being the ultimate professional that one is. All I'm saying is that sometimes when a person gets down on themselves, it just makes the situation more difficult. The situation that Morten had on himself was he had tremendous shoes to fill and I think he beat up on himself a lot."

The King, heroic. © Wayne Archibald.

Original cover art slated for use on the debut Mercyful Fate album, *Melissa*.

Early shot of King Diamond unmasked. © Wayne Archibald.

Timi "Grabber" Hansen, October 28, 1958 – November 4, 2019. © Wayne Archibald.

A rare picture sleeve for Mercyful Fate: "Black Funeral" b/w "Black Masses" (Metal for Nations 12 KUT 106).

Kim Ruzz hits a brick wall. © Wayne Archibald.

Michael Denner, contemplating de-throning of Judas Priest. © Wayne Archibald.

All hands on the damned. © Wayne Archibald.

Plyer of the fat strings, Tim Grabber, live. © Wayne Archibald.

1983 *Roadrunner* promo photo; left to right: Hank Shermann, Michael Denner, King Diamond, Kim Ruzz, Timi Hansen.

King, with bones, black scarf and crude corpsepaint. © Wayne Archibald.

Michael "Justin Bieber" Denner and Timi Hansen, kicking ass. © Wayne Archibald.

Poster for first US show ever, in Portland, Oregon. The concert didn't happen on the 18th, but took place two days later, same venue, on October 20th, 1984.

Hank Shermann, shredding. © Wayne Archibald.

King sans make-up, with fan and acquaintance of the author, Glen Cunningham.

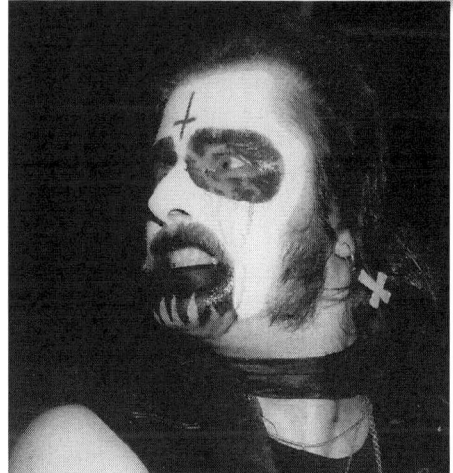

"Turn the cross upside down!" says Ape De Martini, from Oz (look them up). © Wayne Archibald.

King throwing the horns and the crowd throwing them back. © Wayne Archibald.

November '84 in California, left to right: Michael, King, Timi and Hank. © Kevin Estrada.

First US pressing of *Melissa* on Megaforce, care of Jonny and Marsha Zazula.

A boyish looking Hank Shermann in LA, 1984, perhaps thinking about lightening up. © Kevin Estrada.

Tough record label promo photo, with King in full-on evil Elvis mode. Note his *Killing Machine* shirt (the man has good taste).

King and a nationalist Hank. © Martin Rigby.

The debut Fate album; Hank is far right, looking the part.

King Diamond gone solo, Norman's Place, Aurora, Colorado, July 30, 1987. © Bill O'Leary.

King and his adoring fans, Norman's Place, Aurora, Colorado, July 30, 1987. © Bill O'Leary.

Left and right, King on the Mercyful Fate reunion tour, supporting *In the Shadows*, Gothic Theatre, Englewood, Colorado, October 1, 1993. © Bill O'Leary.

Promo poster for *In the Shadows*, the first album of the reunion era.

King Diamond on the LA set of the "Egypt" video shoot, 1993. © Kevin Estrada.

Promo shot taken in LA, left to right: Timi, Snowy, King, Hank and Michael. © Kevin Estrada.

"Egypt" video shoot. Left to right: Michael, Timi, King, Snowy. © Kevin Estrada.

Poster for the Denver stop on the 1993 *In the Shadows* tour.

Looking proud with their instruments of pain. © Kevin Estrada.

Poster for a Minneapolis gig, circa early 1995.

Metal pin featuring *Don't Break the Oath* artwork.

These three shots; Mercyful Fate on the *Time* campaign, Ogden Theatre, Denver, Colorado, February 1, 1995. © Bill O'Leary.

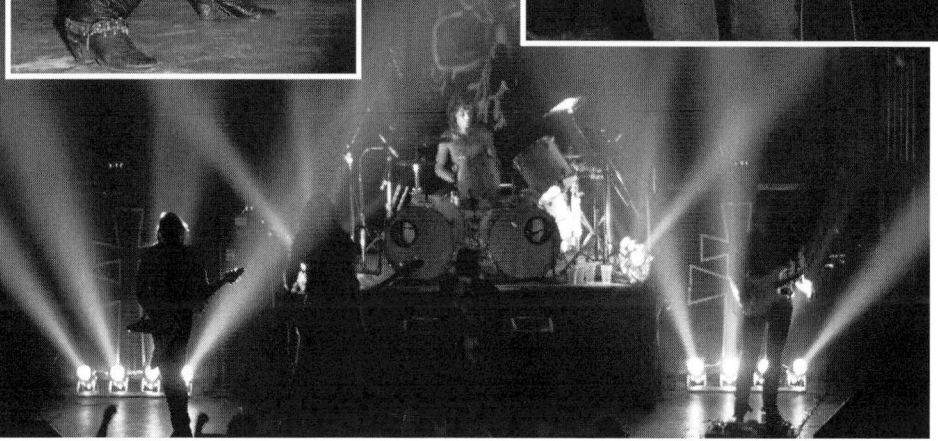

Metal Blade Records promo photo supplied with press kits.

King Diamond in Toronto, 2000. © Martin Popoff.

Take my soul, please. © Kevin Estrada.

Poster for hometown reunion gig.

Mercyful Fate reunion, Hank to the left and the good King to the right, Wacken Open Air at The Holy Wacken Land, Wacken, Schleswig-Holstein, Germany, August 4, 2022. Photos courtesy Wikimedia Commons, © Sven Mandel / CC-BY-SA-4.0.

6.

TIME
"DEATH HAS SO MANY DIFFERENT ASPECTS TO IT, BUT THE SKULL IS FINAL."

By the time Mercyful Fate got down to business of crafting a follow-up to *In the Shadows*, they were a well-oiled machine. The tour for that record was marked by an impressive blanketing of the States commencing September 8th, 1993, and playing almost every night through to Halloween. What would become *Time* was recorded, like the last one, over a long period in Texas, specifically May through August of 1994. Seven live dates in Germany took place over the two weeks leading up to the record's launch date, and then it was... *Time*.

As alluded to last chapter, Snowy Shaw had joined the band already for most of this, but so had bassist Sharlee D'Angelo, representing a Swedish invasion of sorts. As alluded to, the booklet to the previous album includes a full-panel picture of Snowy, with "Snowy Shaw – Drums" in the upper right corner, while the actual drummer on the album gets an "All drums on this album were played by Morten Nielsen" credit (excepting the Lars bit) that is almost too tiny to read.

Notes Tim Kimsey, "Timi I love, but I didn't get to spend much time with him. Sharlee, I spent a considerable amount of time with— gosh, how do I say this? Sharlee is one of the nicest people on the planet as far as I'm concerned, so I also loved being around Sharlee. Great bass player. I watched him grow into the band. I didn't have that same opportunity with Timi mainly because Timi knew what needed to happen. He came in, he knocked it out, he got it done. With Sharlee it was a learning process, of falling into the groove, if you will, of how the band functioned and operated, especially in production. But he fell into that very, very fast and did well. We used to make jokes and have all kinds of fun. Really, all of these guys are class act guys, just a pleasure to be around."

Already a veteran of the King Diamond band, Snowy explains the circumstances of his hiring.

"Both of those bands, people cannot keep them apart of course, because it's like one big incestuous family. But King called me in '91, because, let's say, King Diamond put the band on ice. They were looking for a deal, because they'd gotten out of their Roadrunner contract and all, and they were aiming high, to find a medium label or something. So, Ole Bang, the manager, and King himself, were looking at that. They put Andy and I in charge of finding new members to replace Pete Blakk and Hal Patino. They thought it was going to be a piece of cake, basically, but it took a long time and they couldn't land a good deal. So, as time went on after *The Eye* album, and by '91, King called me and said, 'We're still looking for deals for King Diamond, but now we have this offer to put Mercyful Fate back together and play Dynamo.' Which was a classic landmark for them or something; they did that back in '84."

"So, we got that offer to headline the festival, but they wanted to have the original lineup, except they didn't want to involve Kim Ruzz. I was part of the family, so they wanted me. Because I've been a diehard fan since I was 15 or something, I said, 'Yeah, I would love to do that.' But then nothing happened. I didn't hear anything until maybe one to two years later, when they had decided to get the band back together, but with a Danish drummer, because it was more convenient, based in Copenhagen and all that. King was probably living in Denmark at that point; I don't know. I was supposed to be the first choice there, but they decided to go with a more convenient option, I guess."

"But they called me back for second time," continues Shaw. "What happened to this Morten or whatever his name was, this drummer, they had been rehearsing in Copenhagen and they went to record the album in Dallas, but during the recording, they just realised that this was not going to fly, because they had some serious problems there with his playing, whatever it was. They asked me, 'Do you want to join the band?' 'Yeah, I would love to do that.' But in that case, I also wanted to re-record the drums. 'I could do that easily in a couple of days,' I thought (of note, Snowy has also said in previous interviews that it hadn't occurred to him to ask to re-do the drums). But they were running late and had so much trouble and all that that they had to patch all the drums together, Frankenstein them together. Then Hank had to record all the rhythm guitars. So, they were running low on budget and on time. I just figured, okay, but it's Mercyful Fate for God's sake. If they say it's good enough, it *is* good enough (laughs). So, I just went with it. That's why they have my picture in the booklet, but I didn't play a fucking single stroke."

Snowy was even on board for the video shoot for "Egypt," from *In the Shadows*. Asked what he remembers of the experience, he says, "Not too much, actually, because I was going through a really rough patch personally. I was deeply depressed without knowing it—I didn't know what it was. Wow, going out with Mercyful Fate, that was like... I shouldn't say 'dream come true,' but I never thought I would do that. But when it actually happened, I was so out of touch with myself. So, I don't remember very much, actually; I just felt out of place. Not because of the age difference or that they were Danish guys, but I can't understand Danish, so I'm the only Swede (Timi Hansen was still there for that), and all the crew, everyone, they were talking between each other and making jokes and all that, so I didn't understand shit. So, I felt like a real alien (laughs)."

It was all a whirlwind at this point. Not a week or two earlier, he had been in Copenhagen to meet the rest of the band for the first time and do a quick photo shoot. King was still in Dallas, working on vocals. Snowy had still to hear any of the *In the Shadows* album.

As for his impression of touring *In the Shadows* intensively in the fall of '93, Shaw reflects that, "You could notice a lot of different things from previous tours I'd been doing with King Diamond, like in '89. Heavy metal was fashionable then. Instead of signing a boob from some *Baywatch* type girl, now it was black-clad ladies with cats and Satanic bibles (laughs). It was a whole different scene, the aftermath of the grunge wave and all that. Of course, also with King Diamond, there were... I shouldn't say freaky people, but there was more of that with Mercyful Fate, because they were more underground and more Satanic. But yeah, I could see the difference from a couple years earlier."

"But you could see that interest in Mercyful Fate had picked up over the years, very much because of King Diamond's solo band success, of course," continues Snowy. "They were seen as legendary, pioneers of the early '80s black metal thing. So, there was a lot of excitement and interest for the band and we were doing good. I'd brought Sharlee to the band. When we were kids, at 15, we had discovered Mercyful Fate and all those bands and loved them."

Snowy offered more on his early fandom, in an email interview with *Sick Drummer* magazine. "I immediately became a fan of Mercyful Fate in 1983 or so, when I first heard 'Black Funeral' on a compilation with new up-and-coming metal acts. I loved their style and the way King sang, and from that moment on, my friends and I always tried to imitate his high-pitched falsettos when drinking. 'Hail Satan!' That was just fucking awesome."

"Around the time Sharlee and I must have been 14 or 15, we used to play 'Black Funeral' in our rehearsal room in Gothenburg, knowing little that the two of us would ten years later tour the world playing the exact same song on stage with the original band. That was cool once it hit me one day during the US tour in 1993.

I bought *Melissa* shortly after that, and I was blown away by how complex and progressive the music was with all these tempo changes and stuff. I must admit I even got spooked by 'Satan's Fall;' it was just too damn scary and bizarre. At first, I just assumed they were Americans, British or maybe German, like all the other bands at the time. But when I found out they were from our neighbour country Denmark, I thought that was really cool. I would never have imagined that I would play with the King about five years later."

"When we were playing Toronto (September 16th, 1993), we heard the word that, well, Lips and Robb Reiner are here," continues Snowy, back to the interview with the author. "Wow. Sharlee and I had played 'March of the Crabs' when we were kids, him playing guitar and me playing drums, because it's an instrumental. It was a weird thing there, but maybe because we were the newcomers in the band, we thought we should do a combined drum solo and bass solo.

So, we would just improvise some shit every night, hippie-style. But on this occasion, when we played Toronto and Anvil was there, it was like, wow, we should honour them and play 'March of the Crabs.' We hadn't played that song for years. But just before we went up on stage we decided to do that. Because this was way before the movie and all that, and we thought they deserved so much more."

For support acts on the tour, says Snowy, "I remember it was Flotsam & Jetsam—maybe they were there the whole time—and it was Cathedral, the English band. Kind of funny, they had this big Cockney accent that I couldn't understand shit what they were saying. It was worse than American. Plus, Anacrusis, who I think were also on Metal Blade."

The final date of the *In the Shadows* tour had them playing Halloween at The Ritz in New York City. "From what I remember, we really fucked it up," chuckles Snowy. "Sharlee and I said, okay, it's Halloween, let's have a good time. So, we swapped instruments doing this aforementioned (laughs), jam session. We were just goofing around like we did since we were kids back home. He can't play drums anyway, although I can play bass. We were a little bit tipsy and going at it and we were expecting people to laugh about it, but it was like dead silence (laughs). So, wow, maybe we shouldn't do that. Our sense of humour didn't translate to a New York audience. But yeah, we were just going at it, and we were saved by King who came out and said, like, 'Oh that was a surprise even to me; give them a round of applause' or something. It was really awkward."

The rhythm section's propensity to stretch out in fact got the band an unexpected bad review in *Kerrang!*, for that all important Dynamo performance, the second show of the reunion, with the reviewer pointing out that it was ridiculous that there would be a bass solo and a drum solo at such a showcase, one where sets were curtailed and configured to hit the mob straight between the eyes.

Then it came time to record the follow-up, and not much had changed in terms of the band's writing dynamic, much to the chagrin of Snowy, although Sharlee seemed fine, at least initially, with being placed on the sidelines creatively.

Says Michael of D'Angelo, "He was part of the arrangements. I do believe he and Snowy tried parts to play together—these guys know each other from the Gothenburg area. But he didn't have any impact on... he was not part of the songwriting at all."

"When I came in, I was just the new guy," says Sharlee, "and I didn't have a lot of say about anything, of course. That's a thing you've got to come to terms with when you join a band. It took me a little while. As time went on, it was so much more of a group effort, with not just one or two people steering the ship."

"And Snowy," continues Michael, "the thing is, we became friends immediately. Because he has the same sense of humour. I mean, this guy was just... in my entire people I like to be around... plus he's an absolute excellent drummer in my book. He may be the best metal drummer ever, in my opinion. He could be the No.1 on my list. But he wasn't allowed to play his fantastic drums on the *Time* album. There were limitations. He really had to play... in parts he sounded like a machine, playing on the beat like a rhythm box, really, and that was a big disappointment. Because I knew this guy could play unbelievably great drums."

Remarks engineer/co-producer Tim Kimsey on the making of *Time*, his second now for the band, "By far I would say that is the one record where I think everybody was pretty much on point. We understood one another really well. I had a pretty good idea of what the sound picture was supposed to be. I gotta say, Kim was very good about setting all of this stuff up prior to us going into the studio and recording. There were plenty of meetings that we would have prior to going into the studio. With these guys being so well versed in recording, they knew that trying to figure stuff out in studio would become very costly. So, I would say that was probably the record that I understood the best."

But still, a Mercyful Fate record would take a long time. I asked Tim about how the economics of how this worked, relating to him the times I had talked to more recent era members of the Dio band, and how they would lament that they would go broke working with Ronnie on a record with no income coming in. The point of comparison is that neither of these bands were massive commercially, and yet they burned up writing and studio time over the course of weeks and months, without regular gigging or outside jobs going on. In Mercyful's case, there was the added strain of having to set up house thousands of miles from home.

If there were issues, they weren't apparent to Tim. "I don't think there was a problem. A lot of it had to do with maybe having the discussions with Brian Slagel up front. Brian would come and visit at least one visit per record that we were working on. That was between Brian and King Diamond. A lot of times folks don't understand that we would be six months on, let's say, a Mercyful Fate record, and literally six weeks later we would be crossing over into King

Diamond. Still, Hank and Michael, being Danish, they maybe needed to go back home. But I think that these guys were very, very smart with their money, and knowing that they needed to get in and get done as quickly as they could."

"But at the same time, no one was in a huge rush," continues Kimsey. "In other words, no one was ever watching the clock. I think Brian Slagel helped contribute to that, visiting occasionally and just reassuring everyone. It's like, 'Hey, this is what we're doing, and I've got y'all's backs.' So first and foremost, I think that all of them are excellent businessmen, very careful, and definitely weren't out partying or anything of that nature. Money wasn't being spent on just goofball stuff. It was always, 'We're here to make this record.' It was pretty much right down to business, even though at the same time we had fun in the studio."

Said Snowy on the subject, "When I did my drums and Sharlee did his bass, we were there maybe two weeks. When King is doing his vocals, nobody is allowed to be in the studio. When Hank is doing his guitars or Mike is doing his solos, I wasn't there. Everything was done separately."

His point is that even if a Mercyful record takes months—and fortunately sounds like it as well—it's not like all these Europeans were in Texas the whole time. Asked what he did there however, he says, "From what I remember, we weren't hanging out so much in Fort Worth, where the studio is. We went out for dinner a couple times, but we were mostly working in the studio. It was a big complex. But for a Swede it was weird. It's such an American thing I think, but people are obsessed about air-conditioning. So, the studio was ice-cold. For me to just hang out and watch TV and play pool or whatever, I could not fucking do that. I had to go and sit outside. That is my most vivid memory, I guess (laughs)."

Snowy remembers Metal Blade boss Brian Slagel visiting with the band on the road but not in Texas. "Yeah, he did. I know he was there for the festival we did, Dynamo, and when we opened up for Metallica. Because I sang Uriah Heep to him (laughs). Plus, we were hanging out when we did the shoot in LA. We also had a release party at the Rainbow, and then we were also hanging out at Metal Blade, the office, doing interviews and photo shoots."

Back to Tim's comment about switching witch's hats between the two bands, I asked him how the experiences differed. "It had everything to do with the members of the band," reflects Kimsey. "There were members of King Diamond that were trading out and it was a progression finding the right members to be in King Diamond, although we pretty much knew who was going to be involved with Mercyful Fate. We didn't really frame things any differently for King Diamond versus Mercyful Fate. There was always a roadmap for every song that was done, whether it was Mercyful Fate or King Diamond."

Creatively though, "The storytelling might be more of a King thing," ventures Tim. "More keyboards in a lot of cases. With sequencing and stuff of that nature, that allowed the keyboard playing to take shape. Actually, a lot of those parts were already established. One of the first things I learned a long time ago, two things that matter most is what key something's going to be in and the tempo. And that roadmap had already been established prior to us coming into the studio. Plus, keyboard parts were typically... you'd say it's going to be a harpsichord part or something, which made it more gothic. Those keyboards were definitely thought-through parts coming in. So the roadmap would have been laid. That's typically what we would do on a King Diamond record is we would establish what the tempos were and we would establish the keyboard parts we wanted. Kim would absolutely make sure that those keyboard parts were exactly what he had in mind."

Tim agrees also that there would be more sophisticated vocal arrangements and even more double bass drum on a King Diamond album. "Yes, definitely—both. When I think about Mercyful Fate, I would say it's probably more guitar-driven and maybe not as much production as it is with King Diamond. Lts of stacking of vocals and extra vocal parts would be a part of a King Diamond record. Mercyful Fate? A little more straight-ahead."

Explained King to Tim Henderson at the time on getting the ball rolling on the record, "We don't think very much with respect to planning. When we realised that the final European leg of the *In the Shadows* tour wasn't going to happen, we started writing new material and began sending tapes back and forth overseas. Eventually Hank came over to the US to start arranging and we went into the studio on May 23rd. We had more songs than we did last time. Simply, we just went in there and did it and what you hear is what happened. The album is very much Mercyful Fate within the framework, but at the same time, we've stretched ourselves out a bit, especially with a song like 'Time.' I feel this album is closer to the original Mercyful Fate than *In the Shadows* was, and I love that album still. But I can hear that we've been on tour and we're getting a lot closer. We're more of a united band on *Time*. When I listen to the songs, it puts me in the same frame of mind that some of our older songs did. I just get that same feeling from it, even though it's different in many ways. I'm very happy."

Time got off to a cracking start with a great album cover. Featuring a photograph of a skull in part shadow and some simple old-school text, this was arguably the classiest and even creepiest cover art for the band to date—illustration will always embody that limitation of being illustration.

"I don't purchase skulls; they are given to me," explained King. "One was given to me by a doctor in Denmark. Trust me, I'm not out digging graves when the moon is full. This is some people's first thought: King Diamond, the gravedigger! I may look like it on stage, but not when I'm at home with myself. I have a very special feeling about them. The first thing that you think of when you see a skull is death. Death has so many different aspects to it, but the skull is final. There's always been questions of where the rest of the body goes when the skeleton is left behind. On *Time*, we chose one of the skulls I had at home. It has the in-your-face appeal that *Don't Break the Oath* had. With a simple skull, it's a point in time where we are all the same. It doesn't matter what colour you are, what you believe in or what you do. We all end up like that together. It's one part in life where you can't distinguish each other. There's a lot of meaning to that cover. I've never supported any type of racism and it has a little bit of that in there too. It's a final stage that we all have to go through, and that idea definitely affects *Time*."

The record busts open with a straight-ahead rocker called "Nightmare Be Thy Name," quick to boil, not a lot of words and almost curt and phrase-like. King brings all of his vocal arsenal, all three gears along with a thoughtful harmony choral. But even before we relax into the song's mid-paced groove there an instant confrontation with an uninvited guest (to quote NWOBHMers Demon), or an unexpected guest, to quote King himself. Sharlee opens the album with a Cliff Burton-like bass squall, rapidly accompanied by a twin lead and then a modulation, change of key. This happens over a slow section and then we're into the song, with Snowy exacting and signalling as much by hitting the bell of the ride in conjunction with these nice bass drum/snare and cymbal combinations. Later there's echo added to King's vocals and wah-wah added to the axe solo.

"I think it was one of the more aggressive pieces on the album," notes Michael, penner of the music on this one (Denner is also credited with "Mirror"). "Of course it made me proud, because to open the album with my track, that was very satisfying. I also am very fond of the guitar piece I do, the lead guitar work, in that particular song. It was even released as a video, for MTV. So, I was quite happy about that song, to open the album, because of the video, and because that was one of the better songs on that album, in my opinion (laughs)."

The video for the track is fairly basic, with the band miming to the song in an underpass / parkade environment. Smoke-shrouded, King is the focal point, captivating in black hat, expressive with his hands and eyes.

"Angel of Light" continues in the same gleeful headbanging vein as the opening track, quick to get going but then briskly mid-paced, punctuated by a haunting chorus with King avowing over a creepy modulating prog melody, "I have seen the angel of light... Lucifer!" Again, like the first track, there is fulsome full speed and then there are switchbacks into half time. Late in the sequence there are new riffs as well as a return to the earlier ones.

The groove is absolutely locked down by Snowy, although Shaw had to rise to the challenge of playing to a click, by virtue of Hank's rhythm guitars already having been recorded that way. "Yeah, I haven't thought about it, but that's absolutely the way it was done. I had to play a lot to the click and I don't like that. It was like playing to a rule book or something. You have to play tight to a click track. People could listen to the album with a metronome, which is bullshit. I have no problem playing groovy to a click track, but why? We can play together and do like the '70s style. But yeah, I had no problem doing that; it's actually pretty easy."

"But it's because it was written out on the guitar first," explains Shaw. "It's an old myth, I guess, that bass and drums should be the foundation of things. Mercyful Fate write songs based on the riffs and stuff. Generally, since the invention of click track, the whole scene has changed when it comes to recording. I don't remember exactly, but I suppose that King wrote his songs and programmed songs on his drum machine or whatever. Then I could do my own stuff, come up with my own ideas. What I can remember—which I thought was weird—was that he wanted to please me, in a way. He'd say that I could do my version of the song. We'd run through it and he'd say, 'Could you try something else? Can you try something different here?' It would become a mishmash of everything. 'Oh, you like that thing with the tom-tom? You can do that a little bit, and then could you start off with the hi-hat?' I was thinking, well, this sounds weird. I don't have to do this specifically. It's your song. You're in charge, I'm just taking a backseat here. But overall, I'd say the drums ended up more '70s style than anything."

Fleshing out the process in his email interview with *Sick Drummer* magazine, Snowy explained that "I spent about a week learning and trying out various arrangements and versions in advance before I went to the studio and quickly ran through each song down on tape so that King could hear my take and ideas on it. Then we started from scratch, discussing every bit back and forth, trying out different things. I would come up with tons of variations to meet King's wishes, meeting halfway, compromising. We started from the top and just worked our way through the songs. Once we had agreed on the arrangement, I would record as far as I could into a song until I made a mistake or forgot. Then we just punched in from there and worked our way through the song."

Further explaining this idea of playing along to the guitars, Snowy said that he "had to try to match Hank's timing; I can actually hear in the middle of a song that we took a two-hour dinner break and continued the recording after that. In my opinion, one should always try to keep the same vibe throughout the whole song and therefore try to do it in one good take or as few takes as possible. But then again, these days and with most metal bands, everything seems to be edited and corrected and sounds replaced and triggered so much afterwards that it doesn't matter at all. One might just program the drums from scratch and save yourself the trouble. I hope that trend dies soon."

In fact, it's gotten worse, and indeed many metal albums now feature fully programmed drums, to the point where having a live drummer in the studio is considered an extravagance, like a real string section instead of synthesizer strings, when that got easy to replicate in the 1980s.

"One thing that I find a little odd with King," continued Snowy, "is that you never get to hear the vocals on pre-production or demos, so you have no clue where it all is gonna end up. The vocal lines and melodies have always been important to me, and that's what I'm listening to mostly once there's vocals over a part. I'm not sitting there thinking, 'Okay, this riff eight times then that riff twice' and so on. But I never at that point heard any of the vocals. King might say, 'Oh, you can't do that; that's going to be in conflict with the vocals.'

A Dangerous Meeting: In the Shadows with Mercyful Fate

'Well, what are the vocals?' He wouldn't tell me."

Next up is "Witches' Dance" and admirably the trend continues, with the band punching out accessible songs in a mid-tempo zone, not too many parts, quick to get going, strong choruses. This one is arguably too melodic this soon in the sequence, although it's a purely sobbing, sorrowful melody—horrific, or, if one wants to be disparaging, Hammer horrific.

Incredibly, the little label that could; Metal Blade, had proffered enough budget to make a second production video, not to mention incurring the expense of making such a plush album. Over and above the video for "Nightmare Be Thy Name," now we have a desert shot location, flames and a bat-themed throne from which King gesticulates.

Notes Diamond, "'Witches' Dance' was shot outdoors because we needed a bonfire and we couldn't get permission to do it. So, we had to go over the mountains and into the desert to find a proper location. It was shot at nighttime; in the middle of the wilderness and the only light we had was from a generator. We were told not to go outside of the light because there were rattlesnakes everywhere, and you could hear them as soon as you walked to the edge of the light. It was cool because we had girls come out that actually knew witchcraft and they were dancing the witches' dance within the burning circle. It turned out really well."

The actual witch dance segment of the video is performed to the part of the song that is essentially a mellow break framed neatly by violins. Amusingly, for the harmony vocals, there's a nod to "Bohemian Rhapsody" with King's four band mates portrayed as disembodied opera-singing heads in black shadow, eyes closed. The witches' dance itself is even more amusing, with a bevy of babes dressed in pure-as-the-driven-snow white dresses twirling around like ballerinas from a Whitesnake video.

Remarks Snowy, "The particular occasion for those videos was actually the only time in my life that I've used such a standard setup of two rack toms in-between two kicks. I just did the best with the equipment I was provided and it looked good. In fact, for those videos that were shot in LA and somewhere in the Nevada desert, I remember I requested a cool spectacular Ludwig kit with three kick drums with a big number six on each front head, which our manager questioned and said would be unfair to the fans since I didn't have three legs and wouldn't use that live (laughs). How stupid is that? Who gives a shit? You've already recorded the music in the studio and a promotional clip is exactly just that: something that will promote and hopefully attract people to go buy the album."

There's a memorable snare roll in "Witches' Dance" that transitions into rapid-fire bass drum. "That's just something I ripped off of Ian Paice's drum solo on *Made in Japan*, and it's done on a single kick with one foot," notes Shaw. "I remember thinking that some of the material for the *Time* album was progressive. Hank's songs especially even reminded me of—for lack of a better word—fusion/jazz rock in an old-fashioned style, and that allowed me to play accordingly, a little bit like Ian Paice and Neal Peart in some places, maybe."

Reflecting back on what could have taken place on the previous record, he reiterates that, "The drums are boring as hell on *In the Shadows*. I would easily have done a way, way better job, no doubt about that, unless King wanted it to be exactly like that. I remember when we were shooting the video for 'Egypt,' I even refused to play that silly elementary school fill and be highlighted in a show-off style like 'Look at me,' so I played it with one hand and they edited it out."

Coming back to his strange crediting on that album, i.e. proper explanatory wording but a full-panel picture within the *In the Shadows* booklet, Snowy says, "I never had anything to do with the cover or what's written on it, but I certainly never intended to pretend that I played that crappy drumming. At some point I got a demo cassette of the album. Or at least so I thought—it was actually the final thing. When King asked what I thought of the album, it got awkward, and finally I managed to squeeze out a rather lame, 'Good.' I certainly didn't have the heart to reveal that I thought it was just a demo. But I'm a terrible liar and King's a smart guy, so I think he got the message anyway. So, in retrospect, yes, I wish I'd have had the chance to re-record the drums for *In the Shadows*."

"It says clearly in the liner notes or credits who played the drums on the recordings on the album. I think I would definitely have objected or protested otherwise, because there's no way in hell I would want to take the blame for that boring, lame-ass drumming. Lars Ulrich's contribution was great though. They decided to do this old 'Return of the Vampire' song and I think he really killed it. He did such a good job, compared to Morten, who was lukewarm, or lame, in my opinion. Lars did a killer job on that song. But Lars has always been a huge fan of Mercyful Fate and goes way back with them long before he moved to the US and eventually formed his own metal band... who did pretty well (laughs). But Lars was a couple years already younger than them, so when they were going at it in Copenhagen, he wanted to join the band, but they just laughed at him or something (laughs). Then he moved to Los Angeles whatever and started another band."

Back to *Time*, next up is "The Mad Arab," and after three songs in a row in the Western/Christian Satanic tradition, King goes for a Middle Eastern tale, but one sprung from H.P. Lovecraft and the fictional book within his writings, *The Necronomicon*. Later, as there became a cottage industry of carrying on where Lovecraft left off, *The Necronomicon* was brought into being as a properly published grimoire (magical textbook, essentially), written by the mysterious "Simon."

Remarks Hank, who wrote the geometric, Middle Eastern-melodic music to the song, "I know King has a copy and 'The Mad Arab' is about it. I read it a bit too, but I'm not too much into it," with Tim Kimsey adding that, "I like that one because it just takes me to a place. When I think 'The Mad Arab,' I think about being in the desert. Plus, the guitar parts in that just drive me crazy. And vocally I think it's pretty amazing. Actually, everything that goes on with that song in general is great."

Asked about this one, Snowy reflects that, "I'm just doing my job, doing the best I can and helping make the song the best it can be. If I write the song, I have a certain vision in my head, but with these songs, I have to be a tool for King and Hank so they can realise their vision. I have no problem with doing that. With 'The Mad Arab'... Hank doesn't write any vocal parts at all—he never has. He's like a riff-meister or something. He leaves all the vocals and melodies and vocal arrangements to King. Which works, very good. But for me, personally, I'm more song-based—I like vocals. I think that's the most important thing that people listen to and that's what makes a song good. Instead of adding something on top of it. So, I tend to like King's songs better, for some reason, because they're based on vocals."

With "My Demon" we are back to pure Satanism in the Western tradition. If you hadn't noticed, the notion floated with *In the Shadows*, the idea of steering Mercyful away from occult practice more toward storytelling (song-by-song, not concept album-style like King solo)... well that's been ground to dust. It's what made the band notorious in the early '80s and here it was back again, just in time for the ascendance of Norwegian black metal.

"This is a thing that we were talking about back during the tour in '93," relates Snowy. "I sat down and spent a whole evening talking to King about that. Because like in '93, maybe he didn't hear... I updated him about what was going on in the underground. He hadn't heard. I think he was living in America at the time. But I said, 'Have you heard what's going on in Scandinavia? In Norway and Sweden with this new wave of black metal? All these black metal bands, they're burning down churches and you are their fucking hero. They idolise you, as the first outspoken Satanist and a member of the Church of Satan and all that. I don't want to put any blame on you (laughs), but do you feel any sort of responsibility for that? I mean, they're killing each other.'"

"And he was totally shocked about that. I guess he missed out on that whole thing. So, we spent the whole time talking about religious stuff, and he said, 'I don't want any part of that. It isn't... devil-worshiping is a different thing from Satanism. There are different branches in Satanism.' He didn't want to take part in all that. Because he's a decent guy, of course. In a way, you can be fascinated and excited about occultism, but you don't have to have animal sacrifices and kill each other."

Which brings up the point, why was King living in—of all places—Texas? "The thing is, they decided to move to Los Angeles," explains Snowy, referring to the King Diamond band. "Because everything was happening there; it was a melting pot back then. So, they moved there from Scandinavia in '87, I believe, and I think the plan then was to establish themselves in America and stay there for two to three years or something."

"So, in 1990 they all moved back to Scandinavia, Hal Patino and King to Denmark and the rest of us to Sweden. But I think he met this girl, Debbie, and she was from Dallas. So that's why he ended up there. She lived with him in Copenhagen, but she couldn't speak Danish. She felt isolated and wasn't so happy about that. So, they decided to make a move to Dallas. That's how he ended up there. Because I don't think he's the guy who wants a suntan and he's not much of a cowboy (laughs)."

This woman is not the long-time mate he's with now. "No, they broke up after a few years. I shouldn't say too much, but I think she thought maybe she was marrying a rock star, a David Lee Roth or something, and King is not that type of guy (laughs)."

When I asked King to contrast Texas with Denmark, he said that "The contrast is big, but not as big as with Los Angeles or New

A DANGEROUS MEETING: IN THE SHADOWS WITH MERCYFUL FATE

York. It has a lot to do with where you grew up and what you feel comfortable with. I love going to New York or LA, but it's too far away from what I grew up with in Denmark. Texas is a lot more laid-back, I'd say. It's easier to relate. But if you grew up in New York you'd probably be bored if you lived in Texas. There's such a pace. When I go there I can just feel it in the cab ride from the airport. It's like, whew! Things are going fast! But before, we'd been to Texas on so many occasions, and when we've had days off here it's always been a very nice place. People are very down-to-earth, open-minded. They seem to have that southern hospitality, and it's a nice, relaxed feeling I can relate to."

I asked Snowy if King's various pacts with demons—it's pretty much what most the songs are about: sending out invitations—resulted in any paranormal visitations.

"Let me see; I don't want to ruin his image or anything, but I know when Sharlee was doing his bass... if you play a certain chord on the guitar, either it's a fifth or fourth or something, then which one is dominant? Which is the dominant note? He was playing the right notes on the wrong strings. It's hard to explain, but King said, 'Well, that's weird—it's got to be some omen or something.' No, it's because he didn't go to school. But he'd come to the conclusion, like, wow, something's happening (laughs)."

Back to the record, in conjunction with the evil lyric, at the music end "My Demon" is also by King, and so it's logical that we've got a utilitarian rocker that's not too complex. Also, as with previous tracks, "My Demon" utilises a brisk mid-paced tempo but breaks down to half time regularly. There's a shuffle-like, Sabbath chug to the main premise, but given that this is Mercyful, there's a substantial amount of prog metal-minded action throughout, just not excessively.

"'Time' is probably the song that sticks out the most," remarks King, on the dark ballad style of the title track. "I remember when they first heard the four-track demo of the song, they couldn't really picture where I wanted to go with it. I knew exactly what I wanted it to sound like. That song is very special."

The harpsichord, the whispers, the modulation, the elegant twin leads, the ticking of the clock (which both opens and closes the song)... this is an ambitious outlier on the record, with zero Satanic content, with King rather lamenting the passing of time but then like a good writer, also presenting the positive, that a moment shared between two people can be a beautiful thing.

"The title track is very unique," continues King. "There's a lot of different stuff on that album. You might say that song should have been a King Diamond song and I might agree with that. But the few times I do put that album on, I'm very surprised. There is a lot of raw stuff on that album. I do hear from fans who say, 'Oh man, that album is killer!' Which is good; I'm glad that the fans have different favourites. Because that means that you have not done just one good album and the rest are crap."

"I hear that with King Diamond too, that people have all kinds of different favourite albums. Most people say *Abigail*, but a lot of people say *Conspiracy* and *The Eye*, even *The Graveyard*. But it's hard for me to have that objective look. I know how every little single sound was put on the album, you know? So, I can't sit and listen objectively to these albums. I just can't relate to it the same way other people can. Like when I listen to an Ozzy Osbourne album I don't say to myself, 'I wonder if they arranged the kick drum a certain way right there, or whether they added some reverb in that passage?' I just enjoy it and experience it."

Back to his dastardly deeds, with "The Preacher," King sneers hatefully, relishing the death of a preacher who, humorously, may not end up in Hell because he's got no soul to sell. This one somewhat fits the narrative involving Melissa, King's beloved female foil who was killed by a priest and last lamented on "Is That You, Melissa?" At the music end, "The Preacher" is aggressive and nasty, framed upon a barrage of double bass drums and strafed by dissonant, noisy, crazy guitar solos.

Next track, "Lady in Black," bears the same title as a song by Uriah Heep, one of King Diamond's favourite bands of all time. Through "time" in the other direction, Swedish melodic death metallers Dark Tranquillity capably covered the song on a Mercyful Fate tribute album in 1997, drawing many younger fans to the original. The music on this one, by King, is mournfully melodic, like Sabbath crossed with Maiden, with King stringing long open notes overtop to underscore the sombre effect of this tale, one which essentially recreates the front cover of Black Sabbath's first album.

"Mirror" comes from Michael musically, and it's an obtuse rocker, slightly dissonant, further made obscure and inaccessible by its halting one-and-three beat and increased use of falsetto. If the verse strikes an odd melodic note, the chorus goes one step further toward the obtuse, with the break even sounding off-putting yet sophisticated. Then there's a creepy mellow bit and we're back into the barrage of guitar, bass and drums. At the lyric end, the narrator is captivated by a tormented woman trapped in a mirror, and wonders that if he breaks the mirror, will she be set free?

Michael freely admits that he's not a prolific songwriter. As Snowy relates, "He never really spoke about that, but you are right, he's not. He may have a few riffs here or there but I never saw him as this songwriter who has a big passion for doing that. Mostly it's Hank's thing, to write a lot of cool riffs." In this respect, he's somewhat analogous to Dave Murray and his role within Iron Maiden.

Shermann's "The Afterlife" is next, and this one has King acting thespian much like his hero Alice Cooper doing "Steven," with Diamond playing convincingly the character of a ghost trapped in the graveyard, wondering if this is what the afterlife is like. Quiet music does battle with metal like a Metallica power ballad, and the sense of diversity it represents across the album is welcome (to my nightmare).

Says Snowy on album closer "Castillo Del Mortes," "That was the most complex song on the album; with so many time changes, it was like Frank Zappa or something. King couldn't come up with any vocals. He was singing basically jazz scat (sings scat). I said to him, 'That's weird. You can be quiet instead?' (laughs). 'Or just sing long notes, with grunge, like Alice in Chains did or something, instead of doing the scat thing or whatever you call it."

Indeed, this one is all over the place, a Mercyful Fate epic appropriately put at the end, just to drive home the point how seriously this band takes their work, established all the way back on *Melissa*, one of the great pioneering progressive metal albums of all time.

But Snowy at this point in time was ready for the drumming challenge presented by such geometric writing from Hank. "Yes, well, I gotta say that when I discovered them in '83, I thought what is this?! There were so many time changes—how can they remember all this shit? They must've rehearsed together so long. But then I was 14, 15 years old, and compared to AC/DC or whatever, sure, it was really extreme. But then of course, I developed and got better at my trade, and I found myself thinking that the '90s version wasn't as extreme or wasn't pushing the limits anymore. It was a little laid-back, from my point of view."

"I think that says more about me, because I had developed and they were slowing down a little bit. It's hard to describe. But that's the feeling I had. I was reacting to certain songs that I thought sounded like Lynyrd Skynyrd or something (laughs), more bluesy. But they always had that. Maybe I saw it differently from a distance when I was a kid than when I was involved, which is tricky. A lot of people I ended up playing with later, like Messiah (Marcolin, in Memento Mori) and King… I put them on a pedestal—'Wow, they're gods'—and then I get to know them and it's like, they're just human."

Reflecting on the record as a whole, Snowy says that "A lot of people from what I've heard, think it's one of the better Mercyful Fate albums, or the best one. I couldn't say, because I cannot be that objective about it, of course. I think it's a decent record. From my point of view, again, I hate myself for not being more persistent to King in asking to record the drums for *In the Shadows*, because I think the material on *In the Shadows* is superior."

It was inevitable that Shaw wouldn't last long in Mercyful Fate. As his future track record would indicate, his creativity as a songwriter, vocalist and multi-instrumentalist across many projects, would doom him to unhappiness in a band where there were already more than enough writers.

"If I'm not allowed to contribute, it's choking. I just have to get out of that situation. I tend to take over the bands that I join, like Dream Evil, where I ended up writing the whole album. I don't know why, but it's just my personality or my true nature. I want to create or I'm not happy. So, to be perfectly honest, that's why I didn't feel so good being in the band. I expected to be in heaven or something. It wasn't said in so many words, but this is Hank's and King's band, and Denner on the side, of course. I wasn't allowed to contribute in any way, in anything. I had a lot of song ideas and stuff, but I felt shut out. I'm not just interested in playing drums. I've tried that so many times. It doesn't work for me with the band. I can do it for a short while, but if I'm not allowed to be creative and have more input in any way, it doesn't work. I get fucking depressed (laughs). Hank called me and I quit. I quit when he told me that they were going to do a European tour for *Time*, like in late fall or something like that, '94. I got cold feet and I said fuck, I can't do this anymore, so I wasn't there to tour *Time*, no."

Tim Kimsey could see that Snowy had a lot more to offer, but it wasn't really causing any problems with respect to moving the record along and getting it out the door. Nonetheless there was a wee bit of healthy friction on tap, as Tim saw it.

"No, first off, Snowy brought just awesome drumming to the

project, immaculate. But there was also conversation between Kim and himself as to the parts that needed to be played on these records. What I mean by that is, not always does everyone agree as to what the parts should be. After I had met Snowy and we were in session, there was a pretty big—shall we say—disagreement. That would be a good word for it. There was a bit of a disagreement between Snowy and Kim as to some of the parts that needed to be laid down."

"If I'm being very, very truthful about it, that was the point where Kim basically said, 'Why don't you excuse yourself?' He goes, 'You might want to get out, take a walk for a little bit; we've got to hash this stuff out.' Probably thirty minutes later, I'm a little bit concerned as to how that discussion was going on. As a hired gun coming into all of this, I'm hoping the guys got this worked out well, Kim and Snowy and just the band in general."

"First of all, these guys are class acts. They're not going to get into a fistfight over something like that. But they will certainly have a discussion about things. So being the gentleman that Kim is, he basically said, 'Look, this is gonna take a minute. You might want to take a walk around the block or whatever needs to happen. We're going to get this ironed out and figure it out.' Sure enough, I mean, it would happen that way. I was a little concerned about it because I've seen this stuff happen in the studio before where a disagreement happens and it goes to blows over things. Well, this never happened that way. They got it ironed out and we just continued on. But the question was, what did he personally bring to the session? I think he brought immaculate drumming and amazing drumming ideas. But not always did they line up with what Kim wanted."

"I think they just agreed to disagree and I don't necessarily think it was anyone putting anyone in their place. If anyone was going to be put in their place, it would've been me being put in my place, which was, 'Look, we're gonna have a discussion about this and then you come back and we will have gotten this figured out.' The drumming when it comes to *Time*, maybe the overall big picture was 'Does it make sense?' Because a lot of the stuff is going to be lyric-driven. The intent of the drum parts needs to allow for that vocal stuff to happen. Snowy might have had a difference in opinion as to what to play, whereas Kim's like, 'Well, right here is a vocal line. Why do you want to throw this in there?' Typically this storytelling is taking place with the vocal. Whatever the vocal was bringing to the table, all of that that needs to be heard and clearly heard."

As Snowy explained to *Sick Drummer* magazine, "Gradually, more and more I had started feeling unhappy with my whole situation, and all I wanted to do was to write my own music. I remember spending most of my free time playing guitar in the studio's relaxing room. Also, I wasn't too crazy about some of the material either. But I tried to ignore those negative impulses and convince myself I was just grumpy and had a bad day. After all, I was a fan of old Mercyful Fate, and I knew people would kill to be in my position, so I didn't wanna make any rash decisions. Despite all this, I still I think my drumming on that album is pretty good and suits the music well."

"Before I joined King Diamond, I had no previous experience with the business or touring whatsoever," continued Shaw. "I was totally green, young, and perhaps must have seemed annoyingly naive. But make no mistake, I knew my music, and that's why I got the job in the first place. It was a really good learning experience, and everything seemed to happen for me overnight, pretty much. But I guess it was my time. I had paid my dues and surely was qualified for it. I just had to take the passenger's seat, keep a low profile, absorb, and learn. I'm very grateful for that opportunity. I'm not a businessman and I definitely didn't have any posters of Bill Gates and shit on my bedroom wall when I grew up. I'm an artist and couldn't be happier if someone else could take care of all the crap so that I could concentrate on making music and putting on cool shows and putting out great records."

"When he left it broke my heart," says Michael Denner. "I slowly lost interest in Mercyful Fate. It really broke the band. My favourite of those '90s records, personally, was *Into the Unknown*. I was quite satisfied with the guitar parts I did and also some of the songs were very good. I was quite disappointed with *Time*. I thought there were some weak songs. I thought it was weak and more pop-ish, compared to what we did in the old days. But luckily enough, a lot of people came afterwards and said, 'Oh, I like this song and I like that song.' So, I mean, that's the most important thing, to note that the fans liked the album. But I was very disappointed when we released that one."

Curiously Hank concurs. "The one I don't like so much is *Time*. We did *In the Shadows* and that was the comeback thing, cool, and everybody did their best at the time. But when we were recording *Time*, suddenly King was wanting to experiment and had these other types of songs. I threw in a ballad here and there (laughs). Then afterwards, the production went wrong and we had to remix it. There were a lot of things wrong about the record. But a lot of fans really like the *Time* album, even though it's the one I don't like that much because the material is not that Mercyful Fate-like. There are only a couple songs that you can say, okay, that's true and genuine Mercyful Fate. It was a little too experimental. The best one I like after the reunion in '93 is *In the Shadows* and then the last one, *9*, I think is pretty cool."

Then Sharlee says the same thing... "I actually like all of them in hindsight, now, but there are things I don't like about them and things I do like. But no, I didn't like *Time* very much. That had something to do with the whole process of recording it, which was very long, and it was my first album with the band. Just the process of getting into how you work with all these people took a bit of time to sink in. Now, listening back to it, it's quite melodic, but it's got a bunch of good songs."

"What we wish for is for us to get a little more exposure," mused a hopeful King just after the album was done, speaking with our magazine *Brave Words & Bloody Knuckles*. "To get that special support tour with Slayer or play for a bigger audience. That's what we need because I think there's a lot more people out there that have not been exposed to us fully. We look into the audience and you see a lot of different shirts. I've seen everything from death metal bands to Bon Jovi and that's quite a crossover of people to hear our music. I think we do have the potential of breaking big, if we get the proper exploitation and get the right chances. We just want to make other people aware that we are there and to try and make them take the chance on you. I don't hear other bands sounding like us and vice versa. We just write what we feel inside and whatever we feel at the time we wrote the songs, then that's what you hear on the album. I think that has a lot to do with us still being around so many years later. We've created our own little niche and it's not affected by time."

Despite how busy King was, now juggling both bands at once, Mercyful Fate mounted a robust campaign in support of *Time*, beginning with seven dates in Germany, November 13th through the 23rd of 1994. The North American tour kicked off in Boston on January 18th of the following year, and went through February 19th, with a couple of isolated European dates in July.

Wrote Jane Scott, in *The Plain Dealer*, reviewing the Cleveland show, "Just then, lightning flashed on the Agora screen. Thunder cracked and a red upside-down cross lit up the darkened stage. A black-cloaked figure descended from an upper level carrying a cross of human bones attached to a microphone. This was King Diamond of the Mercyful Fate quintet singing 'The Oath' and beginning almost an hour-and-a-half of black metal, not to be confused with ordinary heavy metal, you understand. Mercyful Fate's shtick is Satan and witches, demons and the dead. Some call this Danish group cult metal. Call it entertainment, too."

"The band—Hank Shermann and Michael Denner on guitar, Sharlee D'Angelo on bass, and Bjarne Holm on drums—kept up a pounding sound that was hypnotic. Much of it was similar, but the steadiness of it was a perfect for foil for Diamond's voice. Diamond swings from falsetto to a bellowing baritone sometime in the same song line. Much of his words are hard to make out, but the feeling comes through. Halfway through the 16-song set, Diamond asked if there were any headbangers, those who swing their long hair around in circles, out there. A few banged in response. That motion seems too tame for today's mosh pit. Some of the fans were too busy body-surfing—being tossed up in the air by fellow fans. Others clustered towards the stage and listened."

"Diamond surprised many by wearing a black top hat," continued Scott. "The effect was a little mixed. Coupled with his white-painted face, *Clockwork Orange* eyes and painted chin marks, his look was more Broadway than creepy. His chin designs have been more extensive since Gene Simmons of Kiss sued him for applying makeup too similar to his.

"Surprisingly, the four new songs from the current *Time* album were among the most effective. The powerful 'Nightmare Be Thy Name,' the Middle Eastern-flavoured 'The Mad Arab,' the glorification of Lucifer in 'Angel of Light' and the song that he said was about his people, 'My Demon,' stood up well to the old favourites, such 'Melissa,' 'Come to the Sabbath' and the finale, 'Evil.' Diamond's solo band, King Diamond, is more theatrical with scenery such as haunted houses. He wants to keep the acts separate, but a little more variety would pep up Mercyful Fate."

Reviewing the Cincinnati performance was Rob Hartzell, who informs us that, "Mercyful Fate's show Thursday at Bogart's went off without a hitch. That's not a bad thing. Several years ago, at a solo performance at the Corryville club by Fate vocalist King Diamond, a fan was stabbed to death. If there were any injuries at Thursday's show, they were hearing-related. The Danish heavy metal quintet was punishingly loud throughout its 90-minute set. The music spanned the band's 12-year career from 'Don't Break the Oath,' the opening number, to the 12-minute 'Satan's Fall.'"

"How things change in a decade. In the mid-1980s, at the peak of its career, Mercyful Fate was at the forefront of the then underground metal scene, along with Slayer and Metallica. Back then, King Diamond's avowed Satanism was as shocking as his music was novel. Since then, the horror shtick has been done—with even more revulsion—by newer bands. By comparison, Mercyful Fate came off like the backdrop for a late-night TV horror film fest. Diamond certainly dressed the part, wearing a bowler hat, a Dracula cape and his trademark Kabuki-style makeup. Factor in the candlelit altar in front of the drum riser with ghoulish images projected on screens above, and what you get is close to high camp. The 325 fans who came weren't laughing. They headbanged and slam-danced throughout a set that focused more on older material than on songs from the band's newest release, *Time*. Although Diamond's voice, a shrill falsetto, is an acquired taste, the band was musically as over-the-top and energetic as its theatrics. All this satisfied the crowd enough to keep them chanting for more even after the lights went up."

As alluded to, in the thick of promoting Mercyful Fate, June 5th of 1995, King Diamond issued *The Spider's Lullaby*, his first solo record in five years. From this point forward he would be conducting in real time the experiment to determine which band would yield him personally more bang for the buck. As we'll find out later, Mercyful Fate would come out on the losing end of this battle.

7.

INTO THE UNKNOWN
"YOU NEED TO FIGURE THIS OUT AND GET THIS TO STOP."

Soldiering on through what was a tough time for heavy metal, Mercyful Fate put together a third reunion album, all while King was doing double duty with his solo band. *Into the Unknown* would emerge on August 20th, 1996, after having been recorded at the beginning of the year, in January and February. A month later, we'd also have *The Graveyard*, from King solo.

"Different members make it quite a different environment because of different personalities involved, songwriting included," said King at the time. "Also, Mercyful Fate has always been a very '70s-influenced band, and I think that's still there big-time. King Diamond is more modern, and there's also a wider variety of instruments used, although both bands are very much based around guitars. But with King Diamond we'll use any instrument to enhance a certain mood, which can be done successfully when doing these full-length stories."

"Which is also a big difference between the two bands," continues King. "That creates a difference in the music. When you're doing these full concept stories, you get into more extreme moods than when you're just doing individual songs. Because you'll have certain things occurring in the story which you have to underline, which is also why the King Diamond records are longer than the Mercyful Fate ones. That's because in my mind the story behind *The Graveyard* was so intense that I really had to try recreating the different moods as best I could. You need the album a bit longer to still have the normal song structures in there as well. Really, if you had both bands record in the same room with the same sounds, it would still sound different, and that's because of the players of course, who make up the two different lineups."

Delving deeper, asked to contrast Hank Shermann and "first guitarist" for King Diamond Andy Larocque at this juncture, King figures, "Both certainly have a lot of their own input into what they like to hear. Both guys I would say always have all their gear in top condition, every pedal, all of it. They always have everything planned out. They know exactly what they're going to do. Equipment-wise, everything works and guitars are being balanced and in synch in all kinds of ways."

"Herb (Simonsen) in King Diamond is like that too, everything right-on. But Andy and Hank are two players that don't do much spontaneous playing. It's very planned out, what they're doing. It happens of course, that they'll say, 'All right, I'm just going to go for it and we'll see if I catch the right feel.' But most of the time even their solos are planned to the smallest detail, with harmonies etc. Whereas Michael Denner's playing is very free flowing. I'd say 80% of his solos are played on feel, whatever comes to mind. Then he will later learn his own solos. Andy is very music-oriented, whereas Herb is more theatrical-oriented, in the way that Herb will go so deep into the story before recording. In his solos he's trying to reflect what's going on in the story at that point. So that's a nice difference between the two. Michael Denner on the other hand is more about feel. He reminds me of Michael Schenker a lot, and Hank is more into aggression, not that Michael can't play aggressively."

Back co-producing Mercyful Fate with King was Tim Kimsey. "The biggest difference was that we were in a different studio," explains Tim. "It was still a part of Dallas Sound Lab, but we were in a much smaller studio. The approach was very strategic and honestly pretty brutal. We got sounds on every instrument—we actually did samples. When I say samples, it was every instrument from kick drum to snare drum to hi-hat to rack toms to floor tom to overhead left, overhead right. You did about a minute-long check of every instrument that was played. So, at the beginning of every day, if we were tracking drums, well, probably the first hour to hour-and-a-half was making sure that nothing had changed."

There we are, back at the theme of his tale, really, that Mercyful Fate was as good as they were because they worked hard. As Michael Denner said, the band's benchmark was Judas Priest in the '70s. *Into the Unknown* was going to be as meticulous and fastidious as the last, as considered, as literally planned. It's almost as if in the back of the guys' minds, they were ruefully cognisant that we've got these off-putting vocals and these off-putting lyrical themes—or limiting, let's say, in terms of commercial reach—that we'd better be the best band in the world behind it.

"I was not used to that," continues Tim, "going through the perfectionist side of things. It was brutal in the sense that we knew every day when we stepped into the studio, we were going to be spending that first hour to two hours just checking to make sure nothing had changed. Now the flip side to that is that when it came time to mix that record, it was almost already mixed by the time that we got there."

Besides the slight change in studio environment, Mercyful Fate had for themselves a new drummer, Bjarne T. Holm, little known before now, save for his connection to the band through Hank's pop metal outfit Fate and second side-gig Zoser Mez, led by Hank and Michael Denner, who says "Bjarne is so versatile; he could play all kinds of music, blues, jazz or whatever and he's an extremely easy guy to work with."

Beginning with the break from Snowy Shaw, Tim believes that "The decision had been made while Snowy was there on the *Time* album, but I think that was kept close-vested. I didn't want to overstep my boundaries and get up into anyone's business. But thinking back on it, I had been told, look, this will probably be Snowy's last tour with the band, so that was the last I saw of Snowy. Bjarne brought a freshness, a fresh new outlook."

Reflects King, "Every studio you work in will give you a different sound, and different contributions from different players will do that too. Snowy brings in one kind of drum kit for *Time*; Bjarne brings in another kind of drum kit for *Into the Unknown*. That's one difference, but there's also a difference in their style of playing. So, these nuances make a difference, even though in the end it's the compositions."

Speaking with MTV for *Headbangers Ball*, King said, "The new album brings Mercyful Fate closer to what we're all about. I think it's more of the old-fashioned Mercyful Fate, but at the same time there are some new areas that we have not been involving ourselves in before. I've used the voice in some different ways that I haven't sung before, and we get into new areas which I think is important too, as long as you keep it within a certain frame. That will always be the case for Mercyful Fate and King Diamond, because we've always played straight from the heart; we always write music straight from the heart. So that means, we're not going to change overnight and you'll hear us play a punk album next year or something. That's never going to happen. We feel so strongly for what we do, and it's honest. We don't try to be anything we're not. We know what we are—we're just a heavy metal band and that's it, you know? But maybe in a special way, because there are so many bands out there today, and there's not many that have done it our way. I think we've had a very unique, special sound, always. There are no two bands out there that sound like Mercyful Fate or King Diamond; I don't think so."

Commenting on the construction of *Into the Unknown*, King said that "When we were recording albums, writing songs, back in the early days, we were more immature. Fighting each other a little bit more to get our own songs on the albums. Today we have a totally relaxed relationship about that. We know who's going to write how much before we start an album. So, in a lot of ways, we can really feel now that we've matured and we're not the little kids we were in the beginning. We know what the business is about. You know a lot more about how you record, and we're producing ourselves now, and those are some big differences."

"Also, touring. We've reached another level, from back when we started. We were touring in a very rough way in the early '80s, and '84, over to the United States. We were living... We had three dollars a day to live off, so that was McDonald's. 'Do you want a pack of cigarettes and a doughnut today or do you want a pack of cigarettes and a sundae ice cream?' We had no money at all. It was hard to make the bus go to the next city. We even borrowed money from the Mafia in New York, to make the bus move. It was tough days, but we got through it and it was very healthy and good to have those experiences because you learn a lot."

With no Mafia tribute to pay in Dallas, now it was down to business, and not with many visitors, other than the occasional look-in by Metal Blade Mafioso Brian Slagel. Noted King at the time, "We do everything ourselves, but Brian had some time and I always like his comments. I might not agree with him, but that's not the issue. He likes what we're doing and I like his company. When he comes in, it's for the sake of the music. We'll always try new things. He was only around for three days but I'd be the last one not to try out any ideas he might have. He got the first impression of the songs and that's what helps us."

"Everybody knew of everybody, but we separated for a while, so no visits from Pantera, for example," continues Tim. "The Pantera thing for me was '93, '94, so I had already been doing Mercyful Fate and King for a couple of years. But we had all different kinds of artists walking through the doors at Dallas Sound Lab. Even, dare I say, rap was walking through our doors at that time. Sterling Winfield and I, we were getting to do all kinds of different genres. Pimp C from UGK was wanting to see if there could be a collaboration with these metal guys crossing over into the rap thing or vice versa. That just never really came to fruition. But everyone kept to themselves when we had work to do. Mercyful Fate's and King Diamond's budgets were very good budgets, but we knew that we were going to eat up every penny of the budgets that were there, just simply because it was going to take time to get through it all. So, no sir, not even the Pantera guys visited."

"It was really meticulous detailed work, and long hours, but I just can't say enough about how all these guys were tremendous human beings, wonderful people. I hope people that are growing up in the industry right now can listen to these records and have an appreciation for the effort that went into this stuff. I teach school and I teach 5.1 Surroundsound mixing nowadays, and we're living in a society where it's instant gratification. I gotta tell ya, as an older or aging producer, I'm telling these kids, you guys need to go take a listen to some of the older stuff that's out there to have an appreciation for what it took. It's not the same anymore."

Into the Unknown opens more like a King Diamond album, offering substantial keyboards and voice and nothing else. What is King saying on "Lucifer?" Well, it's essentially a "Lord's Prayer" to the dark lord, 1:29 of overt Satanism.

Shockingly, this "song," which is essentially a throwaway track, an intro at best, was to cause a rift big enough between King and Tim to the point where Tim would not be back for the next record.

"This was where I drew the line with Mercyful Fate," explains Tim. "We always started with the music first. There were never any lyrics exposed until it was time to sing. The way I looked at it, we're telling stories, but this one was a Satanic prayer. It's nothing shy of that. That really creeped me out. I told Kim, I go, 'Man, to me, it's really crossing the line; I'm uncomfortable with this.' King explained to me, 'Man, we're really just poking fun at the holy rollers.' I said, 'Well, I'm really super uncomfortable with this and I'm going to ask you... I understand, if you guys decide that it's going on the record, but I'm going to ask you, basically, if you will not put this on the record.' The answer to that was, 'No, it's going to go on the record.' That's when I gave them an ultimatum. I was basically, if this goes on the record, then this is gonna be my last album. 'It's not that I don't like you guys, it's not that at all, it's none of that stuff. But it creeps me out just a bit.'"

"So, to this day, we still remain friends," continues Tim, who did in fact follow through on his ultimatum. "I've been over to Kim's house and we've had some pretty in-depth conversation about the spiritual side of things. I get asked all the time, is that real? Is he a Satanist and so on? I don't know if he was or not, but I think that there's mutual respect wherever that may fall. But as far as us having discussions in the studio about Satan worship, that never happened in the studio. He would have his little figurines and skulls and stuff, but that was all part of just setting the vibe for what the record was going to be."

Further on King's motivations, Tim explains that "There was an interview with King about dads and their kids, talking about little children, stuff of that nature. There were moments where literally the lyric content would get you to think as a human being. It's like, oh man, I need to go call my dad; I need to go check in with him and check for sure that he's okay. I've had discussions with Kim about that too. That's what these stories are all about, to get people to think about this stuff. I'd tell him, 'You're a master pro lyricist, man, because what you write will get to you if you're in the right mood.' It will make you think and it will make you want to call mama and daddy to find out if they're okay. But for the most part, we're telling ghost stories and we're telling stories about stuff where you can let your imagination run wild and have all kinds of fun with it. That's literally what we did: we let our imaginations run off with us, which was so much fun."

But Tim put his foot down. He would not be on board—or on the board, so to speak—for 1998's *Dead Again*, but rather replaced by his understudy, Sterling Winfield.

"I had to think long and hard about that," reflects Kimsey, "before I put that ultimatum out there. Because you've got to think about it like this: for six years, between Mercyful Fate and King Diamond, that was my living. I did nothing but those records. So, before I put that out there, I just felt like I needed to really think about it. I needed to be prepared for what the answer to that was going to be. The answer that came back was exactly what I anticipated. I did not want to be a missing cog in the wheel that needed to turn. So basically, I told the guys, 'I won't be your engineer on the next record. However, I will help you find the person who will be your next engineer and help you guys through all of this.' That's where we made the decision that Sterling would be the engineer on the next record."

Once "Lucifer" is dispelled with (or summoned onto the studio grounds, as it were), *Into the Unknown* explodes into view with a double bass drum barrage and some howling guitars before King enters centre stage, singing sonorously the opening verses of "The Uninvited Guest."

"There's a little old man" becomes this year's hook line, at least for those paying attention to Mercyful Fate at this time, which frankly is a rarefied corner of the potential heavy metal audience. Nonetheless the song is a rousing rocker, buttressed by fulsome, red-blooded production.

As if on cue, an uninvited guest of sorts made his presence known on the sessions. Relates Tim, "There was a time where we were recording onto digital tape. It was DA-88 tapes and the lights were down. I'm laughing about this now, but something happened where this is no joke. The tape machines went into slow rewind. When that happened... first of all, usually when digital tape goes into slow rewind, you don't hear audio that comes off of that tape. But it went into slow rewind and it was making this really eerie, spooky, weird sound. Lights were down low... I could not get the tape machines to stop doing that."

"Hank was in the control room with me. As a matter of fact, Kim was out in the studio doing vocals when this happened. I looked over at Hank and I go, 'Hank, what do you think this is?' He goes, 'I don't know, man, but I'm gonna tell you, you need to turn the lights up. You need to figure this out.' So, it was nothing shy of just like, oh my gosh, what is going on?! Then that's when Kim—through the microphone; I could still hear him and everything—he goes, 'Well, they're here.' So that just made the situation even more eerie. Hank was... I don't know if he was kidding around with me or anything, but I want to say he was half-serious about it; he goes, 'This is really creepy, man. You need to figure this out and get this to stop.' 'We'll get it done somehow or other. I'll figure it out.' It was really creepy."

"The Uninvited Guest" was the subject of the band's most elaborate and classy video yet, with multiple sets including farmers' fields, a creepy house (for the "little old man" narrative) and a church. Woven throughout the colour-splashed tale, the band looks impressive rocking out, cameras panning to guitar solos on cue, as well as capturing punctuated drum whacking. As usual, King's expressive actorly gestures really bring the singing to life, in essence, making his falsetto parts look more natural.

Strength to strength, next is "The Ghost of Change" which sounds like bracing uptempo Black Sabbath. Second song in a row and the music comes from King. It's impressive that while writing even more of the music for the solo situation, there's still enough in the well for top-shelf Mercyful material. The verses and half the chorus of this one are in falsetto but it works well. Along the lines of what we are being trained to expect with a King contribution musically, there aren't too many parts and the song is sturdy and hooky.

At the lyric end, there's a reference to the old oak tree, which was fully depicted through a song called "The Old Oak" back on the *In the Shadows* album. There, much hanging took place but there is no mention of a woman resigned to that neck-breaking fate. Here the inference is that King is consorting with a passed-on woman who might have been hung there bathed in moonlight. Of course, we always ponder fondly on Melissa, but the cast of characters has been growing, subtly.

"It's like describing an old thing that happened but in a new way," King told Hardradio's Sheila Rene, when asked about this one. "I told you the story about the incident where we're all sitting around the table and this glass flows up into the air. It has something to do with that. The ghost that came that day could be seen in many different ways. It gives you these two paths you can go by. You're at a crossroad and there's a lot of interesting stuff for you if you want to take the other road, or you can stay where you are. At that time I definitely took the new road and experienced a lot of things that I never imagined were possible to experience."

INTO THE UNKNOWN

"In this song, 'Ghost of Change,' this spirit or ghost came back to me and gives me another chance to change my path. I'm actually being given the chance to relive my life, and as it all passes by I'm sure that I don't need that ghost of change anymore. This is where I want to go and the road that I was shown back then. The self-manifestation for me as a person and what I believe in and how I see the world as well as the music which you hear on this album... we are where we want to be. We will always hopefully be able to put new aspects into the music, but there is a certain aura and frame that Mercyful Fate belongs in, and within that frame there are still a lot of corners that haven't been explored yet. It's self-confirmation musically and also to the fans because you're not going to hear a disco album or something crazy like alternative. We are what we are and we're not pretending to be anything else."

"Listen to the Bell" is more proof that this is a special album, although—let's face it—"under-rated" is a term that could apply to the complete Mercyful canon of the '90s. Still, this is groovy, dark, well-written and well-constructed traditional metal. Not a fast one, "Listen to the Bell" is a doomy grind. Lyrically, it's a deliciously dark story: there's a black church, dead trees, "them," a bell, a belfry... King is weaving connections throughout his canon, creating what is almost an extended conceptual film noir narrative across the years.

Commenting on the composition process, King told Rene, "Hank wrote that song. Hank and Michael both write stuff on their own and record them on four-track tape with a simple drum machine and a little bass. They send the tapes to me and I listen to them. It's gotten to the point where Hank knows very much what goes and doesn't go with me. He has turned into a person that can write a song with the vocals in mind. It's much better than in the early days. There was very little that had to be changed on Hank's and Michael's songs this time. It happens often that it could be that the main part of the song is all right but the chorus isn't quite there, so we work it out."

"Before recordings and tours," comments Bjarne, "Hank and I always rehearsed, just guitar and drums, to open up the new riffs and arrange a little, so the band had something to work with right away. It did happen that you already had a long day, but I remember many times arriving and already in the parking lot hearing Hank and his Marshall stack, loud—very loud—playing riffs so great that it filled you up with energy and you just couldn't wait to get behind those drums and play. This particular song was dark and very Mercyful Fate but had a flow to it, and at that point made me think that it might even have a chance on Danish radio, who did not have a passionate relationship with occult metal in the mid-'90s. My bank manager tells me that didn't happen (laughs), but it is a great album track."

"Fifteen Men (and a Bottle of Rum)" finds King impinging on Running Wild's pirate metal terrain, usurping Alestorm. But true to mandate, it's pure (and well-paced) storytelling. King was trying to do this repeatedly throughout reunion-era Mercyful, while, as we've seen, not giving up on Satan. At the music end, this one comes from Michael and it's admirably outside of the box, more atmospheric and bluesy, although as bluesy as Mercy gets is basically arriving at Sabbath and no further.

King called the song "slow and sad," also telling MTV, "A song like 'Fifteen Men (and a Bottle of Rum)' we haven't seen from Mercyful Fate before, really, talking about an old ship in the Caribbean Sea that has a bunch of drunken sailors on there. They can't sail the ship when the storm comes, grabs the ship, and throws it into the Antigua islands, and everybody goes down and drowns. You can hear this captain still singing at the bottom of the ocean, 'Storm is coming.' But that's a different subject."

"I'm lazy as a songwriter," admits Denner. "I can do one song a year or something, because if it's not there, I would just leave it, compared to just making twenty songs and eighteen of them are terrible. If I cannot feel the song, then I would just leave it, and I can leave it for six or seven months without doing anything about it. But this time I had two songs ready and it worked out; it fitted in with the rest of the songs for the album. So that was a pleasure to be able to write the songs."

Then it was over to King, who Michael says, "turned out the lights, to get in the right mood and atmosphere. We just left him in there doing his shit. We would play a game of pool or grab something to eat. He preferred to just be in the darkness in there doing his stuff. Then he could bring us in and say, 'What do you feel about a choir here? Or the chorus I made there?' and so on. To get our opinion. But we just left him in there, because this is a special moment for him, to be able to do what he does. We just left him there in the dark (laughs)."

It turns out the lyrics are generated in the dark too. "Yes, I like to do them at night," King told me back in '96. "If they're 70% done, I can continue during the day. I could if I wanted to, but I prefer doing them at night. I have a better feel and I think better. There are not so many disturbances and I like the darkness; that's the best environment for me to be inspired in. But in terms of subject, you are inspired by so many things. A lot of what you hear on the albums, of course it's not original. It might seem original, but it's taken from so many different things. Not that I'm aware of taking it from elsewhere, but everything you see and hear around you is stored, put into your brain in some way. It's like a factory. You get a lot of raw materials in and then something is manufactured. That's what's happening. It's just a matter of taking out the right things. You get in different moods and you start remembering this and you start remembering that, a conversation between two people… 'That's right; that guy was treating that other guy like that because… that's right. Interesting.'"

Then everything has to be just perfect to convert his words into sounds, including all of the music surrounding them… "In the studio, I have to be there every single moment that we're recording anything," explains Diamond. "That's the way I feel, that I have to be there to make sure to myself that everything goes down with the right feel. Because a few kick drumbeats can really change the whole feel of a riff. The same goes for laying down the vocal tracks. There'll be days that I get a lot done because I'm in exactly the right mood to do these things. There'll be other days when I can't catch the feel and I can hear myself—I'll be in there singing for an hour-and-a-half and I've got nothing on tape that is worth listening to in my opinion. Then it's like forget it, give it up, let's go on to some solos or other stuff, because it's not working today. Then the next day I can do the same thing in like an hour and have everything done. It's very up and down, a matter of being in the right mood at the right time."

Next is the record's title track, exemplified chillingly in the abstract by the record's classy, understated cover art. Here King uses successions of simple words, no proper place names or Christian (!) names, as he spins a tale of human sacrifice, with much of it reporting on the short but gradual process of death. The music is groovy and traditional and King sings it in kind. He's thespian but also very human, reflecting the two sides of the ritual gathering. "Into the Unknown" is one of the band's most atmospheric and "loose" songs in a long time, despite the many parts, which sound like they've grown into place like a cyst more so than planned on a whiteboard.

Reflects Bjarne, "It's possible that some songs on this album could have come from other bands, but the great weirdness of the title song is a good example of something that could only come from Mercyful Fate. There are dynamics to make the more powerful parts stand out, but all the time there is an undertone of some sort of danger. I love that all of this is done with a couple of guitars, vocals, bass and drums. 'Now my finger points at you;' that's King at his very finest."

As Diamond told *Terrorizer*, "The harmonies in the song are probably the most complex of any song we've done in the past. I think the song would have been at home on *Don't Break the Oath*. Try to count the timing in this piece: it's so screwed-up."

Any Satanic intent on the title track remains veiled, but that resonance is stronger on "Under the Spell." At the witches' dance, "He" arrives and drinks all the wine.

"That song is very much about people who have a relaxed relationship to religion," points out King. "But there are a lot of people who are hysterical about their religion and won't tolerate anything else. In that song we ask the question, 'How come you're so sure you're right? It's an inner thing that we can't all believe the same. It's a mockery in a way, where I'm standing outside the church and seeing the Holy Ghost with these witches who are partying. This is pretty heavy stuff. It's blasphemy."

"What I have always thought seems confirmed more and more," King told me at the time, in one of our periodic spiritual check-ups, or check-ins. "Of course, I've had a lot of experiences that have made me think of things spiritually. But also, in everything we do, there is very much a down-to-earth life philosophy. You know, how does the human mind react? How do we behave towards each other? Are there societal problems we should think about twice, or do we throw them out because they don't really concern us? A lot of these issues we're raising are what is going on today. But it's within a story, so people who don't want to get too involved don't have to."

"But I still have the same view I've always had, and that is, I believe we all have a power inside us. I don't care what people call it, maybe a soul or spirit. That power, at some point, was unearthed for the first time. Each power exists to experience all possible feelings and experiences there are to be experienced here on earth. I think that it probably takes many lives for one power to experience all the feelings. But these feelings can be experienced in many different ways, even if doesn't mean that you have to experience all actions. Like feelings of killing other people: it could be in a war or in self-defence, but there is a certain feeling if you've done that, I'm sure. Being in prison, or being punished, and even being punished for things you haven't done. But that has to be experienced at some point."

"I may have experienced these things in former lives. Maybe I was a witch-hunter at some point. That's why I wrote *The Eye*; I don't know. But I do believe we have to go through all kinds of feelings that there are to be experienced, and that might take several lives, where this power will be unearthed within each human. We will learn a lot of things."

"And when this power dies, it goes to what I just call 'beyond,' where knowledge or experience is stored," continues Diamond. "Then a very little bit of it is taken with it back to earth, where it will go through another life, where it's stored up and built until it's the fulfilment of the experience that you have to have here on earth to arrive at a complete form of life. I believe that it has a lot to do with the questions you ask yourself. There's a certain balance in this world between good and bad, and it shifts all the time. I believe that that shift has to do with things that need to be experienced. At some point, a lot of good things will be experienced by a lot of these powers, and it will seem like the world is a little better. Then next time around, oops, it's time for most of those that have gone through the good stuff, they're not going to go through it again. Suddenly there are certain shifts taking place."

"Things like why an innocent little kid gets run over by a truck running after its ball… it makes no sense in many ways. The usual reasoning for that is that God's ways are mysterious. I personally can't accept that. It's personally okay that others can, because I always have respected—and always will—other religions, and people who believe different things. Because individual means exactly that: one-of-a-kind. There is no one else that is the same, and therefore everybody will have different thoughts from everybody else, and different feelings and different needs. We have to respect that. But we don't, and we probably never will, as a world. That's why we have all these wars. People love to judge others by what they believe or even by things like status symbols. You'll believe the mayor over the common worker any day; that's the way society is. In most cases, it's not a good position to have."

"Back to the spiritual thing, that kid that gets run over, to me that power in that body, that little kid, has finally reached that experience level of having experienced everything there is to experience here on earth. Therefore, there is no need to be here anymore. Sometimes you hear about a plane crash and there will be 200 people, and 197 killed and three survived. No way. There again, it could never work for me that oh, God was merciful to those three. Well, what about the other 197? But to me, there were a lot of these powers gathered in one place, ready to go on. There were also three that were insufficiently experienced that will carry on."

Mind sufficiently blown, when I asked King if this corresponded to any philosophical readings he's come across or any religions he's heard of, he says, "I don't think so. Not closely. I don't know about too many different religions very much. I've never had the urge to actually get into it. But for as long as I can remember I've had these kinds of thoughts, asking myself a lot of questions about things and trying to answer them in a logical way. But still, religion can never be completely logical because you're talking about beliefs, and a lot of these things you can't prove to anyone. No one can prove that their god is the right one. That's impossible. You can't stand there with your closed fist and say, 'I've got my god in here, in my hand. Now I'll open my hand and show you exactly that he is here, so you will believe too.' You open your hand and there's nothing."

"So, it all comes down to beliefs. Everybody's different and we all have different needs because of where we come from and what's been happening in our childhood. We all have pictures and images which have been shocked into our brains, and at all times they will influence us. Sometimes you might change your view, and at other times you might stick with it because you've never had any proof that would make you think differently. Then you can start talking about life philosophy, which is a whole different point, the way you live and interact with others."

"But good and evil... one doesn't come without the other, or we're not alive. We have to have those two other points to everything to express our feelings. If everything was perfect you'd be nothing, because how would you use that for anything? Everything is perfect. You're in limbo."

Arcane and deluxe treatise on reincarnation fully unfurled, it's back to the album. Noted King on the "Under the Spell" musical vibe, "When I listen to 'Under the Spell,' it has the same beat as much of the early material. But nothing on *Into the Unknown* is a copy. We decided to use two rhythm guitars, one on each side. That was a challenge in a big way."

An additional note on the lyrics, King refers amusingly to the "southern witches," making the story sound local to his experience now as a Texan. In the song, they busy themselves "turning every single cross around and upside-down."

Another brilliant musical configuration forms the rock bed of the album's next track, "Deadtime," this one being a rare Michael Denner composition and therefore rarefied in its fit to the catalogue as a whole. Like its predecessor, it's uncommonly melodic and groovy and King sings it just as uncommonly, putting atop it an Ozzy Osbourne-like vocal melody. Lyrically, King retells the tale of *Little Red Riding Hood*, adding an extra jolt of implied child abuse, which was fully on his mind given the concurrent writing of *The Graveyard* where that is central to the theme.

King framed this one as "a joke, like what we had on King Diamond with 'No Presents for Christmas.' I misunderstood *Little Red Riding Hood*, where you hear about Little Red Riding Hood. She's a little bitch in this story, where she's bringing poisoned food to her grandma, trying to kill her off. It's Mercyful Fate so we have to have a werewolf in there, not just a normal wolf. It ends up with grandma not only eating the wolf but Little Red Riding Hood. So... I'm sorry kids, I didn't mean it (laughs)."

"You can barely get around what that is about," explains King, speaking about *The Graveyard* but tacitly addressing why there are echoes of in "Deadtime" as well. "It's a subject that is maybe taken lightly, or at least something people don't like to talk about. It's such a taboo that it gets pushed away. It's like if people start talking about it, people will start pointing fingers and suspect *them*. But if you don't talk about it, we won't solve it. There are too many cases in the judicial system. Or it can be that the way we bring up our kids is wrong, where we might just take the slightest little effort that might help in these situations."

"A little kid going to school on its own. It might only be 500 yards, but those 500 yards can be extremely dangerous. It doesn't take very much for a perverted criminal or psychopath to stand in the bush and say to a kid, 'Hey, your mom's calling over here; can you hear her?' That kid will react to things like that because it's natural. But if those instincts can be changed a little bit, or if you can find maybe an elder lady or elder man who's not working anymore, with free time on their hands, to just follow the kid to and from school for a few dollars... just seeing an adult with a little kid will deter perverts from approaching them."

"Of course, the whole game is luring them," continues Diamond.

A DANGEROUS MEETING: IN THE SHADOWS WITH MERCYFUL FATE

"But there are so many things involved. Andy and I talk about it a lot—because he is a father of two kids—just how in society we're very suspicious of each other. Andy says of his little boy and little girl, he says, sometimes I'm actually scared to go pick them up after kindergarten. Because you can be scared that something has been said, and some adult with a perverted mind has misunderstood or read something into it. It could be a little girl saying, 'Daddy gave me a bath this morning.' The teacher might have a bit of a suspicious mind and start digging and saying, 'Really, oh, how does daddy bathe you? Does he touch you?' and all this crap."

"I mean, hey, you can't even have a healthy family where a parent can't even bathe their kids?! It gets so dirty just because people have dirty minds and dirty thoughts. If you don't talk about it, it's going to remain hidden. Like it says in the foreword to *The Graveyard*, we all have dirty thoughts and that's okay—as long as you don't act upon them. But if you can't admit that you have such thoughts, something might be wrong with you. Something might be nagging you deep inside. I'll admit it any day, that God, there are some 13-year-old girls that look killer walking down the street. You're like, 'Wow!' Every normal guy will look at it that way. But all those who are normal will also not act upon that thought, or that picture in their mind."

"That's where decency comes in. But people who say, 'Me? Never!' You're a liar! Why don't you admit it? Maybe you're the guy out there with your binoculars watching the kids in the playground? I think if you're more open about these things, you'll be able to take more of these lunatics who are walking around out there off the streets. But with our judicial system, it can't be right that you can take a child molester—which I consider the same as a murderer completely— and he can be released six years after committing the crime."

Asked if he had little princes and princess Diamonds of his own, King said, "No, but I would love to have kids eventually. But we tour so much. I do spend a lot of time away from here, you know. I want to see my kid grow up. I definitely want to be there. I don't want to come back after five months and say, 'What happened?! Oh God, is that really mine?!'"

Come "Holy Water," really, we remain in a very melodic place, with this song being arguably the hookiest yet across the album, with Bjarne rocking it mid-paced, hi-hat a little open for extra groove, riding his ride cymbals in other parts, some of them on half-time breakdowns. Lyrically, King couldn't get much more gleefully

Satanic, snarling over a mournful chord sequence, "I'd rather drink from the Devil's well and then I will go straight to Hell—oh yeah!"

As for the reference to the "valley of Blankenstein," "That's a real place in Germany," explains King. "A lot of stuff in that song is taken from real places. There is that myth that the devil keeps a lot of souls captured in this one lake, and if you throw things in it, they'll come up and turn everything upside-down."

Into the Unknown closes with "Kutulu (The Mad Arab Part Two)" which reprises the geometric, middle eastern musical riff and structure from "The Mad Arab" from 1994's *Time* album, but played tighter and a little quicker, less of a slog, snappier. Plus, King is slightly more aggressive on the vocal. It's a little jarring hearing King go full-on death metal for the "Kutulu! Kutulu! Kutulu! Kutulu!" bit but then again, death metal was doing pretty good at the time, especially on Metal Bade.

"That's based around the story of the person who supposedly found this ancient book called *The Necronomicon*," King told Sheila Rene. "It's only two songs we've used from that book. It tells of the exciting or interesting things that happened in his life. Was he a real person? Was Jesus a real person? It doesn't matter because it just makes for an interesting story. It's supposedly the guy who wrote *The Necronomicon* that Clive Barker and H.P. Lovecraft got a lot of their stuff from in his writings. Not exactly the story itself, but the powers that are described in it. The elders and the ancient ones."

The Japanese release of the album got a bonus track, Mercyful's sparkling, vital and immediate version of Judas Priest's "The Ripper," which also can be found on the fine *Legends of Metal: A Tribute to Judas Priest* album where Mercy was joined by other bands well within their class.

"Mercyful Fate was very inspired by Judas Priest," reiterated King, speaking with Scott Hefflon. "So, this was a way of paying tribute. That was a perfect song for Mercyful Fate. Each instrument, the vocals and the production really recreated the sights and smells of the alleyways being stalked by the Ripper, down to the bit of swagger in his walk. I had a really good feeling with that song. It's very rare that I can get into the mood of someone else's lyrics. In the very early days, I was in a three-piece that Hank and I helped do a demo for. He had a song about being a truck driver that he wanted me to sing, and I was like, 'Are you serious?!' He said, 'What? I don't think it's that bad!' I felt so stupid singing that song. I couldn't relate to it."

A DANGEROUS MEETING: IN THE SHADOWS WITH MERCYFUL FATE

Sadly, *Into the Unknown* would be the last Mercyful Fate album from Michael Denner, who had been there from the beginning. "The thing was, my wife, our first child was supposed to be born at that point and there were complications before the birth, and I had to make a tough decision to leave the band and support my family. I really enjoyed playing with the guys, so that broke my heart, and they're dear friends of mine. That was a big and sad decision to take, but that was the only thing I could do."

"The thing is, with that album, it was a step up or two. We went back to what I loved about playing with Mercyful Fate. There are some great songs on it. I was in shape and I did some work I was proud of doing. To have Bjarne Holm in the band, he's an old friend of mine. I've known him since the early '80s. I actually tried to get him to join Mercyful Fate because Kim Ruzz was out of the band for a short while. So, I tried to get Bjarne Holm in the band, but he was busy doing something else. That was way back in 1982 (laughs). Bjarne is a very easy guy to work with, and that helped me not to be too sad about losing Snowy at the time. I do believe the band's songs were a bit stronger again. I was quite happy with that album, compared to *Time*."

"But yes, I was about to become a father for the first time and my wife had complications right before the birth and it was very serious. We thought she would be crippled. When my son came, he had this handicap, he's special needs, so I had to use all my spare time for that. It was a very, very tough decision. I recall when I saw the band for the first time with Mike Wead when I left, it was very painful experience. Because I picked him out as a replacement for me. He had the feeling and he could play my solos. But when I saw them live, I had to call a cab and go. It was like seeing your old girlfriend with a new guy."

On the tour trail back in '97, Hank acknowledged Michael's absence, explaining that, "Mike Denner is not playing tonight. He decided to be back with his child, in Copenhagen, which was something that also happened with the US tour last year. He wants to take care of his new-born child. We have a new guitar player called Mike Wead, who's been in Memento Mori and Abstrakt Algebra. He's a really, really good guitar player, and his playing style is very similar to Mike's, so he is the perfect fill-in."

Addressing extra-curriculars at the time, Shermann added that, "When Bjarne and I are not doing Mercyful Fate, we're doing a side-project called Gutrix, which will release an album on Dzynamite

Records. We have a CD ready and a video ready. King Diamond lives in Dallas and we live in Copenhagen and the bass player lives in Gothenburg, so we don't see each other on a daily basis. We have a lot of time off, so we have time to do other things to keep ourselves occupied."

Indeed, Gutrix issued an album in 1997 called *Mushroom Songs*, and as with all these guys away from the central tenet, Hank and Bjarne opt for more of a '70s vibe, a little psychedelic, a little grungy, but generally rocking out retro.

Eager to hit the road, King was calling *Into the Unknown*, "the strongest of the three reunion albums." When I asked him about sales over the years, he answered more so in terms of the King Diamond catalogue, saying that "Every single album has been at least 100,000, especially *"Them,"* which was over 200,000. *Conspiracy* must have been up there too. *Abigail* was also there, but it was *"Them"* that put us in the Top 100 on the Billboard charts. So, it varies with album to album, but it also depends on whether you tour or not. Mercyful Fate is going to start a short tour now and I know King Diamond will come back after we've done the European tour. The King Diamond album has just hit the streets. Mercyful Fate is on Metal Blade worldwide, who also have King Diamond for everywhere but Europe, where it's Massacre Records. Both labels are really excited. They're getting more orders than expected, so that's very good news. The touring should help. We are doing the double headline tour in Europe (note: this was Mercyful Fate and King Diamond, with the front man obviously pulling double duty!), starting the 27th of February. Once the album works itself in a little here, hopefully there will be the basis for doing a really totally crazy King Diamond tour."

As he told *Terrorizer* at the time, "The tour has been well planned. Each band will play for over an hour. It seems like a new thing to do. The tour is going to be so special. Right now, King Diamond has a new stage being constructed in Copenhagen with a complete graveyard including headstones and coffins. Mercyful Fate will have a full production as well."

King didn't think putting both Mercyful Fate and King Diamond on one bill in America would work. "No, it's not that feasible or possible to do the double headline shows over here because the sites just aren't there to fit the tour. If you want to put both bands on the same bill it's hard to get the money out of the promoter. He can't put more people in the place and all he could do is raise the ticket prices and I don't believe in that."

"I think Europe and the US are much the same," answered King, with respect to where the band(s) did best. "It's been a long time since we've toured Europe. It's only been a few festivals by Mercyful Fate. Now it looks like we're going to do a tour that's bigger and more extensive than the last King Diamond tour for *Conspiracy*. But it will be different for Mercyful Fate. We've done separate German and Italian tours, and shows in Holland and Belgium, but there's not many places Mercyful Fate have played. We also just did the Monsters of Rock in Brazil. That was both bands. We did four shows in Brazil and one in Argentina. I played four shows in 24 hours and then did six shows in 48 hours. But the voice held up—that was amazing."

Curiously, King remarked that the contrast between the two solitudes for him personally is that, "It's the same, except I'd say that King Diamond is a character who is performing these things on stage, which the rest of the time it's pretty much me letting go of my feelings."

Indeed, the band played Monsters of Rock in Sao Paulo, August 25th, 1996, to an audience of 49,000. There were six South American dates in total before the band transitioned to the US, beginning that leg in Old Bridge, New Jersey, ground zero for metal on the eastern seaboard, on October 19th. With a lone Canadian date in there, in Montreal, the band covered the eastern half of the US winding up in Houston on November 9th before a one-off gig in Mexico City. Says King, "The Mexico City show was the best ever. It was an old opera house with a 3,000 capacity which sold out. It was so cool."

A robust European campaign followed, with the band working its way across the continent (mainland only—no UK shows) from February 27th through to March 30th of 1997.

As always, the legend of King Diamond preceded the band arriving in your town.

"I mean seriously, man! You have no idea the rumours I've heard on the road. There was once the crew guy that said, 'You should hear what we told one of the fans.' It's like, you gotta stop that stuff; you're just fuelling all this weird stuff. But this time, I was not even there. I was at the hotel room sleeping. They said, 'Don't go to that room; Diamond's sleeping in there. He brings his coffin from Denmark. If you wake him up, he's guaranteed going to kill you. So, you've got to be quiet.' It certainly doesn't help when they tell them these stories!"

"Of course, by now people know from interviews and all that that it's not that kind of thing. Now I can counter when people ask me things directly. I was once in San Antonio on a radio show and a fan was asking a question, 'Is it true you sleep in a coffin every night?' I said, 'Seriously, not every night.' Then they can think what they want. Can you imagine my wife's parents? When they saw pictures for the first time. Like, 'This guy would like to marry your daughter.' 'Uh, I don't think so.' They don't know what the person is like."

Of note, King later in fact found his "soulmate," marrying the Hungarian-born Livia Zita-Bendix, 28-years his junior, born Livia Zita Lokay. Livia is active in King's career, as his business partner but also as guest vocalist both live and in the studio on King's projects. She is also a graphic designer and photographer. The couple had their first child together, a son, in 2017.

"A lot of people unfortunately treat the fans of metal as if they're stupid," continued King at the time, on being perennially misunderstood. "They are super-intelligent. That part they've got so wrong. Our stories are not that easily absorbed because there's a lot of twists and turns. Those who are into really getting out of the story what they can, they find all these sub-layers and connections and stuff and they get it—they absolutely do; they get it. But still, there's an entertaining story for those who don't want to go too deep. But those that do, they certainly get it. Going up on our coven website there's a forum where fans are talking together. I often go there to see what they're talking about, and there were discussions where they'd be talking about religion or music or the military or daily life, jobs or whatever. Man, they get it. I mean they get it! So, it's a misconception that metal fans… yeah, look at them, long hair, scraggly this or that, they can't be smart people—they've got it all totally wrong."

"It's not so much to give them a shock," continued King. "It's more like to put them in a mood of some kind. I've learned with the lyrics that sometimes it's more effective to suggest things than to actually say exactly what it is you want to say. If I want to describe a certain sinister winter or a face from outside, instead of saying exactly what it is and looks like, and that it had these hollow black things, teeth coming out of the mouth, I'll just say that behind there in the darkness suddenly there was the shape of a human face. The listener can make it much scarier than I can, because he will pull from all the things that he feels most scared about and use that. But so many things on the albums come from real things. They twist and turn a bit but it's those inner nasty feelings. Some people hate spiders and they probably hate some things that were on *The Spider's Lullabye* because it was not described in super detail to where they could associate all the worst fears themselves. You know what I'm saying? You suggest something up to a certain degree, but then you leave it to their imagination because they can much better scare themselves."

"We're not thinking of packing it in yet," said King, framing the state of his affairs at this juncture in 1996. "It's very much a matter of the fans. As long as they want it, we'll probably try it. The day the fans aren't there and we're playing for 50 people in a bar somewhere… you don't want to get to that stage. Then we'll start doing something else, movies or whatever. I'd love to see some of these stories turned into a movie."

8.

DEAD AGAIN
"DARK IMAGERY AND NIGHTMARISH SITUATIONS AND GHOSTLY THINGS."

In 1998, King was at it again, virtually pairing the crafting and issuance of a King Diamond record with one by Mercyful Fate. February of that year saw the release of *Voodoo*, with King explaining to me at the time that, "Maybe *Voodoo* is a little more upbeat and aggressive, more of the traditional King Diamond style, compared to *The Graveyard*, anyway. It was never meant to be a story about voodoo. I had started writing music for the next album, I had some ideas about calling the next story *The Plague*, but that almost took me right back to *The Eye*—it was the same time period. Suddenly we were talking about witches getting burned again and all that stuff. It was like, I've already written about this; this is ridiculous! So, I change my mind, and I do that a lot. But I'd always wondered what voodoo was about. I only knew what everybody else knows—chicken feathers and blood, blood, blood—but not really what it was about. So, it was okay, I'll check that out. When I started reading about that religion, it was like 'whoa!' I said, I've got to write a story with this in it. It was actually inspired by the actual song 'Voodoo,' because that song was written before I looked into this. On these demos I had these tribal drums, and that's what made me start thinking about voodoo."

Once *Voodoo* saw release however, King was very quickly back to work on what would be the fourth of the Mercyful fate reunion albums. The big difference this time is that Hank would have for himself a new axe partner for the first time, given Michael Denner's exit from the ranks. Enter Stockholm shredder Mike Wead, who by this point had built a long discography for himself through such esteemed acts as Hexenhaus, Candlemass, Memento Mori and Abstrakt Algebra.

"Some of that stuff was great and some of it wasn't," remarked Wead, speaking with Abner Mality. "I like some of those old records a lot. We had a good time doing them. I've worked with a lot of talented musicians through the years, so I'm pretty happy about how they turned out. I've actually been talking to the other guitar player in Hexenhaus, Marco, about doing something again. Mostly just for fun. We have some songs we've been kicking around. When it comes to playing, Hexenhaus was the most progressive one. It was the most fun playing those songs."

Asked if he prefers more so progressive metal, Wead says, "Sometimes, yeah, but overall I prefer the more melodic parts of a song. It's easier to play my own style during those parts. I've been playing for such a long time that I've developed my own sound. It should be fairly easy to tell when I'm playing a lead." On the topic of whether he plays "on an instinctual level," he answers, "Yes, I'd say so, but it also depends on what parts I'm playing. If you're playing a really complex lead and the backing music is complex as well, I have to really think about what I'm doing. But if it's a more ordinary rhythm part, it's easy, it's second nature."

Assesses Snowy Shaw, now out of the ranks of Mercyful but a co-member of bands with Wead, "Mike is a phenomenal guitar player. It's also a shame that he's not... going back to all this talk of contributing in the songwriting, I bet he has a whole bunch of classic songs to do, that he could bring to King or Mercyful Fate.

We were working at the same time that I was doing Mercyful Fate — he and I were in Memento Mori. But yes, he's a phenomenal guitar player, and also a good songwriter and could come up with catchy titles and all that. Really talented. But nowadays I guess he doesn't write that much. He's just playing guitar."

As for Wead's influences, Snowy figures, "the obvious ones, like Yngwie Malmsteen (laughs). All the guys from that period were hooked on him. But also he goes way back to Uli Jon Roth, the predecessor to Yngwie, of course, plus Michael Schenker and some of the fusion guys."

"They both cover about the same ground," says Sterling Winfield, concerning Mike's and Hank's roles in the band — Winfield would be co-producer on the project, credited first along with "Mercyful Fate." "I remember having a discussion with King on *Dead Again* about, well, their tones are different and I don't want it to feel lopsided. That was one thing that King did speak up about, and we had that talk a couple times. I told him, 'I understand what you're saying, but I don't think it's going to be a big deal because I will try to shape both tones where they are not completely sounding like each other, but that they complement each other.' I think that's what we did and he was happy with it in the end."

"Not everything is all puppy dogs and rainbows and kittens in a recording studio," continues Winfield. "You have discussions; somebody sees something one way and the other guys sees it another way. From what I remember, Hank was always a Strat player. He played with a single coil into a Marshall, an old vintage Marshall. Mike always had that humbucker sound, going into an amp that was probably a little more modern. That's the contrast there; Hank was more the vintage guy, the Ritchie Blackmore influence single coil Strat sound going into a Marshall amp, and Mike was a little more modern humbucker going into something a little more modern like a Marshall, but like a 2203 or something like that. But we did actually work it out."

"As far as their playing styles go, they both pulled about the same weight, as far as what they did. They both did a rhythm track on each side, left and right. They usually would trade off and have a lead on each song. Sometimes on the Hank-written songs there would only be a spot for him to have a lead. Or if there was a song where Mike wrote the riff, then there would be just a spot for him to have a lead. But most songs, there was a spot for both of them. Actually, they have similar styles. When it came to knocking them out, they both took about the same amount of time to get their stuff done. They always had all their parts mapped out before they even showed up. It was all charted out. We always had these charts in the studio as to who needs to do what where. Very well-organised. That was one thing that I absolutely love about working with those guys. Even though things might not go perfectly according to plan, they did have everything mapped out and thought out before they even walked into the studio."

Reflects Hank, "Especially after *Time*, we thought wow, that's a mistake. We knew it was a mistake, even though it sold pretty cool. From there we headed to the old style from the '80s and you can certainly hear that on *Into the Unknown*. Then we went to *Dead Again* with Mike Wead as a guitar player and we changed again!"

Continues Sterling, "We were coming off of *Voodoo* and when I say we were coming off of it, we went directly from production on *Voodoo* straight into *Dead Again*—we had no days off. We were working 12 hours a day, and our production on *Voodoo* went over. We were supposed to have a ten-day break in there or something, if I remember correctly. We went over as most projects do, because they never go how you planned them."

If Mercyful always seemed like a hermetically sealed shop, at least the guys managed to get Dimebag Darrell in on the King session. "Yes, geez, man, I remember the night that we had Dime down for the solo he did on the title track 'Voodoo.' There was definitely a hangover the next day on that one. But no, Mercyful, it was such a gear change and breath of fresh air, because we had a different drummer come in. It was night and day. It being Mercyful Fate and not King Diamond, King was really willing to hand over more control to me as co-producer and just say, 'I want you to do this.' He let up the reins because it's not King Diamond—it's Mercyful Fate."

"I remember it being really, really fun, with a lot more creativity coming from my end. As far as the sonic things go, the drum sound in general, he left that up to me. He was like, 'Just do it, man. Just take the ball and run with it. When it comes to my vocals, just let me come in here and do my thing and I'll be happy, you know?' But it was gruelling because of the hours and because we were coming off of that other project and going straight into it without a break. Still, the atmosphere was a little lighter, a little more carefree."

Asked if given his long history with the band, there was a little bit of Pantera and Vinnie Paul in the drum tones this time (indeed the sounds are steelier than ever) Sterling figures, "I would be crazy to say no. Definitely not miking techniques, but as far as the actual sound, that was going to come through me by osmosis anyways. So, I think there's a little bit of Pantera influence in there. There's two people, two or three people in my life, that taught me just about everything I know about sound. Tim Kimsey was one of them and Vinnie Paul is the other—I learned so much from those dudes."

"But it was really easy going," continues Winfield. "You're dealing with a different band except for King, who's the one commonality here, but it's such a different vibe, and not in a bad way or a good way, just different. I remember having a blast 'cause I'd already worked with Hank before. We would have our days where things would go great and you'd have your days where certain things wouldn't fit in. You're not sure things translate from preproduction into real production sometimes. You just have those days in the studio. But overall they made my job easy. We got sounds really easily and we just kept trucking through it, getting it on tape. Brian Slagel would always come down for a day or two during the production of both King and Mercyful Fate. We'd go out to dinner and hang and he listened to the tracks. We'd play him what we had and we'd always be sending him cassettes or DATs or whatever as we moved along. In fact, I just saw King and Brian the other night at the first show of this new King Diamond tour at Bomb Factory here in town."

Asked about the difference between King when he's writing the music and Hank's methodology, Sterling figures, "The King stuff tends to be more story-driven. He has this vision for things. Nowadays, which is King Diamond more so of course, him and Andy do everything in Pro Tools and they bounce things back and forth between here and Sweden, where Andy is. But back then he would just bring his little four-track recorder in and he would already have a keyboard idea and a structure. He'd have this rudimentary rhythm guitar riff thing going. But the music would work around the story, because King would come up with the story first and then weave the music around that. Whereas a Hank-written song is more riff-oriented, more like pulling from his influences that he loves, which are numerous and many. So, he's more that style: heaving rockin', guitar-driven."

"No, it's all King, all day, all night," chuckles Sterling, asked if any of the backing vocals included any of the other members of the band or indeed any outsiders. But, as he relates, Diamond maintains a difference between what he does between the two bands. "Yeah, the Mercyful stuff was always more straight-ahead rock album type stuff. King, again, more story-driven, a lot more theatrical, a lot more the big choirs and operatic-type stuff."

Over to a touchier topic, Sterling reflects that, "The falsetto, people will say, 'Oh, he's just doing this falsetto thing and he's layering that in there.' But he's singing that falsetto louder than most people sing. He's got a very powerful voice. A lot of people don't realise that, namely how much this dude projects. We would do ten-, 12-hour vocal sessions. He would go home and his throat would literally be bleeding. He would just take care of it as best he could and we'd be right back in there the next day. He really works hard. You hear King singing and you immediately know it's him. He's got his own signature. It's a wonderful contribution to the music world. King is King and there will never be another."

"I would say that he's probably right on the edge of a low alto/high tenor kind of thing," answers Winfield, asked to describe King's middle gear, that gorgeous Glenn Danzig-like singing voice he shows us in doses, between the half-spoken snarl and the falsetto. "I think you're right with the Glenn Danzig comparison. King's got a wonderful straight voice, if you want to call it that, his full chest singing voice. Absolutely. I think it's much under-appreciated and underrated. When that dude starts singing, you know exactly who it is—it's a signature."

With respect to the *Dead Again* album cover, we're back to illustration, but it's the esteemed Kristian "Necrolord" Wahlin who got the call. The most prolific illustrator in black metal and other genres for many mostly Scandinavian bands, Wahlin went with a tribute to *Don't Break the Oath*, showing the Devil from that cover on a faux framed painting, in the form of a silhouette, filled with King and clutter.

Into the music, the album opens starkly with a geometric riff rife with pregnant pause. Then we're quickly into the meat and muscle of "Torture (1629)" which finds King relating all manner of witch torture and execution as it related to the mass witch trial in Wurzburg, Germany, 1626 – 1631. In the spaces created either side of the riffing we clearly hear the bright and steely drum sound conjured by Bjarne and Sterling.

As we learned last chapter, Sterling was there because Tim Kimsey had taken issue with King's overtly Satanic lyrics and here we are in that space again, although really King is essentially telling a story of Christian brutality.

"I knew he had had some issues with that," muses Sterling, "and

I knew that he couldn't see doing the next couple of albums. I didn't know that that ("Lucifer") was the particular rub until after I had gotten into the production on those two albums, *Dead Again* and *Voodoo*. It's not quite my bag, but I understand where he's coming from and that is completely within his right."

Next is "The Night," a swaggering mid-paced rocker with a call-and-response vocal, mirroring the duality of the lyric. The narrator—easy to imagine as King—plus his friend "Old Nick" are on the prowl, in fact riding a snake, to find God and find out who he or she really is. User-friendly this one is, especially at the riff end of things, salt-of-the doomed earth like Sabbath. Or Pantera, really, because this isn't far off Dime at his most groovy and accessible. Perhaps as a clue to the headbang-ability of "The Night," a video got made for it, although it's a straight live performance theme, i.e. no props to underscore any of the narrative.

"Since Forever" continues in this huge stadium rock mode, with a thumping mid-paced beat and simple riff, even if there are creepy recurrences of the mellow intro music. King's lyric is enigmatic, vague through the use of the awkward phrasing of "since forever."

A reunion of two old souls is taking place, but then the last verse has King piling upon the listener fully four mysteries across five lines. Ultimately what we have is an elegant example of King's idea of not giving too much away—he can go both ways, i.e. highly descriptive with proper names or like this, and both have their merits.

"The Lady Who Cries" isn't particularly long, but it finds the band back to celebrating their progressive metal roots, offering various speeds and multiple breaks, many of them complicated in their own right, some of the riffs like top-flight Tipton and Downing. Seems like a Hank tune but King gets the music credit, as he does on fully five of the album's ten tracks.

"Very preparatory," is Sterling's answer on how the band can make such crafted complexity and not break the Metal Blade bank. "It wasn't like this organic thing of free-flowing ideas. It was fairly planned out, down to the day. We had our charts up on the wall the first day in and we were knocking stuff out. Financially things were taken care of up and down, down to the minute, and you made sure things got approved and all that. Just like being on tour. They ran a really tight ship. King had a lot to do with that—he was a highly organised person. Without that, it would have been pandemonium; it would have been chaos."

So, no pandemonium, and nothing paranormal either. "No, but

I think there's always some energy around places like that, artistic places. I always wonder about that. I'm not sure if I ever witnessed anything, but I hear stories from other folks."

"There's always weird stuff happening around us," countered Mike Wead, speaking with Abner Mailty, "like VCRs going on by themselves. I think everybody in the band has had their share of weird experiences. I remember one time when we were in Dallas recording one of the Mercyful Fate albums and I was in the lounge. It was somewhat like this, with couches, tables and VCRs. I was just reading a magazine and all of a sudden the VCR starts playing for no reason. That was a very odd thing."

There's no surprise however that something spooky happens in the lyrics of "The Lady Who Cries." In the song, King chalks up what is an almost amusing win for the Devil, taking the tale of the weeping Madonna statue and turning it on its pointed ear. At night, clues are made available that the Devil is in fact inhabiting the stonework, with the implication that all the prayers showered upon the statue day in and day out are going straight to Hell. "Great vocals," comments drummer Bjarne, "and haunting guitar solos, which gives the track some metal/blues tone that I like."

Adding to the richness of variety across *Dead Again* is "Banshee," an act of pure doom, and, given the mournful harmonic riff, doom even of the newer ilk practiced by the likes of Paradise Lost and My Dying Bride. Lyrically, King is back to painting pictures with simple words and in this case, representing a simple concept, howling banshees "under" the window, unsettling enough that the cats have taken off. As it turns out, the banshee is not a threat in itself, but a sign that before the night is done, someone will die.

Instantly with "Mandrake," we hear why Hank should be heralded as one of the great riff masters of metal. Again, there's a sense of history to what he does, where here on the verse as well as the galloping portion that occurs come chorus time, he evokes Glenn Tipton and elliptically, Tony Iommi. Let's also not forget the production as well as the performance at the drum end. Bjarne sounds live and aggressive, even if the song is in a relaxed tempo. All told, across the writing and the sound picture, *Dead Again* is arguably proving itself as the best Mercyful Fate reunion album thus far—again arguably, because on all of them, the band are sweating blood to deliver quality.

At the lyric end, King reveals much of the dynamic and the lore of the mandrake root's magical powers through time—there's even a mandrake connection to Hitler—but the treasure here is in his rhythm, his cadence, the words spilling out, falling upon themselves as if the teller of the tale is in a fever caused by mandrake root poisoning.

"Sucking Your Blood" is somewhat of a vocal showcase, with King using all his guises, including vocal harmonies.

Describes Sterling, on setting King up to do his thing, "We would turn out all the studio lights, and he would just have a music stand set up, where he could set his lyrics. He would have a little table over to his right for his cigarettes and coffee and stuff like that. We'd set up a mic and he'd just have a little red light out there so he could see the lyrics. He would set the mood for himself. It's a lot of dark imagery and nightmarish situations and ghostly things, so he's trying to set a mood for himself to really get into these characters and these lyrics. King is the man when it comes to these things. He has a vision and a certain way that he wants things to be, and so we do our best to make that come to life for him."

Affirms Sharlee D'Angelo, "He liked to do his vocals on his own, with the engineer or the producer. He usually blacked out the studio completely and had a lot of candles and a few skulls and things, his own little dark good luck charms. That's basically how he gets in the mood."

And the mood is definitely as dark and as dead as can be for the album's nearly 14-minute title track, with "Dead Again" going to extremes, from grinding atmospheric doom to frantic velocities of gothic speed metal. Straight horror music too, as the band work their way, sometimes surreal, past King's descriptive and action-packed lyric reporting on the moment of death and what might happen during that indeterminable stretch of time.

Sterling's understudy on the project, Kol Marshall explains how his work on this song helped to move him into the producer's chair the next year, on what would become Mercyful Fate's last album to date.

"I'm very proud of having been involved in 'Dead Again' because I think the one thing that sold King on working with me was when Sterling wasn't available for that. Sterling had, for whatever reason, been unavailable during part of 'Dead Again''s production and so I ended up doing the vocal recording for just that 14-minute-long title track. That was the last song for which King had to record vocals. He really didn't want to have anybody but Sterling recording vocals and he was steadfast about that. But when it came right down to it and that was the last one to do and Sterling had to be somewhere else, I was second engineer and it was my job to step in. I did and it went really well. So, we'd developed a rapport in the studio with me behind the controls while he was singing that, and I think that led to him being willing to let me take the driver's seat for the whole project the next time around with Mercyful Fate's *9*."

Relates Winfield, who indeed was there for the music, "I remember the discussion being that the whole thing was this journey of this guy dying. I had to put myself in the mind of this psychedelic journey to grasp what King was doing. We sat there and it took us a whole day just to get the tempo mapped out, because they were doing it by feel. Hank Shermann and Mike Wead were in the control room and we were building this tempo map so that they could play to it, so that Bjarne would have a track to play to. There were several different tempo changes in the song. But the only reference to 'Satan's Fall' that they ever made was just the link that it's going to be a long one, like 'Satan's Fall.' It had nothing to do with that song lyrically or story-wise. I also remember it didn't really start to come to life for me until I heard it with vocals. Then I was like, okay, I'm getting it now."

Bjarne T. Holm on drums helped the process as well. "Yes, amazing. I love that dude; he's top notch. Whereas we really struggled on the King Diamond album, with getting sounds and getting drum parts nailed (note: that album features John Luke Hébert on drums, as does the follow-up, *House of God*). That was one of the reasons we were so far behind on production on that album—we spent too much time on the drums. So, Bjarne comes in and instead of taking three or four or five days to get drum sounds, we had drum sounds in about two hours and he was nailing the songs, even this really long, epic title track. He nailed that in two takes. That's it. That's a 14-minute song and he nailed it."

For his part, Bjarne calls this one, "a heavy metal opera or something; 14 minutes of dark madness. One has to send wholehearted warm thoughts to Metal Blade for giving the band absolute artistic freedom. There are lots of mood changes and chances being taken from a composition point of view. But no timpani, no 110 violins or giant production, still only a classic band setup. I think I dubbed a triangle though."

"Fear" demonstrates the band's ability to push melodic boundaries, second bonus to this one being the cantankerous and bashing performance welling up from the rhythm section. King's lyric is an unshowy treatise on the concept of fear, which he recognises looking at back him in the mirror. The vocal melodies consist of long notes, but the distinguishing feature is the song's mournful, slightly atonal guitar riff, not loveable but hooky because of its oddity.

Dead Again closes with "Crossroads," a song credited to Sharlee D'Angelo at the music end. Amusingly, the riff sounds like a slightly uptempo variant of old Mercyful classic "Gypsy," and pointedly not the type of thing a bass player would tend to write.

Lyrically, King manages a considerably poetic telling of the standard tale of the crossroads, the place to consort with the Devil as it were. Helping shine it up, he injects into the equation a quartet of female gods, namely Hecate, Diana, Selene and Persephone.

Reflects Winfield on the D'Angelo credit, "The thing about working with King, especially on a Mercyful Fate record, was that everybody came to the table with things and they were always good about helping one another. 'Hey, I got this riff. Can I put a song on the album?' And then working out the business details later."

"But, yeah, it was awesome to work with Sharlee, great to hang out with, funny. He had a monster bass tone that I absolutely still love to this day, one of my favourite bass tones that I've ever recorded. Just monstrous. At that point he was just running a big, Classic Ampeg SVT with the... they didn't call them Classics back then, but they were just the old, big, giant, 150-pound bass heads, going into the big Ampeg 8x10. Then he had a couple of really cool foot pedals that we used to make the thing all distorted and huge sounding, just really big and monstrous. It had a lot of teeth in it: smooth and big and fat, you know?"

"King's a really good guy to work with," adds Sharlee. "Of course, I've had a lot of arguments with him in the studio, but it's usually just musical things. He's of course very particular in what he wants, what he wants out of something, and so am I, at times. But he's not impossible at all. He'll say, 'I want you to play like this.' 'Yeah, but that's not going to be very good.' We would try both versions out, and he might actually go, 'You know, you're right. Let's go with your version of this.' So, there's a lot of back-and-forth. But I suppose like anybody who cares about what he does, you take a stand and you fight for it, if you think that you have a good point. I mean, he's in the studio constantly, monitoring things. He would sit in the corner and scribble out some lyrics and do whatever, but as soon as something happens, he's there all the time; he listens. You hardly notice him, in a dark corner somewhere. But no, he's very good to work with."

"Crossroads"—and therefore the album—ends with a harsh and hard stop, and this after the tension builds as the band bashes and Diamond shrieks. Tucked way at the end, it's testimony as to how many top-quality songs are on this album everywhere you look, and that's lyrically, by music structure and again, through the power and passion in the performances. On this one it's everybody, but in particular it seems like King and Bjarne are having the most fun.

"I think it was mostly Hank and King that got into the odd quarrel about things," continues Sharlee, "but I didn't really have much of an argument with any of them.

What does working on a Mercyful Fate album entail? In the end, it's all very much a band effort. But King's very much into the production side of things. He sits down and listens very carefully to things way more than the others of us do. But on one song, one person might be the leader, and then another one will be different."

"I'm biased because I got to work on it," says Winfield, asked to assess *Dead Again* across the reunion albums, "but it's definitely one of my favourites. I would get a different charge out of it than a fan might get, which, I'm a fan as well, but at the same time I was there; I got to be a part of it. That was my first big co-production break right there, with King saying, 'Hey, I want you to co-produce this.' That was him being nice enough to let me have control of the ship for a while and let me drive things. I'll always be grateful to him for giving me that opportunity."

As for Sharlee's assessment... "I think *Dead Again* had a lot of good songs and a lot of potential, but some of them just didn't come out right in the end. Be it the recording, playing, mixing and all of that. So, I would have to say that my favourite of the albums I did with Mercyful Fate has got to be *9*; I like that a lot. I think *Into the Unknown* is a little too dry-sounding. I don't know what it is, a bit stiff and a bit dry. *Dead Again* I thought had a pretty good production. But just some of the songs are being performed, I don't know, slightly stiffly. It's just something I remember compared to what I thought it would be, to what it became if you listen to it with completely fresh ears and you don't have an opinion of what it's supposed to sound like. That's the thing: I'm too involved to say anything, to be objective about it. Anything I say will of course be extremely subjective, because I had an idea before we started about how it was supposed to sound, when it was done, and of course, it's not like that."

The album did not exactly penetrate the pop culture bubble and make much of an impression. *Kerrang!* predictably gave it a brief and dismissive review. But less predictably, that review was by Malcolm Dome. This proves that even the old guard, those who were there from the beginning and get it, even they can feel a sense of cringe-factor at their heroes being out-of-touch with the fresh music of the day, even the fresh hard music, which at this point was Marilyn Manson, Rob Zombie and Coal Chamber.

What's interesting there is that these acts are all, in a sense, scary music—and what a different level of scary that was, compared to the traditional themes and tales and conservative backing soundtrack utilised and patronised by King and crew.

Hit Parader's uncredited three-star *Voodoo* review struck the same tone, indicating that, "The King lives! Love him or hate him, you've got to hand King Diamond one heck of a lot of credit. Working with what would appear to be no more than a modicum of talent, this Danish rocker has constructed a long and successful career for himself as both a solo performer and as an integral part of the fright-metal act, Mercyful Fate. This time around the King is on his own, producing an album, *Voodoo*, that presents all the "classic" King Diamond effects—loud guitars, screeched vocals and songs that chill to the bone. Most likely *Voodoo* isn't about to win any new converts over to the King's dark musical visions, but if you liked him before, you'll probably still like him now."

The first date of the *Dead Again* tour campaign was July 24th, 1998, at one of Jack Koshick's infamous Milwaukee Metal Fests, the 12th, in fact, with Mercyful sharing the headlining slot on the first of two nights with Death and Cannibal Corpse, who ultimately did not show due to bus trouble. The author was in attendance and got to witness a changing of the scary metal guard of sorts, with all the excitement and buzz surrounding Emperor's headline set on the second night, the Saturday.

Crestfallen after the show backstage that they had to play without their keyboardist, Emperor nonetheless got across to the rapt crowd their next-level black metal aesthetic. King was a known quantity and his music was starkly polished compared to the disturbing wall of sound emanating from the dour Norwegian crew. As a result of this polarity of approach, press for an act like Mercyful Fate had proven to be thin on the ground right from *In the Shadows* in '93, through to the band's upcoming last album, *9*, in 1999.

After Milwaukee, it was pretty intensive touring through the rest of the summer up to September 5th and that was it, a full dance card for that stretch but nothing more, and all of it in clubs and the odd theatre in the United States, with Europe ignored.

On November 24th, 1998, Metallica issued a two-CD covers album called *Garage Inc.*, which gathered up all their old covers and added a pile of new ones. Track seven on the first disc was something they called "Mercyful Fate," which was in fact a medley of five Mercyful classics, namely "Satan's Fall," "Curse of the Pharaohs," "Evil," "Into the Coven" and "A Corpse Without Soul."

"That was so well done," King remarked, speaking with Scott Hefflon from our mag, *Brave Words & Bloody Knuckles*. "I was amazed. You can tell they really dug into the songs. They stayed authentic to the tempo and melodies; they just used a lower harmony in those places where the vocals get too high. Kirk didn't copy the solos, but he got the feel. It made me feel really good to hear someone get in that close to the original, yet it still sounds like Metallica."

Telling more of the story, speaking with *Metal Hammer*'s Chris Chantler, Diamond explained that "I didn't know they were planning it. Lars called me up at home and said to me, 'Hey, what's up? We're recording stuff right now; you wanna hear it?' I said, 'Wow, I get to hear stuff from the new one? Cool, man!' Then he played me the whole Mercyful Fate medley down the phone. He said, 'What do you think?' I said, 'Are you kidding?!' This was really, really an amazing take on those songs; it just sounded killer; it was so well done."

As King recounted, the love from the Metalli-cats didn't stop at *Garage Inc.*: "I've sung it with them at least three times. Once was in Italy while touring in 1999, and the last time was for their 30th anniversary show in 2011—that was my first time playing live after my heart surgery! On one occasion, Lars phoned while I was buying a car, asking me if I wanted to do the medley live the next day. So, I flew home in that new car and I ran in and put their version on, because it's different than ours—they have chosen certain verses to play. I can't just say, 'I'm singing a part of this and a part of that.' It's really their own take on it."

As with all the unsung bands Metallica chose to support on *Garage Inc.* (and earlier on *Garage Days*), there was a bump in recognition for Mercyful as well as a nice payday. I've talked about this with guys from Holocaust, Diamond Head and Budgie and the royalties were indeed much welcomed across the board.

9.

9
"THERE IS NOTHING HELD BACK, JUST LIKE THE EARLY DAYS."

"We wanted to do something different than just make another *Dead Again*. We really tried to find some new inspiration and make it a bit harder, more up-to-date, contemporary, make the production heavier than on *Dead Again*. I think that's the big difference."

So says Mike Wead, curiously revealing a truth that he might not have meant, and that's in the phrase "up-to-date." What would be Mercyful Fate's last album as of this writing would indeed sound rougher and harder, and yes, there's something up-to-date about that, but it's a focussed and even obscure up-to-date: *9* sounded a little more thrash 'n' roll, with a touch of black metal, a touch of thrash and a touch of NWOBHM as seen through the lens of younger bands beginning to revisit that era.

But it's emphatically not up-to-date like nu-metal, black

metal or even power metal, or whatever Coal Chamber, Slipknot and Marilyn Manson were. So maybe it is up-to-date with respect to something Mike Wead would understand and feel in his metal bones, something Scandinavian and underground. Maybe he did imbue that comment with meaning, rather than something you toss off on the press trail.

The fortunate point however is that 9 would indeed stand apart from the other four reunion-era Mercyful Fate albums. As good as they are—especially for this writer *Dead Again*, but everybody has their picks—they are of a state-of-the-art set, studied and storied collections of songs made by meticulous craftsmen trying really, really hard.

"They're individual songs," said King at the time, speaking with Scott Hefflon. "That goes for all Mercyful Fate albums, with the exception of *In the Shadows* which has a three-part song. King Diamond is the outlet for concept stories. In the beginning, Mercyful Fate was not that theatrical a band, so King Diamond was created to tell stories. It uses any instrument that'll enhance the feeling. Mercyful Fate is much more direct—there's no need for additional instruments. One thing many people don't realise is that the 'two classic albums,' *Melissa* and *Don't Break the Oath*, are very different from one another. People group them together without remembering that they're very different. But the thing about 9 that reminds me of those two albums is the attitude. There is much more aggression and attitude in the performance than there has been recently. Without losing the melodic aspect—there's a really good balance on this record. And the lyrics are much more direct this time out. There is nothing held back, just like the early days."

Further on the comparison between bands—he's said this before, but it's as if every time he says it again, there's something new that pertains to the current situation—King figures, "Mercyful Fate is very Stratocaster and King Diamond is very B.C. Rich. King Diamond is more modern and theatrical whereas Mercyful Fate is more '70s-influenced. Even if both bands played the same song, they would sound very different. Mercyful Fate's lyrics are about Satanic philosophy and raise a lot of questions about religion, and King Diamond is more horror stories focusing on human actions and reactions."

Here the guys were in Texas again, making a record, repeating the pattern where the understudy takes over as co-producer, with Kol Marshall on board for the roughshod rendering of what would become 9.

"I'll be honest, Martin; I wasn't that well versed in black metal and I wasn't all that familiar with King Diamond," said Kol, about first becoming part of the coven, one record back. "I'd heard a couple of songs, I'd seen images of him in his facepaint and I'd seen him at the local Guitar Centre store at times, but obviously without makeup. But I didn't really know him or know his work until I found out that he was coming to Nomad with Sterling. Sterling was bringing him in and that I was going to be working with them. I said, 'Oh, I need to get familiar with this.' One of my friends who was more familiar with his work hooked me up with a bunch of music. I've got to be honest; I'm not really from a metal background. I just happened to be in the right place at the right time to work with this particular metal act. We got good results and so it's been good for me. But it wasn't what I started out doing."

"You're right, though. What was great about that is that I came up under Sterling and assisted Sterling on some work before being first engineer myself. Sterling had done the same thing under Tim Kimsey and my assistant J.T. Longoria was next in line and took over and did *Puppet Master* and beyond. It really goes to show his more traditional work effort and work ethic and that he liked to bring up people who understood his process, started out helping out and then taking charge."

"But I don't know that we set out to do anything differently," continues Marshall, "other than the fact that it was me in the driver's seat that time instead of Sterling. King's approach was always very methodical. If anything, I think that he was letting some of the other members of the band bring more to the table. I may be wrong about that, but I was under the impression at the time that it was very much a collaborative effort with a lot of the music writing, certainly more so than a King solo project, which he usually demos out in great detail before he reaches the studio stage."

Sound-wise, says Kol, "I know that it's very different from previous releases by both Mercyful Fate or King Diamond, the stuff that we had done together at Nomad previously. The studio had digital tape at the time and an Otari console and that tended to get a very crisp, clean, and more detailed sound than some of the earlier productions, to my ear. So, I think that coming to that studio and going digital had an impact on the sound as much as anything else."

"What I remember enjoying the most was tracking the vocals. The basic tracking was done very systematically. We had a regimented system for how the tracks were produced because one of the main things, whether it was Mercyful Fate or even more so with his solo work, is that King wanted the consistency in production from the first note to the last. He wanted everything to sound like it was all recorded in the same moment. So, we were meticulous about making references and checking reference recordings before we would start a new project to make sure that the drum mix hadn't moved or the pitches hadn't changed or the tuning or things of that nature."

"But when we got to working on the vocals, I got to see King being creative, because he would work a lot of the melodies out in his head in the control room while we were working on the tracks. But he wouldn't actually really try them against the music until he was in front of a microphone. So, a lot of times he'd have some ideas, but then he'd fine-tune them once he got in the booth. That seemed to be his process."

The music was done the usual way, contrasting against Snowy Shaw's story about making *Time*. "Yes, they recorded in a traditional style with the rhythm section, bass, guitar and drums, just basically banging up the rhythms and then rerecording the bass and rhythm guitars as needed, if needed. But to get that feel, they were definitely getting the rhythm tracks live. It's my preferred way to work. Every time the drums were always the foundation and often with rhythm guitar and bass at least playing along with the drummer. Brian Slagel came by a couple times, but I don't know if it was that project or another. He always seemed like a jovial guy, very excited and very happy. I think we went out to dinner once or twice. But yeah, he did seem to be very enthusiastic about the project."

I asked Kol about Kim Petersen, the King we get outside of music. After all, take the makeup off and he's almost just another guy, albeit in the Glenn Danzig "evil Elvis" vein, retro looking, maybe a little Lemmy to him as well, with the commonality between all four of these personalities being the big sideburns.

"He was really into racing. He liked both his racing video games and he enjoyed going to NASCAR races. I think he had just started getting into it at the time I worked with them and got progressive more deeply into it." For his own ride, King had a black Corvette. "He did. He used to love the sound of the engine. It was one of the newer models." As for his house... "It seemed pretty normal and traditional other than the few eclectic items that he might have on display, and he had the biggest TV I'd ever seen."

When I asked Glen Drover, guitarist for King from '98 to 2000, about the Diamond domicile, he said that "He's got a really nice house, actually. When I first got into the band and did the *Voodoo* tour we did the rehearsals in Dallas and the first show was in Austin, but I was down there for a couple of weeks doing rehearsals. The first night we got there, we all went out to dinner and then went back to King's house and hung out there for a while. Man, he's got a large CD collection, thousands. It's a really cool place, but it's pretty normal, not what you would think. He's got a few pictures here and there, and some stuff drawn by fans. My memory is a little funny, because I was just dead. I'd been travelling all day and there was the stress of, 'Are they going to like me being in the band?' and stuff. But yes, he had a couple artefacts here and there. I think he's done quite well for himself. He's got both bands going, and Mercyful Fate did well. I'm sure the Metallica covers album helped out Mercyful Fate too in terms of exposure."

One additional spot of trivia from Glen: when King recorded his vocals (for *House of God*), he says, "It was pretty dark in there in the live room where it was set up. No crosses or candles or anything like that, just a few red floodlights. As far as the rest of us, we cut a lot of our tracks right in the control room."

I prodded King himself, back in '96, on lifestyle away from rock 'n' roll, with Diamond commenting that, "I hated American football when I first got here, because I didn't know the rules, the strategy that goes into it. I thought, how could people watch this? They play for ten seconds and then they take a minute's break. What the hell is that? And then it's called football, but everything takes place with the hands. But when you get into the rules and the strategy and stuff, then, wow it's intense."

Early on, like Steve Harris but not as seriously, King dreamed about being a professional footballer. As well, unsurprisingly, "When I have some spare time I like to collect CDs," offered King, "especially from the early '70s. There are so many bands that never made it from that era that are just killer. Even Scandinavian bands. One of my all-time favourites is a Norwegian band from '72 called Aunt Mary. Their first album was called *Loaded*. Killer stuff on there. There was a three-piece band from Sweden called November. Very heavy. They were singing in Swedish, but killer stuff. There's a German band called Zarathustra, also from 1972, guitars, keyboards and stuff. There was a Scottish band called Bodkin. There are so many obscure bands from that era. Lucifer's Friend had an album—I actually have it on CD—from before they were called Lucifer's Friend, five out of those six guys, a band called Asterix, and it sounds just like the first Lucifer's Friend."

"So, it's mostly old '70s stuff," continues King, clearly warming to the topic (again, putting him so much in synch with Michael Denner, who still to this day runs a record store). "Like Captain Beyond. I finally found their third album on CD. I look for most of these old bands, Atomic Rooster, and a band called Jericho that I used to have on vinyl. They're an Israeli band but they recorded in England. Dirk Steffens, who was the producer for some Accept albums, he recorded his own stuff back in '76, and has a record called *Seventh Step*, which sounds very much like Captain Beyond's first album. That's the stuff I'm hunting down when I'm out there."

"Mountain, for instance. I've been looking so hard for the first one which wasn't even called Mountain. It was Leslie West's solo record, but the album was called *Mountain*. But that has some of the songs that were released on some of the live albums. But I had no idea how to find the original record. But new stuff, definitely Metallica and maybe Pantera too. I'll buy the new Jethro Tull (laughs). But it's an old, old band. I went and saw Ozzy Osbourne yesterday. That was killer. I've seen him twice now. He's changed the set quite a bit and I've never seen him play as long as he did yesterday. It was unbelievable."

I'm sure this has changed since then, but when I asked him in 1999 whether he was into the internet, he said, "No, I'm not, and I don't even want it. Same thing with TV. I don't even have cable here. If I had it I would not do what I'm supposed to do—I know it. I like composing music but it's so easy to go, 'Oh right! That Formula One race is on at four in the morning because it's direct from Monaco.' I should be playing instead, but that convenience of just flipping around and seeing things I enjoy for relaxation would take away from it. To be honest, I haven't read many books in the last few years. Having both bands going, there's been very little spare time. Mostly I relax by watching sports. Soccer, motor car sports, Indy, Formula One."

And smoking. Remarks Kol, "Yes (laughs). I do remember him saying that he didn't think he could accomplish the same thing or sound the same without smoking. He proved himself wrong. He smoked some very, very strong cigarettes and he smoked quite a bit of them. It didn't seem to hold him back in any way."

"The only cigarettes I can smoke are from Denmark," said King at the time in an interview with Mike Coles. "They're very genuine tobacco. They're stronger than Camel or even Marlboro, but they're a lot smoother. I've tried smoking the others, but it really hurt my throat. If those were the only cigarettes, I wouldn't smoke."

Asked if he's ever done any drugs, King replied, "I have tried hashish twice, when I was extremely young, but that's it my entire life. We always try to make an extra effort to keep the band members drug-free. In the early Mercyful Fate days, Kim Ruzz was allegedly smoking. He was fired once from the band. He came back and had promised that he had dropped it and he obviously had because he got all his energy back."

"Later on it actually happened with King Diamond. I had noticed that the performance of two members had gone down, not being reliable when they were supposed to appear in the studio. Then finally someone else told me that now that they were fired, they could now tell me that they were on coke. That they had done coke on tour and it had really affected them. So, they were fired. I don't want to see it. It's a thing that affects my life and my work and I can't have that. I need people that I can depend on when I work. There was a crew member that was doing coke on our last tour, and when I found out one night, the next morning I got everyone off the bus and I didn't want to mention names, but I told them I knew who it was and that I didn't want to hear it again or that the person doing it was going to go home real quick. They don't realise what they are doing here. If there is one gram of that shit on the bus and we get pulled over and someone finds it, that bus will get impounded and then two or three shows go down the drain. Maybe even a week's tour. Or the tour stops. I mean don't you fuck with my tour, you know? Don't even try it."

9, Mercyful Fate's seventh studio album, was issued June 15th, 1999 and came wrapped in the band's deathliest, most dastardly and simply greatest album cover of the band's long career. The Devil bathes contently in a lake of fire, rendered by the band's long-time designers Studio Dzyan, in rich earth tones and metallics.

"Absolutely," agrees Sharlee, with a chuckle. "It just seemed like everything was just coming into place at that time, having that album cover, coming up with a bunch of great songs, and at the same time Metallica doing their Mercyful Fate covers and all that, and then getting asked to go out on the road with them, and to go all over the world by ourselves. It was a good period of time for us."

"Yes, this same artist painted *Melissa* and *Don't Break the Oath*," confirms King. "Actually, there were two guys who worked at the company at that time, a painter and an artist more into airbrushing, and they were all there from the beginning. If you look closely, the cover of *9* almost blends the two covers together."

As for the title, explains Diamond, "Aside from the obvious, that this is the ninth studio album Mercyful Fate has done, including *The Beginning* and *Return of the Vampire*, nine is a magical number. It's a number that's used repeatedly in *The Satanic Bible*. Everything you multiply by nine, if you add together the digits, you return to nine. Three times nine is 27, two plus seven is nine and so on. And nine multiplied by 74 is 666, and if you add six plus six plus six, you get 18, and one plus eight is nine. It also relates to human life, the duration of pregnancy being nine months. There are many, many connections with nine. It's also the number of Satanic philosophy, not 666. That's a number taken from the *Bible*."

Which naturally diminishes its significance for a guy like King. "Yes, Satan is a Christian god, one that appears in the *Bible*, and yet many have chosen to throw away that part of their own manufactured religion. That's not to say that Christianity is bad. I don't think that anything a person believes in is bad, as long as they don't try to force it down my throat. My religious beliefs, my spiritual beliefs, are different from everyone. I've not found what I believe in any book, but I can totally relate to Satanism as a life philosophy as described in Anton LaVey's bible. It has nothing to do with spirituality; it's more a book of logic. It gets into human instincts, not spirituality. I think most people know that I'm not a Satanist in the Christian sense. I don't believe in their Satan any more than I believe in their God."

Back to the new record, *9* opens with a heart-racing Hank Shermann number, with "Last Rites" spurred on by a double bass drum maelstrom from Bjarne. King's lyrics are just as pointed and direct, but also smartly questioning. Our protagonist lies on his death bed not a Satanist or a Christian but an atheist, wondering what's next.

"I especially decided not to do any long, involved songs," says Hank. "I just went for short and effective metal songs for the *9* album, and King went that way as well. Also, I wanted to take it a step further in aggressiveness and being a little harder and also pressuring King to be a little more heavy, instead of being routine. He was also pushed to the limit."

"You are right," King told me. "It is a dirtier sound, but that just comes from the songwriting. It comes straight from the heart. The rest is getting a sound that complements the sound right, a sound from the studio that fits the compositions. But the overall aggression of the songs is coming from the songwriting."

Hank elaborated, in conversation with Robb Chavez from *Robb's Metal Works*, explaining that, "After the last tour in '98, we composed songs for *9* and then went to Dallas in February, recorded the album in forty days, and we did the European tour, the festivals with Metallica for about thirty shows and then we went to South America, Brazil, Chile and Argentina, and then we went over and prepared for the US tour. So, it just never stops—we're on the fifth US tour, altogether since '84."

When Chavez points out the record's heavier vibe, Shermann says, "We didn't exactly plan it come out like that, but we were planning to be much more aware and focused and alert about the outcome. We said okay, we need to get out of this routine, with recording. There's much more melody going into it with the vocals again, but they're a little more straightforward like the earlier ones. It's still complex songs but there are no long songs this time, so for the next record, it gives us some new direction to work with."

But like King, Hank doesn't want radical change record to record. "I don't know, the old songs are pretty good, but I never go back and compare. But I could easily do that and I could easily imitate that kind of the songwriting. But for me, when I write songs, they're still in the same area. I'm not trying to encourage too much of a style change. I'm basically keeping it the same but trying to make it better and better. Sometimes I succeed, sometimes I might not."

Musing about how the band has adopted Texas as its second home in a sense, Hank tells Robb that, "from '93 to '99, we've spent about twelve months, one year, within those five, six years, in Dallas recording albums. It's because King is living in Dallas, but it gives the other guys, who live in Scandinavia, an opportunity to get away from home, get an apartment, just relax and have a car and drive around the Dallas area. It's a little boring, but it's okay (laughs)."

Next on *9* comes "Church of Saint Anne," a chilling tale of a priest whose eyes go black as he's possessed, soon to be found in the church tower hanging from the bell. Hank's music track for this is a slow and ruminating burn, made all the creepier by his mellow chorus over which King croons. Bjarne occasionally goes double-time on his drum track, turning the song kick-ass like Priest.

King writes the next one, "Sold My Soul," which is one of the most memorable tracks from the entire reunion era, hypnotic, frighteningly direct of lyric, simple with pregnant pauses. Also memorable is the song's opening sequence, where drums and unusually clean guitars are accompanied by gnarly effect-drenched bass. It's a huge sound, which, as Kol explains, is quite understandable given Sharlee's methodologies.

"Sharlee, he was there the whole time and he and I hit it off very well. Mr. Holm on the other hand didn't speak a lot of English when he was there; I don't know if he spoke more later. But his visit was the briefest, because once he was done with this tracking, he left. So, I had the least amount of time getting a chance to get to know him. But Sharlee just seemed like one of the coolest guys. And he did something for me—I have to tell you this story. First of all, Sharlee plays very aggressively. He plays a... I believe it was a Rickenbacker bass through an old Traynor tube amp and a big Ampeg 8x10 cab. And he's a monster. I mean, the guy's like six-foot-six or something. He's huge."

"So, I found out that he tunes his bass 20 or 30 cents flat. He doesn't tune it to pitch because he plays so hard that he pulls it into pitch. I also discovered he had to change his bass strings between every song to maintain that consistency of tone that King was after. He played so hard that a lot of bass players don't change their strings hardly ever. They may go ten years without changing their bass strings (laughs). But in this case, Sharlee was changing his bass strings between every song. You'd work on a song, when his track was done, he would be restringing before we did another song."

"That's a big investment in bass strings," continues Marshall. "I'm sure he had an endorsement deal with somebody. But anyway, what I didn't know is that he was saving them. At the end of the project he presented me with a crown of bass strings. He came in front of the console, with his very Jesus-like appearance, put it on his head and raised his hands to a cross, took it off his head and handed it to me (laughs). I still have it to this day. I have Sharlee D'Angelo's crown of bass strings, which was all the bass strings he used for Mercyful Fate 9. I display them proudly. But that one, yeah, I really liked, 'Sold My Soul.' It's a simple melody with simple lyrics, but I think it's powerful."

Besides Sharlee's thumping bass throughout, there are some ripping riffs and solos between the plainspeak verses, as well as a ton of vocal arranging from King, who in fact finds another gear, this resigned, depressed low and ruminating croon. Given the sentiment of the lyric, it's some of the most emotionally devastating music in the entire Mercyful catalogue. There's a sense of regret there—about the whole thing, maybe—that is visceral and soaked in loneliness.

"I can really recognise the sound of my own voice again," said King at the time. "It was because the words were right. It gave me the inspiration to do more vocal harmonies as well. 'Sold My Soul' has more going on vocally than I've ever done before. That's more like what we did in the old days as well. But while much of this relates to the early days, the production is very modern and heavy. We used detuned guitars on two songs on that album, something we never really did before."

"Sold My Soul" would have been perfect to push as a single, or at least serve as a song for video treatment, given its irresistible pull. However, as Hank told Robb Chavez, "Unfortunately I don't think we were invited by Metal Blade to do another video. I don't know why. I think they think it's useless. It's pointless. It's not worth doing a video because there are so many countries that don't show those. But I think it's bullshit. I think it's very important to show. The only thing that's happening is that the countries or the stations that show Mercyful Fate videos now will only be showing all the old stuff because we don't have a new one. We can only wish that we could do another one, but it's something to do with money and stuff."

"House on the Hill," like "Sold My Soul" before it, begins with Bjarne and Sharlee. Quickly we're into a speedy rocker which adds to this notion of *9* being Mercyful Fate's *Painkiller*. Indeed, time and again across the album there's a frantic energy as if the band may not be long for this world, as if life has to be lived in a blaze of glory because the flame is about to die.

This approach was being received well, said Sharlee at the time, asked by Chavez if *9* had been eliciting good reactions. "Oh yeah, very many, actually. Especially with all the reviews that we've seen. We came pretty high in all the sound checks, in the magazines, like No.1 in *Heavy oder was!* But really, we do whatever we feel like at the time. One album might be a little more melodic, one album might be a little longer with more epic songs like the last one was, of course, and the new one is a reaction towards the last one. So, this one is much shorter, with shorter songs and much faster songs. We got enough of the symphonic crap on the last album, so now it's just metal."

When I met up with Sharlee in Toronto at one of his shows with Witchery, his well-regarded "thrash 'n' roll" side-project, he told me that, "I always wanted to push it in that direction. One thing that was funny, that I read in *Terrorizer* in their review of *9*, he wondered if I took a copy of *Restless & Dead* (Witchery debut, issued October

2nd, 1998) into the rehearsal room (laughs). Which I didn't, but he does have a point because it is a lot rougher, especially sound-wise. I'm really happy with that. It's also shorter. It's a good 40, 45 minutes. The last one was about an hour, and it was a bit too long, too boring. But what I like is mainly the material, and that it sounds quite organic. It wasn't overproduced. I think that's the one we put the least time in in the studio, so it's a lot fresher in that way."

With the title, "House on the Hill," King reminds us of both "House of the Rising Sun" and semi-famed old Audience album, *The House on the Hill*. But Diamond's tale is of course much darker than either of those—in this house there is a cellar... with a well. In that well are kept stillborn babies, "souls that God didn't hear."

"Burn in Hell" is another bodice-ripper of a "Painkiller," although the central riff sounds like Iron Maiden's "Wrathchild" on speed. Seductive melodies unfold one after another, with King accenting them with falsettos and harmonies. Again, you can't get more in-your-face Satan-loving than "Burn in Hell."

"Lyrically, I'm going back to the style of the earlier albums," King told Scott Hefflon. "No holds barred, say it as it is. So, I'm using the Christian words and both gods, God and Satan. I personally don't believe in either of those two gods. That's just my personal view. But people say, 'Then why did you use the words?' I say, 'That's what a lot of people relate to.' They are like labels. Like if I said Johnnie Walker to you, you would think of whisky. If I say God, most people would think of good, and if I say Satan, most people think of bad. But when you put those words in there, that's the initial thought people get."

"I use those words to formulate those questions, like, 'Are you so sure you are right?' 'What proof do you have?' 'Do you think you are better than other people because you think this way?' Even people who believe in the same God have vastly different beliefs from each other. Within this same framework, they hate each other. I can't understand it. I can't believe that people who believe the same God can't just accept each other for being different when it comes to thought. Because that is all religion is: thought. Nobody has the proof to show to someone else, and say, 'Hey look here. There's God. There he is. Look at him!'"

"I have my own very spiritual, personal beliefs, but it doesn't mean that I will have disrespect for other religions. I accept that people think differently, and they have different ways of experiencing spirituality. Because it's just like anything else. We experience what colours we like and why. It's not like red is a bad colour and blue is a good colour; it depends on who is looking at it. That's what you need to respect and that's what you have to accept yourself. Therefore, there are no wrongs and rights. I see good and evil as one thing. I can't really explain it in a few minutes, but I believe in the powers of the unknown. I believe there are many powers and influences, and some of those come from within, from what some people term the soul. I believe that we live several times to achieve a certain amount of experience. I think you have to experience a variety of things, all the experiences that there are on earth, and that will take several lives."

Continuing, King adds flesh to the explanation concerning cumulative experiences he gave earlier in the *Into the Unknown* chapter. "I do believe that that soul, that power within you, is stored somewhere, and a little bit of it goes down and starts again to gain more experience. It will pick up where your first experience was in your first life, and it grows. But those experiences, those powers, are still around us. Sometimes you can tap into them and get some benefit from them in your normal life. I think that—and it might sound crazy—that you have to experience killing too. There are many different ways that that could come. It could be a war. But there is a certain feeling associated with that. I think that will happen to you before you are ready."

"But that can happen in any of your lives. This lifetime I live now, I live according to logic as much as I can. I'm not thinking, 'Oh, wait a minute, according to what I believe, I should also kill someone.' I might have done that two lives ago. I need to live according to my logic and my senses and get as much as I can I out of my life that way for what makes sense to me in this life. Because if you think about having certain experiences, you might waste your time not living according to your own logic. You might repeat yourself."

Back to the topic of letting it all hang out on this record, saying things like "I sold my soul" or "Burn in Hell" or "Where is your Jesus now?" King figures, "I chose different phrasings and words because people often misinterpret what I say. People relate different things to the same words, so you sometimes try to say the same things with other words. For some reason, if you use words other than the straight, direct words, it weakens the whole. I use the traditional Christian words because they have impact, they make people think. When I say Satan in the lyrics, it doesn't mean I believe in Satan the way the Christian church has created him. I don't. But I am willing to use their words to get my point across. It will instantly make people think about a very specific image. If I said, 'The powers of darkness might give you knowledge without your knowing it, powers you can use for yourself in positive ways,' that's very different than saying, 'Satan might give you more knowledge than you could ever imagine, and maybe you could use it positively.'"

"The words do mean something to me, but not the same thing they mean to others. Satan, to me, stands for the powers of the unknown. That's what it's always meant to me. But I can't use it thinking people will know I'm talking about the powers of the unknown. That would be foolish. So, starting now, again, just like in the early days, I'm using the words that will make people think about what I want them to think about. Things I think are important to think about, and then people are left to make up their own minds."

It's an important point King is making here: re-read the above, as well as what he said in the *Into the Unknown* chapter. Keep that considerably obscure philosophy in mind when reading his lyrics dotted with Christian characters. Above all, as he's directly told us, try imagine that when he's talking about Satan or the Devil or Lucifer (or Baphomet, from the next song on the album, "The Grave"), what he really means is something revolving around "the powers of the unknown." Which could refer to a couple of things: 1) the experiences we haven't yet piled up over the course of our multiple lives (and therefore the wisdom from them is yet unknown); or 2) the mystery of the entire and enveloping reincarnation concept King believes.

"The Grave" also lives strong on bass guitar, given its low-toned slow boil framed by a unison walking bass line riff conceived by Hank. Says Kol, "Hank's style was maybe a little more traditional. King liked to use whole tones, whereas Hanks was leaning more towards a pentatonic style. But they all seemed to work well together. But 'The Grave," that's totally a blues riff (sings it)—it's a pentatonic scale. It's absolutely a blues riff but a heavy metal version. Very Sabbath-y in a way. Yeah. But it's a blues when you boil it down at the end of the day with the flatted fifth—it's a blues note."

"So, when we were working on the vocal for that, that was the first time I really realised the difference in their creative styles because King wasn't feeling the blues thing, from listening to that riff. I said to King, 'It's a blues riff and you've got to sing a blues melody to work.' He did come up with a minor scale blues-like melody: 'There is a cemetery...' That's how that song came together.

But yes, it made me realise that Hank's style was more bluesy and the King style might've been more, like I said, using whole tones and flatted notes, things that give it less of a blues feeling, more Halloween-y or horror-like."

Not much to the lyric here, except for the slight twist that there's a certain grave that can produce the devil. Again, it reads like a standard, brief horror tale, but upon reflection, one realises that rarely do you hear about the conjuring of the Devil taking place at a grave.

At the music end, there are many slashing textures across this one, plus there's a speedy double bass break imbedded within, lest one fall asleep at the cemetery never to wake. The intro to "The Grave" sounds buried alive. Explains Kol, "They said, 'We want it to sound like a jam room recording, like a rehearsal room recording that breaks into the studio recording.' As opposed to setting up a 57 and having them play it in the room live, which would have made no sense logistically but would have achieved the desired result perfectly, what I did instead was I just had them record it but then I made a mono mix of the intro of the song and I pumped it through a little Marshall practice amp and miked that with like a little battery-operated... and you've got this really cool lo-fi sound that they loved. I was really surprised that they wanted to do that."

King calls "Insane" "the fastest song we've ever done" and indeed Bjarne's beat is military precision double bass at high velocity. But the riffing is relaxed, just chording placed up top, while King mirrors the guitars, singing long notes and ignoring the freight train that is Bjarne. Hank and Mike periodically do break into palm-muted madness, adding tension to King's lyric about a mind beset by torment possibly of a supernatural nature, possibly not. It's all over in three minutes, with "Insane" serving as microcosm of the album's flash bulb personality as a whole.

"Kiss the Demon" alternates creepy quiet passages distinguished by bass chords and King using that low, sad, almost speaking voice of his, with triumphant metal riffing somewhere between Sabbath and Maiden. In contrast, "Buried Alive" features an aggressive and vengeful King, shovelling on the dirt as his victim recovers from the poison slipped in his drink. Diamond wrote the music to this one as well as "Kiss the Demon," and here we're revisiting the Egyptian riffing of "Gypsy," which, despite its derivation, offers contrast to the rest of the record's slower and faster conceits.

As we draw to a close, Mike Wead gets a writing credit, and on the album's title track no less. "9" opens with a pile of scary sound effect music before collapsing into a claustrophobic and experimental doom topped with a philosophical and enigmatic lyric from King that asks more questions than it answers.

"I love the title track," says Marshall. "I had so much fun working with Mike on that. It was often something that we would get to when we weren't working on one of the other songs. I think it was something Mike was still composing even when he got to the studio. What I remember most about it was his finesse as a guitar player and the interest he has in being really involved with getting the tones and effects just the way he wanted on that song."

"I used some unexpected equipment to get what he was looking for, actually, in a number of cases. I did unusual things to achieve the desired result they had. Our rack effects in the studio that are more often used for vocals and other things ended up in the signal paths for some of the guitar effects. So, we had a lot of fun with that particular track, doing some unconventional things. One of them was the little soundscape that appears in the middle of the song. My assistant Vince Rossi and I stayed up 'til the wee hours of the night doing that. The sun was just coming up when we left the studio after making that, that soundscape. King wanted the sound of Hell, what it would sound like in Hell. So, we had a lot of fun overnight making that for him."

"He had some edits when we showed it to them the next day and we remixed it. But the slowed down… I put a straw into a glass of milk and blew bubbles and slowed it down because I wanted the sound of bubbling lava. He ixnay'ed the bubbling lava (laughs) but most of the rest of what we did stayed in there. They let us get extra creative on that piece. Otherwise, I know that most of the effects were their own, their own rigs and their own setups. It was only on the title track, '9,' that I recall busting out some other weird things from my own rack to make some of those sounds. The really flange-y guitar was a cheap box flanger but it just has the perfect sound."

"I quote '9' all the time; 'I am nine. You are nine. We are nine. We are all nine.' I like the lyrics of that one. But trying to pick what I like best changes so much and it's been so long since I did that work. My favourite songs have changed. They were one thing while we were working on it and they were another thing after. There are different things I hear ten years later. To me, that's the mark of a really great musical work, is that you keep finding new things to fall in love with. You live with it. It's weird though; even though I was involved in every minute you hear on that record, you forget all those details."

Kol was also allowed the extra creativity of playing keyboards, however sparingly. "I don't remember off the top of my head exactly what tracks I played on," reflects Marshall, "but I probably use my Kurtzweil keyboard, the K 2000 that I had at the time. But it may have been King's own keyboard. He would oftentimes come in and have a part, but he just felt that I could play it a little tighter 'cause I was a keyboard player, so he'd let me play it. Yeah, it was oftentimes his parts and I just performed them."

The spirit of cooperation Kol experienced with the 9 record was most definitely a Mercyful Fate thing, in contrast to King Diamond, which really was a band named properly, deliberately framed as more of a solo project situation.

"Yes, it seemed to me that there was much more of a band environment with Mercyful Fate where the different members were bringing things to the table. Although I think Andy LaRocque did do some writing for some of the King Diamond stuff, it was by and large at least 80% King's own works that he had meticulously demoed at home. So, it seemed more prearranged for his solo work. He had done more demoing and more composing on his own before getting to the studio and so there was quite a bit less experimentation. It was a little more methodical."

"But his work ethic and dedication was so intense. We were so focused that we would become almost psychically connected. We would realise the same thing at the same time and laugh to see who said it first. When you're in the studio 12 out of every 14 days, for 12, 14, 15 hours a day, you get to know somebody pretty well (laughs). We definitely built that relationship and built a really good one. I was sorry that that working relationship had to end when I left, but he wasn't interested in travelling to work and I wasn't either."

Kol, originally from New York, went back there and resumed studio work as well as a career in corporate communications.

"In terms of the sound, it's less raw, much more refined," continues Marshall. "He was more meticulous about consistency with his own albums than he was with the Mercyful Fate stuff I worked on, although he was still systematic and concerned with the quality and the consistency. I know with *Voodoo* and *House of God* and *Abigail II*, we did meticulous referencing so that every note, every snare drum was tuned exactly the same. Every song, we were very careful to create consistency."

A DANGEROUS MEETING: IN THE SHADOWS WITH MERCYFUL FATE

For the release of *9* in Japan, there was a bonus track called "S.H.," essentially two minutes of unsettling layered guitar plus keyboards and no vocals. Take your pick: the initials stood for either "Silent Hill" or "Shermann Hank," penner of this bit of devilish classical music.

"All told, *9* is just more aggressive," muses Kol, asked to compare the final product with *Dead Again*, "in both the writing and the sounds we got. Sterling coming from the background he does, he was much more familiar with the genre than I was, and so he was getting sounds that metal listeners were more accustomed to. I actually read a lot of negative feedback about my production because I wasn't producing that album like a metal album. I mean, I did the same things with them I might've done with a jazz act. I have an approach that's different and I wasn't trying to dial up very processed sounds. I was trying to get very, very natural sounds. It may be more just a difference of experience or difference of approach, but I think they're all great sounding albums."

On the subject of whether the band might have gotten some help—or hindrance—from any invisible forces, Kol answers, "Nothing during *9* but there were quite a few instances working with King over the years where some inexplicable things happened. My favourite example is the story about a little guy we called the glitcher. I think it was *House of God*. There were some glitching noises being produced out of the blue from our digital tape machines. It turned out there was nothing wrong with the tape or the recording, but the machine was having errors. We had a backup and we replaced it and continued to work."

"But when the glitches began happening, it was bad timing. We were under the gun to get work done and it was stressful. We were behind schedule, so we were working late. I have the control room... I have a picture of it in my mind. I was sitting at the console. When I'm sitting at the console, there's a desk to my left and that's where King would sit; that's the producer's desk. Right in front of the producer's desk, there was a door that went to the hallway and eventually to the exit and also the bathrooms. Then to my right, there was also a doorway that led to the booths and the main tracking room. Most people would come and go through the door on my left, not walking through the booths. So that was the main control room door. Sometimes it was propped open for whatever reason. There was no one else in the studio, so we didn't need to close it."

"On this particular night, the door was propped open and King and I were working late into the night mixing and I was feeling a bit fatigued. But I felt like I was doing fine. I glanced up towards the door on my left, the main studio door, and I see this little guy and he was just the ugliest little demon thing I could have pictured. He had an oversized cranium, beady little eyes and discoloured grey-green skin and he had one hand on the door and long spindly fingers."

"As soon as I looked at him, it's as if he'd caught me catching a glimpse of him and he ducked away. I'm sure my jaw dropped. Probably my face went white and everything else—I'd just see this apparition. I look over at King and he's looking at me in astonishment too. He says to me, 'Oh, you saw him too?!' I said, 'What did you see?' He said (in Danish accent), 'A little guy, man!'"

Between wrapping up work on the album in March and the record's June 15th release date, there had been a notorious school shooting and attempted bombing at Columbine High School in Columbine, Colorado. There were 15 dead including the double suicide of the perpetrators. Gothic rock was implicated, with Marilyn Manson getting dragged into the fray. King explained to our magazine many of the same salient points that Manson was making about this tragedy.

"The first two things that always come to mind when things like this happen are: were the people who committed these crimes already somewhat insane, yet it hadn't been detected? The other is the parents: where were they? On the first, some people are simply born wrong. They're sick. They were born that way. Perhaps it wasn't discovered until they were 15, 30, or 60, but that's just when it showed itself. They were always like that; they were simply not caught performing an act that's considered abnormal. But after the fact, when you hear them talking, you see that they've always had a problem—they have a sick mind."

"As for the parents, I wonder where they were that they didn't see the problem before it was too late. Where is the communication, the relationship, understanding and support? So many parents are too busy with their work or their own lives, and the kids are simply forbidden to go see their friends because they're 'bad' or they listen to the wrong music. But if the kid reacts by shooting up in an alley instead of meeting up at their friend's house and listening to records, which is worse?"

"Try to understand what it is your kid is doing and why, instead of blindly forbidding it. It's a parent's obligation to be there for their kids, not just regulate their lives without understanding why it's so important. Honestly, how many times has this thing happened in Jesus' name? 'Jesus spoke to me, so I had to kill the wicked.' It's rare that they report it, but some brave journalist writes about it no matter what the consequences, and when it's out in the open, the church claims Satan must've gotten a hold of him, claiming to be Jesus. It was what they preached that made him do it, but he was insane because he was hearing voices to begin with. We all agree on that."

"So, stop blaming it on music and movies, because you're not willing to accept that religion is to blame as well. These people are sick in the head; they just aren't caught in time. Not everyone is sane. That's a misconception. Another misconception is that kids are stupid. If you see some of the footage of debates and discussions, kids are much deeper and more knowledgeable than they're given credit for. They're mature on a level that many parents just don't understand, mostly because they aren't closely involved in their kids' lives. Why do you think a kid wears a shirt with a skull on it? Because it's cool. Because he's expressing himself. Another kid wears a polo shirt, and maybe he's miserable because he wants to wear a shirt with a skull. Maybe not. Maybe the polo shirt is cool to him and he's expressing himself. There are many, many scenarios and everyone's different and there is no right and wrong. The sooner people realise that there'll be a lot less conflicts."

Before we leave the *9* album for good, I wanted to address once more the frustration I've had picking clear favourites across the Mercyful Fate reunion records, or indeed, articulating clear differences between each of these five records. To reiterate, King and the guys make it hard to pick because they've managed to make all of them pretty much unassailable.

My personal inclination is that *9* is the odd man out and typically the one I get most excited about, triggered by that sumptuous, seductive album cover and then always satisfied at the headbang once I entered the coven.

But, curious at what other smart fans thought, I surveyed my friends through Facebook and pretty much found that the consensus record is the first one, *In the Shadows*. Now, my question posed to the Fate-ful was to pick from the first four, because, again, *9* was the one for which I already had clear and defined opinions. This one sits apart for the reasons articulated by the band in this chapter, reasons I agree with.

So here are the results of this informal survey, presented in reverse order, leaving aside the names of the speakers to protect the innocent!

Dead Again: "*Dead Again* gets a raw deal because Denner wasn't on it, but I loved the raw, real sound of it. Mercyful Fate and King always have a bit of a propensity to overproduce everything. It's part of the experience, I guess. *Dead Again* was so much rawer that it made it seem very fresh to my ears!" "Lack of Michael Denner hurt the songs on *Dead Again* and *9*."

Into the Unknown: "*Into the Unknown* was the closest Mercyful Fate got to sounding like Mercyful Fate since 1984."

Time: "*Time* is perfect! What a killer album. *In the Shadows* is also very good and the other two have their moments like 'The Uninvited Guest,' 'Banshee,' 'The Lady Who Cries,' 'Dead Again,' 'Fifteen Men (and a Bottle of Rum),' and 'Kutulu.'" "I actually find *Time* to be a little more forward thinking and an overall better listen than the others. Just my opinion."

Like I say, most of the love went to the first one, *In the Shadows*... "It's *In the Shadows*: undoubtedly the riffs are very similar to those that you can find on *Vizier of Wasteland* (Zoser Mez album), influenced by '70s rock bands like Captain Beyond. The main difference is the characteristic gothic vibe of the Mercyful Fate sound. Most of the songs from *Dead Again* sounds doomier than those on *Time* and *Into the Unknown*. *Time* is less proggy than other Mercyful Fate albums and *Into the Unknown* is probably the heaviest and fastest Mercyful Fate album—pure speed metal brilliance."

"*In the Shadows* is the best of the lot, just an incredible, partially updated for the '90s, tour de force of metal."

"*In the Shadows* is a lost classic. *Time* is halfway there. *Into the Unknown* and *Dead Again*'s best parts were their artwork. *9* looks classic but isn't."

And there's more... "*In the Shadows* is definitely a classic with *Melissa* and *Don't Break the Oath*. *Time* could use a remix and remaster, while *9* is actually pretty solid, although a couple songs are 'meh.' *Dead Again*, half the songs are solid, and I thought *Into the Unknown* was pretty good; the title track is classic Fate and 'The Uninvited Guest' and 'Listen to the Bell' had good hooks."

"*In the Shadows*, from start to finish, is my favourite Mercyful album. Of course, I love *Melissa* and *Don't Break the Oath* but *In the Shadows* is just so full of incredible songs with catchy and heavy hooks, and not a weak one in the bunch. Also, love the production."

"*In the Shadows* is absolutely brilliant. Not sure if it was just because it was the comeback album, but I love it. The others are good but don't come near it."

"*In the Shadows* is in a league of its own compared to the other three. Far superior. No comparison."

The minions continue... "*In the Shadows* is classic Fate all the way, as is *Time*, which I actually prefer slightly over *Shadows*. *Into the Unknown* is right up there with the previous two releases, particularly 'The Uninvited Guest' and 'Fifteen Men (and a Bottle of Rum).' *Dead Again* and *9* had a few moments here and there, but you can tell that the band were pretty much phoning it in by that point."

"*Time* is an absolute classic, second only to *In the Shadows*, which is an absolute masterpiece. *Dead Again* and *9* weren't as good in my opinion. 'Buried Alive' stood out, and I believe I liked 'Mandrake.' But for sure *In the Shadows* is my cherished treasure from that era."

And finally, "*In the Shadows* and *Time* are by far the best of the last five albums. I remember *Time* sounding odd with strange production when it came out but it is a grower and has more great songs on it than any of the last three. I give *Into the Unknown* a slight edge over *Dead Again* but both are still better than *9*. The start of King Diamond's solo career watered down the quality of Mercyful Fate's reformation material."

Closing out this little thought experiment are a few comments that I felt warranted inclusion but were uncommitted. "*Into the Unknown* has epic songs, dense and complex and classic. *Time* features shorter, tighter songs and I actually think is equally classic, reminding me of an update of the EP days. I never warmed up to *Into the Unknown*, and *Dead Again* shoots for classic status, but misses the mark."

"I dunno, Martin, I remember I loved *In the Shadows*. I was psyched to have them back and I knew a kick-ass tour would follow. That old Mercyful stuff came out when I was a little kid and now I would get to see them. The title track had a kick-ass riff, 'Room of Golden Air' was cool, and there was still Shermann and Denner. But nothing about it screamed 'Mercyful Fate' to me as opposed to a King Diamond solo album. As time went on, the stylistic gap between the solo stuff and Mercyful really narrowed. *Time* had its moments, but by the time *Dead Again* came out, I'd had my fill. As for the new Mercyful reunion? Nah."

"I have a hard time thinking of many bands so distinctly split into pre- and post-reformation eras in terms of impact and quality. Deep Purple managed a reformation album that was almost as good as their golden-era material. But from the first mini-LP to the last

9

note of the second full-length album, with a sprinkling of killer B-sides, demos, rarities and radio performances, Mercyful Fate weren't just one of the greatest metal bands in history, they were a transformative experience for the genre, an occult speed metal band with Schenker/Tipton-level Euro class guitar playing and the most underrated rhythm section out there with a vocalist that sounded like no other. Post-reformation they were simply a solid metal act that sounded like the logical extension of King Diamond solo."

Quite the damning comment, but most damning of all... "They're all like one gooey, four-hour-long, middle-of-the-road Mercyful Fate record to me."

Wrote Brian Aberback from *The Record*, "9, released this summer, reveals Fate playing with a vigour and viciousness that's been lacking in recent years. 'There's probably more melody in there than the past few albums,' Diamond said. 'You need melody and a good song. You just can't play heavy riffs from hell.' Headbangers needn't worry, though. The melody found on 9 renders the razor-sharp riffs and thunderous rhythms more memorable without detracting from the collection's overall vibe. On top of the mix are Diamond's unmistakable—love them or hate them—unforgettable vocals. One moment, Diamond sounds like an opera singer, hitting glass-shattering high notes. The next, he switches to a guttural sound, best described as someone's final, dying breaths."

An uncredited three-star *Hit Parader* review declares that "Mercyful Fate is one of those bands that simply won't go away. Major superstars throughout Europe, the band has always lived on the periphery of mass acceptance on this side of the Atlantic. On their latest effort, 9, King Diamond and his crew put together one of their heaviest albums yet, a disc brewing with quasi-mystical messages and pure metallic mayhem. While the King's voice can still hit registers that only dogs can fully appreciate, it seems as if MF may finally have hit upon a formula that will appeal to stateside hard rock hounds."

In any event, little did the guys in the band realise that 9 would represent the last album and tour for Mercyful Fate, at least to this day, 26 years later. As Sharlee told me back in '99, "It's a small, concentrated tour this time, just concentrating on the major cities. Because within nine or ten months, we've done the album, an extensive European tour, also South America and now North America. So, we wanted it to be short instead of like nine weeks which it was last time."

A DANGEROUS MEETING: IN THE SHADOWS WITH MERCYFUL FATE

But of course, he had other gigs anyway. Arch Enemy would be the big, blasted successful one, but for the moment, he was excited about Witchery, as was the rest of the metal community—*Restless & Dead* was a buzz record, and the product of an extreme music supergroup of sorts to boot.

"Basically, it's just our teenage dream," said D'Angelo. "It's the music we listened to back then, and we just put all that together and whatever comes out comes out. It's a definite rock band theme. It's just a band playing and there's nothing to it. It's very, very few overdubs in the studio and we just go in and pound it out."

But his plans for the renegade band were already being hampered by his Mercyful gig. "Right, the thing was I was already on my way to start the European tour for Mercyful Fate, when we got the offer to do the Witchery tour. So, there was nothing we could do. We tried to figure out something. When the Witchery tour started, it was five or six dates before the Mercyful Fate tour ended, so there wasn't much we could do about it. The only other option would have been not to do the tour, but it seemed important to do it because it seemed to be a good one. With Witchery, there are no egos involved, so I don't care if I'm on the tour, as long as it gets done, you know what I mean? For the best of the band. Although personally, it was a little bit like sending your wife out on vacation with a good-looking man (laughs). But you have to go past that and see what's better for the band."

"Now, just a day or two after I get home, I'm off to Japan with Arch Enemy. Then I'm not quite sure what's going to happen. It's going to be either recording or touring with either Arch Enemy or Witchery. We're probably going to be recording with Witchery. We've been negotiating a couple of tours also though. We really haven't toured Europe yet. So that would be a good thing to do."

Hank's attitude was much the same: just keep forging metal, no matter what the name on the tin. "We have six shows left in the US tour. From there, everyone goes home. I take a vacation. Then the King Diamond band starts writing; they're going into the studio in Dallas on January 3rd and then it's probably Diamond's turn to start a US tour and European tour and Mercyful Fate is on standby position. Meantime, all the other guys in the band have their own bands, really. Sharlee plays in Witchery and Arch Enemy, I have another project, Mike has another project. So instead of just sitting at home, we work on new music. So, we just take that energy and creativity into other bands."

Indeed, both Hank and Bjarne, working together, would be back with another album in 2000 called *Sick in the Head*, recorded for Metal Blade under band moniker Virus 7. Also on board would be Dave Moreno on bass and Edgar Paul Allen on vocals. Allen would be credited with all the lyrics, Hank with all the music.

The live campaign for the *9* album found the band in Europe from May 23rd, 1999 through to a Wacken festival date on August 6th, as King put it, "two months all over Europe, sometimes with Metallica and Monster Magnet, sometimes on our own, mostly big festivals, but we have quite a few club dates as well."

After the fact, asked whether Metallica fans knew Mercyful, King said that, "Actually, those who came to the shows knew very well what we were doing. We have a very big following in Holland. Most of the Eastern countries, people just went nuts. Absolutely nuts! It was between 15,000 and 35,000 people at most of the big shows. It just seemed like we were playing in our hometown every day. That's just what it seemed like. We played in Milan, which was also headlined by Metallica. Later on that night Hank and I were invited on stage with Metallica to do a few Mercyful Fate songs." With makeup? "No, I had the cross-bone microphone and just a T-shirt and jeans on."

King was reflective with respect to the band's influence on the metal of the day, particularly the burgeoning black metal scene at the time, kicked off for real about 1994 as Mercyful Fate was just embarking upon their reunion, but really coming to a boil in 1999.

"I know of the bands, and I know many of them have said kind words about us: Dimmu Borgir, Cradle of Filth, Emperor and more traditional metal bands like Hammerfall. While I'm very honoured, I just really haven't listened to many of them. I'll probably run into some of them at the festivals this summer. You could say that it's good and bad. When I have a little time and listen to albums, I listen to those that I collect as a hobby. I'm not really on top of what's going on in the music scene today. We always do things straight from the heart. Then again, straight from the heart is still influenced by what's around you. So maybe if you listen to a lot of bands around you, you would be influenced in writing songs in that direction."

The European assault was followed by mid-August dates, one each in Sao Paulo, Buenos Aires and Santiago, and then a month of shows in the US and Canada, Mercyful Fate conducting their last show of the reunion era in Milwaukee on October 23rd, 1999.

To be sure, there was no set plan that there would be no more Mercyful Fate, but that's exactly what happened. Seven years later,

A DANGEROUS MEETING: IN THE SHADOWS WITH MERCYFUL FATE

King was telling me that, "There hasn't been too much sitting down. I talk to Hank now and again, but it's like King Diamond is really busy these days. There are some other things that play a role in why it's taken this long time. Some people say, 'Well, is there going to be a reunion? I haven't seen any breakup of Mercy' (laughs). That's not how I look at it. But I can understand why others look at it that way. But the fact is, Mercy has a deal for US and Canada with Metal Blade, and for Europe with Massacre Records, to do an album. So that's in place. It's not like once we find some time to record, now we have to spend six months negotiating a deal. No, the deal is there. So that helps a little bit on the chance that there will be one."

"But there are other things that are against it," continued King. "When we had the last talk about Mercy, it was right around the time *Abigail II* came out. We got the shock that the internet had been straining the profits of record labels and it was becoming really hard times. That was the first album we ever released where we were told by the record label that there was no tour support available. That was a shock."

"Then we had to restructure our deals and this and that and found this new way of recording that actually gives us a better product. We never would have found it—it was good for that—but we never would have found that way unless we were put up against the wall. But now we get better product, because we can spend more time on details. So, it's been for the better in one way, in a quality way, but it would've been nice to have that quality and have that the label spend the money on the band. Not just people stealing the music."

"So, when that happened, these became the facts: it's still possible to do King Diamond and live off of it as a full-time job. Because it's what I love. I love doing it. I'm very, very lucky to live off of my absolute biggest hobby. But it is also a job, and it is what puts bread on the table. That's because of King Diamond. If there was no King Diamond and only Mercyful Fate, there wouldn't be Mercyful Fate either. There is no way. If we did Mercy again, it would be for the pure love of the music that I still have. Because I wouldn't make a dime. Not a dime. Mercy has never sold what King Diamond sells every time. Mercy doesn't have the same contracts that King Diamond has."

"So, in this scenario we are in right now, Mercy would not have the benefit that King Diamond has, of using Andy's gear, from his personal studio in Sweden, and the use of Andy himself. If we had to hire him for Mercyful Fate, that's a ton of money out of our budget there. So, with a smaller budget, higher expenses, it is hard to make a go for Mercyful Fate. Those are the sad facts. Who knows? Sometime it might happen down the road that the guys get together and do one more, but I would never consider it a reunion. I wouldn't want the labels or anyone else to play on that, because I think that would be a cheap trick."

A DANGEROUS MEETING: IN THE SHADOWS WITH MERCYFUL FATE

10.

AN EPILOGUE
"BURN IN HELL"

With no fanfare, Mercyful Fate was delicately placed on the shelf like a grinning crystal skull.

June 20th, 2000, King was back with a new album, a little more than two years since his last one, called *House of God*. Just as Michael Denner had come along 15 years earlier for *Fatal Portrait*, Mike Wead was brought into the solo fold of King's band for the *House of God* tour, after the departure of Canadian Glen Drover, who would wind up, albeit briefly, in Megadeth.

February 6th, 2001, saw the previously discussed release of King's pre-Mercyful Fate material with Black Rose, while the following month, also for Metal Blade, we got a King compilation called *Nightmares in the Nineties* comprising songs from his four solo albums in that decade. Work on *Abigail II* took place from May through August of that year, after which King discovered for himself, alluded to earlier, a life partner in Livia Zita.

"It was quite odd, actually," explained King, in conversation with David Perri, who asked in 2008 about meeting Livia (of note, there's no mention of a romantic liaison here—King is strictly business!). "When we had finished *Abigail II*, she was doing an interview for *Metal Hammer* Hungary regarding *Abigail II*. She was in the US studying in Michigan, so she called me from there to ask about *Abigail II*. We talked for a while and did the interview and then she mentioned to me that she was also a singer. A lot of people have said that to me and some of them are probably pretty good singers, but I never have a chance to hear that. She said, 'I have this demo that I feel pretty good about if you would like to hear it; it would be an honour to hear your opinion about it.'"

"So, she sent it and it was actually a Nightwish song, one of their ballads. She sang that and there was so much emotion involved it gave me goose bumps. I was like, 'Wow!' Then I started writing for *The Puppet Master* and the further I got into it, I thought that this story had the potential to become really theatrical, more than ever before. The problem was that the female character was playing quite a big role in the story. It would be lame on a song like 'So Sad'… can you imagine me singing, 'And then she said to him with her eyes, "I can't see you anymore."' It would have no power compared to a female voice. I can't start pretending to have a female voice—that would be ridiculous."

"So, the further I got into the story, the more I thought, 'Oh God, if we could find a female vocalist, it would really enhance the theatrics here and it would be much more personal and in the face of the listener.' It's much more personal to hear a voice singing, 'Now I feel it, now I hear it' than to hear another voice singing, 'Now she feels it, now she hears it.' It would be something fresh and it would never be used to the extent that it would change the King Diamond style at all. I would never allow that."

"Then I played her demo to the other guys in the band and I played it to the record company because I wanted everyone to be on the same page. They all loved her voice and said, 'You should do it man—try!' Then I talked to her and eventually she came over and recorded and it turned out so good. It also was so well received by the fans. They all loved this new element that came in because it made everything so much more theatrical. A lot of guys and girls like to hear a female voice. She has a lot of goth in her voice and a lot of feeling. The tonality of her voice fits mine extremely well. It was all good and no negative."

"That's why we decided to bring her on the road," continues Diamond. "There were a couple of songs from *The Puppet Master* that she added a lot to, like 'Blood to Walk,' just because she was there. In the chorus with me alone, I would have to pick whether I sing the low lead vocal or I sing the low falsetto choir voice. Neither of the two would have created the mood that the chorus needs. Now with my normal low voice in the chorus and her low falsetto on top, her falsetto is close enough to mine so that the overall feel of the piece comes across in a nice way."

"The same thing went for a couple of the *Abigail II* songs, as well. She does quite a bit on those. In the song 'Mansion in Sorrow,' after the first chorus there is this verse where in the studio, I felt that to get the right effect, I took a low normal voice and then I put a low falsetto on top of it to create a certain mood or feel. There is that same thing right there. That passage would not have sounded good with just one voice. If I just sang a low falsetto, it would totally not have the power. If I just sang a low normal voice, it would also not have the mood. The fact that she was there taking that low falsetto was so cool."

"In 'Spirits,' there are a couple of those melodic pieces, like after the weird acoustic intro, where we sing in harmony. For the first part of that melodic piece, I used the low normal voice and she did the low falsetto and suddenly halfway through I jumped up over her low falsetto to a high falsetto to create the harmonies up there for the second part. It just adds more of what is there on the studio versions. It creates more of the right feel. Some of those could be the make-or-break of a song. I would probably say it wouldn't work. If I take this one, it doesn't work and if I take that one it doesn't work; it has to be both of them."

"It has been rare before that we had to say that we won't pick a song because it can't get the right feel because I have to pick between two totally different lead vocals on the same verse. I have to pick the one melody line that sticks out, the one that the audience can't live without. When I come from a verse to a chorus, I might sing the first three or four words with a lead melody line, then I jump to harmony line one for the next five words, then go to the third harmony line and then back to the lead. I only have one voice."

"That's an interesting to thing to hear how these songs work live with just my voice," continues King. "For the majority of the songs, it's just me there. Sometimes the other voice is just a mood creator and I don't need her—my voice is stronger than it ever was before. On songs like 'Welcome Home' and 'The Invisible Guests,' the lead vocals are cleaner and better than they were originally. In that respect, it's not a matter of 'He needs help,' but it adds a very cool feel to a lot of places. She is used sparsely in many songs and on many she is not there at all. Of course, on *The Puppet Master* and the *Abigail II* songs, she appears quite often with a very good result."

Abigail II hit the shops on January 29th, 2002, while up into September of that year, Hank, Michael and Bjarne were back with a new band called Force of Evil. Vocalist for the project was Iron Fire's Martin Steene, while King Diamond's Hal Patino joined the ranks on bass. The band's self-titled debut was officially issued on January 26th, 2004 (there was an earlier indie 1000-pressing), almost a year after work had begun on the project. In the meantime, the band made their live debut at our magazine's (*Brave Words & Bloody Knuckles*) Six-Pack metal festival in Cleveland, Ohio, June 13th, 2003.

Speaking with Hank two weeks after the fest, I asked him to describe the sound they were going for with Force of Evil. "I'd probably say classic metal defined by the type of riffing, defined by the type of singing, the vocals. So yes, classic metal that originates in the '80s with a touch of the '90s."

"It actually started a couple years back," continues Hank. "I had this theme or project in my mind to make the consummate metal band, where people are happy, they want to drink beer, they just want to listen to metal and have a good party. That was basically the starting theme. Then I contacted Mike Wead. I went to Stockholm, Sweden to record some demos with him. So, we started the project a couple years ago, but then it faded because I went into photography and I couldn't put my mind into the metal stuff."

"But then I came back to it and said wow, it needs to be Michael Denner in here because he's right next door to me. Sometimes the distance, like with Mike Wead being in Stockholm, it creates a little delay (laughs). Also, I thought it would be more right because Michael and I go way back, twenty years and even more as a friendship. So, I contacted him and that was pretty cool, that we would start this together. He was really into it because he had a divorce and all that and he's busy with his son and everything. So now he has the time for all this, to make it really kick in."

"I've got into this problem with King," answered Hank, when asked when we might be seeing Mercyful Fate back again. "Since

An Epilogue

King is doing his solo stuff, he has to think business-wise, of course. He's putting all his effort into the King Diamond band, so that's not to say when he feels like... he's probably very aware of the strategy, how to balance between Mercyful and King. That confuses the fans. Also, to me, having King Diamond in the media all the time, that tires people. So, I think his focus is 100% with the King Diamond project right now. Maybe sometime next year. But to me, it's a lot of years and you lose it. You have to be respectful of King money-wise, business-wise. Business-wise, King Diamond is a better choice for King personally, and of course, he's going after that. So, we just wait and see what comes up. But we have the recording agreement and the recording funds waiting for us."

This echoes the point made by King in the last chapter. It's analogous, in a way, to the discussion that took place around the Genesis reunion in 2007. The harder thing to do, the more creatively exciting thing to do and the seeming the most interesting thing to do by far with respect to the fan base, was to have the band reunite with Peter Gabriel. The hard facts of the matter turned out to be, however, that the easiest thing to do, i.e. go with a Phil Collins-fronted Genesis, would generate the most revenue and so that's what happened.

Although Hank says of King now verses then that, "The beliefs are certainly the same and the personality is the same," he adds that, "the changes are probably a little more business-like and music-wise. Business-wise, he's focused on making money and music-wise, he's also changed a lot. I don't know if it's for the better or for the worse. I'm not supposed to say that publicly. But there's certainly a big change that is so obvious to hear on the later King Diamond albums, versus the '80s ones; there's a huge difference. But with the new one, *The Puppet Master*, he told me it's really close to being back on the level it was at in the '80s. So, I think he really gave all that he had to come back. He tried with *House of God* and with *Abigail II*, but those didn't really hit it, I think. But I think he will have some good stuff moving forward. The quality and the level of the compositions are apparently going to be closer to the '80s albums."

This apparent solid financial footing for King Diamond as a solo artist versus Mercyful Fate makes sense from a branding perspective. It's much simpler and more cohesive to have this complex character in corpsepaint and top hat, and with that voice that no one else dare copy, be the focus of the albums and the live show, as well as the name on the tin.

A DANGEROUS MEETING: IN THE SHADOWS WITH MERCYFUL FATE

To dredge another comparative from prog, Fish in Marillion was almost too much, but Marillion with Steve Hogarth is a sensible and cohesive band and Fish as a solo artist is also an act that is easy to understand. Put another way, King Diamond is the perfect elevator pitch. To explain Mercyful Fate, you'd have to bang on the "close door" button a couple times.

So, Hank now found himself sitting on the sidelines with his baby band, but also taking pictures, becoming a successful and even somewhat famous photographer.

"Yes, especially here in Copenhagen and Denmark. I've always had an interest in photography and then I started doing photography of my ex-girlfriend now and a reporter saw that and said, 'Wow, you must be expensive.' I said, 'I don't know, depending...' and he sent it to a magazine and they instantly hired me. All of a sudden I was getting all these models hanging around and I'm just doing it the way I see it, with this style and taste I have. So, I've been doing that now for about two years. It took all my time and I took about 20 or 30,000 pictures so I have tons of pictures that I still can sell to the world. I've only sold them to Danish magazines. But that's been interesting. Now I'm a bit more into music, but I might do huge photo shoots here and there later."

Continues Hank, "People have to think about the future because being a musician, you're very happy getting the recording contract, but you're basically not realising that you're getting a little screwed. Not sounding pessimistic or anything, but if you're really reading the contract, it's really screwing you all the way. You have to think about different... like Andy LaRocque from King Diamond, he has his own studio. Other people start becoming producers. So, you have to think of a backup, because living as a musician is very tough. Especially nowadays, because there are so many bands and everyone can make the recording of their band in their bedroom and they can release it."

"He's quite a famous photographer these days," affirms Michael concerning his band mate. "He does photos of nude girls, for magazines in Copenhagen. It's not pornography, but in very small swimsuits or nearly naked (laughs). He's very good at it, actually. I'm right in the heart of Copenhagen as well. Hank lives near the outside parts of Copenhagen; he's seven or eight kilometres away from me."

Michael was running his record store at the time, which he continues to do to this day. "It's called Beat Bop and I recently named it that because it's a mixture of jazz and rock, and mostly vinyl. The only thing we don't have is classical music, because I don't know anything about it. We don't have much in the way of DVDs or anything. It's mostly second-hand stuff. Most people don't want to sell DVDs—they buy them and they keep them. We also concentrate on music. We don't have much film and video."

Michael considered Force of Evil, "old-style metal from way back, the '80s. Also, the difference is we didn't want to get it too tight, so we played it live in the studio. Even Martin, there are no tricks or anything; it's only his voice. Martin also did all the lyrics, except for one song. He's more a traditional hard rock/heavy rock singer compared to King Diamond's high-pitched vocals and his more theatrical way of handling the vocals."

Commenting on the band name chosen for the project, Denner says, "It came immediately. The way we started this was Hank and I in my kitchen, drinking coffee. Hank said, 'I must ask you this, Michael: how do you feel about making a band all over again?' He had the name, and he said, 'What do you think about this name?' I said cool (laughs). So, he had it sorted out even before we talked about it. I must say, there are a number of meanings with this name. Of course there's the song, 'Evil' by Mercyful Fate, and Hank wrote that song, so he's Force of Evil (laughs). If you say King, the evil way he acts on stage, he's like an evil person, and the Force of Evil is making Hank and I, behind him. So, there are a lot of little things in this name that remind you of Mercyful Fate."

"We will continue making records as long as we're able to do it, hopefully for many, many years," adds Denner. "Because there is a very strong personal feeling in this band. We are very close together. I've never experienced such close friendship between five people in a band situation. Actually, last night I had the guys home for dinner; so much fun, you know? I've been in several formations of bands where there were musicians I didn't want to have a private life with, so this is a big difference for me."

But as far as Mercyful Fate goes, "Actually, we don't know what's happening at the moment. But I feel that if King and Hank want to do it, they should do it. I hope so, because they make good music together. I would definitely not be a part of that; I would leave that to Mike Wead. He's done a perfect job, and he's a very nice person and a great guitarist. So, I would never interfere. They can do this perfectly. There's no need for me, and I will concentrate on Force of Evil and only be in this band. I'm better to be 100% here than be 50% in two bands."

A DANGEROUS MEETING: IN THE SHADOWS WITH MERCYFUL FATE

September 15th, 2003 marked the release of *The Best of King Diamond* and *The Best of Mercyful Fate*, with matching cover designs, followed on October 21st by an all-new King Diamond album, *The Puppet Master*. Into 2004, Force of Evil came out with a live DVD called *Evil Comes... Alive*, while King answers with a live album called *Dead Lullabyes*.

But King was not done with Mercyful Fate, striving to keep their memory alive with an archival DVD set which, alas, never happened. As he told *Metalrules.com*, "Once we're past the release of the live album, Andy and I will start writing material for the next album. At the same time, I have to look at a lot of DVD stuff, old bootleg stuff. We want to see if we can put together a retro Mercyful Fate DVD and a retro King Diamond DVD to give the fans some of the very early stuff that we were involved with. I'm talking about bootlegs that no one has ever seen before. We do have copies of every bootleg that has been available, but we have masters of bootlegs that no one has ever seen. It's that stuff that I would like to get out to the fans, so even collectors will be blown away. Very good picture quality, very good bootleg sound quality on all instruments."

"An example would be Mercyful Fate in early 1982, before Michael Denner joined the band, playing a live concert in Copenhagen. When I saw it the first time, I was a little stunned. 'Oh my God, that's not Michael Denner there?!' We have even more stuff of King Diamond. I received 35 tapes a few weeks ago where the majority is stuff that people have seen before, the collectors. That is not interesting for me at all."

"But there's Mercyful Fate live in 1983 in a converted church that had become a concert venue in Amsterdam, Holland. The venue was called the Paradiso. We were playing *Don't Break the Oath* songs before we recorded *Don't Break the Oath* and we're burning the cross on stage and all that stuff. It's cool and is very good quality. You probably won't have seen any bootleg quality that good, both picture and sound. It is really interesting. If I were a fan, say it was Sabbath and I could get some of that stuff, I would be right there, I would love it."

"In the end, the fans decide themselves what they will buy and not buy," continued King. "It will be clearly labelled what it is, never before available official bootlegs. We hope to get through that. I have to have another meeting with Brian and when I've been through all of it and found the very best stuff, we have to see how he wants to approach the whole thing. Of course, we will throw all the official videos on that."

An Epilogue

Six years on and there was still no Mercyful Fate reunion, or even the DVD of which King speaks. Force of Evil returned in 2005 with *Black Empire*, a second studio album, same lineup, but the band called it a day the following year.

Meanwhile King was still motoring along, bringing a new banquet of horror in *Give Me Your Soul... Please*, issued June 26th, 2007. At an Ozzfest stop on August 9th, 2008, King joined the Metallica guys for a rendition of the Mercyful Fate medley from *Garage Inc.*. Further high-profile exposure occurs when King garners a Grammy nomination for "Never Ending Hill," in the Best Metal Performance category. What's more, Mercyful is included in the *Guitar Hero: Metallica* video game, by Activision, who also include King as a playable character.

Unable to find the original masters, Mercyful Fate executes a brief reunion and re-records "Evil" and "Curse of the Pharaohs"— this is all the original guys, save for Kim Ruzz, who is replaced by Bjarne T. Holm. The game eventually sees issue on July 14th of 2009. Still, King says that Mercyful Fate is "in hibernation."

Explained King about his impressive, evolved facepaint in this era, "The one I have now with a lot of crosses that are both one way and the other way, I really like that one. That will probably stay for a long time because it was one that started with *House of God*, and it shows very much what the story is about. There is that church for real and these theories about whether Jesus actually escaped there—if he ever was. Mary and him maybe, all these crazy things. There was a person in the story that doesn't know what to believe because he never got any proof, and that's what I'm about. I don't slag any religions, I don't judge people by what their religious beliefs are. I never did that and I finally got that out on that album: I haven't seen proof whether there is one, many gods or no gods. I would be the last to say that there are no gods in this world because, I mean, prove that. There is no proof—that's why it's a belief. That's what the makeup today reflects."

Then, in 2010, King's work ethic, and, apparently, his smoking, caught up with him. Put in hospital November 29th, 2010, he had been informed that he'd had several heart attacks due to multiple arterial blockages, ascribed to his heavy smoking (not to mention countless hours deep into the night in various Texas recording studios for years and years). King promptly had triple-bypass surgery and by December 11th, he was back at home convalescing.

So, what had gotten Diamond to this point? Well, just two years earlier, David Perri had asked him what he did to take care of his voice. Although there were some responsible positives in his response, he confirmed the infernal presence of cigarettes everybody chides him over.

"I smoke cigarettes and drink lots of coffee," scoffed the King. "It's true. I don't do anything special. When we're on the road though, I do take care of it. I don't drink any alcohol whatsoever. Well, people might see me drink one beer, but that'll maybe happen twice on a whole two-and-a-half-month tour. I'll have one beer, maybe two. If we find a nice restaurant on an off-day and we have a dinner, then I might have one. But otherwise, I stay away from it and I try to get my sleep. Getting sleep is not always easy on the road. I try to stay away from partying and things like that so I can make sure the voice is there the next day. You have to do that; you have to be careful."

"That's something that a lot of fans probably know by now, but they've probably misunderstood it, a little bit. At the end of a show, I don't hang around like the other guys do. I have to take care of the voice. I sweat a lot on stage with the coats and the hot lights and all this shit, and once you're done and drenched you can catch a cold, even if it's a summer night. All you need is a little wind blowing and you feel like you're standing outside an open refrigerator. It gets really cold and it's the best way to get sick. So, to avoid that stuff, when the band is on its last note, I'm on my way to a car. Then it's back to the hotel to get the wet clothes off as quickly as possibly and then jump into a hot shower. It's all about preventing getting sick."

"You can have five crew members hacking on the bus, and you're going to get it sooner or later," continued Diamond. "You're spending eight hours on the bus with these guys. They get it easy because they're in contact with so many people. Then when I get it, it can be tough, especially if it goes into the lungs. When that thing happens, it's hard to get oxygen on stage. I had a few times where I was in situations where you almost black out because you're not getting enough oxygen to the lungs. If you have to go up there congested like hell, it's tough."

"You have to remember that singing in my style, I get very little oxygen compared to other guys. You take one quick breath and then you use that breath for singing long lines and then you try to grab another quick breath somewhere. But other guys can take a bunch of breaths and get a lot of oxygen in there. If you're playing in a packed place and it's hot and people have been there all night long, there's not much oxygen left. If you go in a sick condition… there's been a few situations where I couldn't see because of the lack of oxygen. Everything was going black. I could barely lift my hand to bring up my microphone. So that can be tough."

Little did he know that his arteries were blocked. Here he is, a heavy smoker, no oxygen in the room, maybe he's got a cold, and he has to sing the 30 parts he's packed into every song, using all those different gears. Watch a half dozen songs in a row and it quickly becomes apparent how many frantic costume changes King has to perform… just with his voice.

"But you learn on the road, so that's why I've got to take care of myself," continued King, unknowing in 2008 how close he came to death. "I've got to take care of myself doing whatever I can. There might be situations where it's out of my hands, where the other guys are sick and I'm going to get sick too. But you do whatever you can to prevent it so you can be at your best. Otherwise, it's not so good. When we're in the recording studio, I drink a lot of coffee. Coffee and cigarettes are the only things I really have in the recording studio. I'm always with a cigarette and a cup of coffee."

"If I want to party, I can party when I get home. I don't have to party on the road. It's more than just a hobby; it's a hobby that's also a job, you can say. But I have too much pride. I couldn't live with myself if I didn't do it this way. Those times when I've had trouble at a show because I've been sick and I've had a hard time hitting some notes, the fans will usually know it. I might even tell them, because it's just unbearable for myself. I have had so few shows in my career where I felt it was a perfect show. A perfect show for me is where I hit every single note that night dead-on. Even if there are two or three of the higher notes where I pitch a little over or under… sometimes it's not even the singing, it's more that you can't hear on stage. If there's a couple of those that really stick out that I don't hit perfectly… God, I hate myself afterwards. I'm very, very critical of myself."

"But it's the only way to get better and keep it up," continues King. "The old songs, for instance, are much easier for me to sing today than when I was younger. Much easier. I have much better control of my voice. Another thing that plays a role live is that we have a top pro crew these days, and the monitor system that I use for my vocals is specially built. There's no other like it in the world. I tried some of these ear monitors and I couldn't get used to it. I have to feel my voice come blasting at me; I want to feel it. I don't want to just hear it like I'm listening to headphones on a stereo. So, I've tried some other systems and they're not for me. I need to hear the voice full blast. It's all these different things that you get used to. So, I have better sound than I used to have in the old days, and it's much more enjoyable these days. With some of these really high notes I look forward to them coming, whereas sometimes in the earlier days when it was hard to hear because you had a shittier monitor system, it was scary getting to those parts. I just hoped I would get them right. You might know that you could do it, but if you can't hear yourself properly, it gets hard."

"I can tell you with Mercyful Fate, there's one specific song that I love playing live, but I know that we always have problems with it," muses King. "It's 'Satan's Fall,' and because it's so long at 12 minutes plus, there's no opportunity for the guitarists to tune. Then when you're in these hot, sweaty places the tuning on the guitars starts drifting after four or five minutes. So, when they keep playing, they get slightly out of tune with each other. It happens every time we play the song. When you get to the end part, those single notes they're playing where I have to go in and sing some high falsetto... I don't know where to go with my voice. So, imagine if the guitars are each a bit off, I try to go next to one of the guitarists. Then I try to figure out what pitch to sing in. Out in the hall it sounds like I'm singing out of tune! I am out of tune with one guitar, but I'm in tune with the other. I can't split my voice in two and hit both notes."

"Those are tricky parts, I tell you. When you get to those, you feel discouraged and you think, 'Oh no, here they come.' I might sing exactly with one guitar but the other is still a bit off, and because of that, the vocalist sounds like he's the one who isn't right. It's a lot of things to think about, and that's just a couple of them. Then there's all the other cues and when to use this prop or that prop, or is the actress going to make it out as Grandma on time? All these things."

Then it was time to sing with the Metallica boys again, when on December 7th, 2011, they joined in on the festivities at the Fillmore in San Francisco in honour of that band's 30th anniversary. This was a test of the returning King, and he performed with aplomb—you can't kill the metal—dressed in all his splendour, suddenly making the world's biggest rock stars look ordinary, as well as his own band mates, Hank, Michael and Timi. Besides this performance of the Mercyful Fate medley from *Garage Inc.*, King would play no shows in 2013 and only two in 2012, specifically Sweden Rock and Hellfest, both in mid-June.

AN EPILOGUE

November 11th, 2014, Metal Blade issued another King compilation called *Dreams of Horror*, with 2015 marking the return of Michael Denner and Hank Shermann, recording as Denner Shermann, a four-track EP called *Satan's Tomb*, also for Metal Blade but only for Europe. Drumming on the project was Snowy Shaw, another Mercyful alumnus. In the all-important front man position was Sean Peck, from San Diego-based power metal band Cage.

As Hank explained to Anthony Morgan from *Metal Forces*, "Snowy was Mercyful Fate's drummer for the *Time* album. He also did some tours with us—with Mercyful Fate and King Diamond—so we have known him for 25 years or something like that. We said that we had to have Snowy on this album, because we consider him one of the best drummers in the world on so many different levels. It's not just being a metal drummer; it's just as a whole drummer. He has so many layers in his playing, so you can actually enjoy just listening for the drums. He was totally into it, and we were very happy about that since it's a good body of work. Also, we consider him one of the best."

On both the EP and 2016's full-length, *Masters of Evil*, Hank would write all the music with Sean penning (or Sean pecking) all the lyrics. True to form, Michael Denner was content to play his guitar but to sit out the song credits.

As he did with Mercyful, Hank still had the mighty Judas Priest of the 1970s to use as inspiration. "Obviously with the sound, every time Michael and I play guitar together, it sounds like 100%, genuine, authentic Mercyful Fate," Shermann told Morgan.

"That's just how it is, because every guitar player has a sound. No matter what amp or guitar you're playing on, your sound is who you are. Of course, with that aspect and with me being a composer and having so much experience with that—having created all of the music off of *Melissa* and three or four songs off of *Don't Break the Oath*—it's still in the blood. That's the style that we like best ourselves, a little more classic heavy metal."

"Also, being big fans of Judas Priest, from early Judas Priest up to maybe *Killing Machine*... *Sad Wings of Destiny*, *Sin After Sin*, *Stained Class* and *Killing Machine* are extraordinary albums, in my opinion. They're like totally cool, even 30 years later. I still favour those old records, probably because we grew up with them. I would say it's almost inevitable that it will sound like and be reminiscent of our old band, and some of our early inspirations. Compared to when I did the riffs to all of the old classics back then, not much has changed in how I do it today. It's the same guitar; I'm just playing my Fender, jamming, so not much has happened (laughs). It's basically sticking as well to what we created back then, just with different riffs obviously. Also, since I know I'm not composing for Mercyful Fate but for Denner Shermann, we can go other ways that we probably wouldn't have done with Mercyful Fate. Who knows? That should be detectable for any true fans of Mercyful Fate. They should be able to hear where we come from."

A twist of fate, as it were, would result from the band using the original Mercyful cover illustrator for Denner Shermann. Essentially this would have repercussions a few years later, as will be explained.

"Coincidentally," explains Hank, "there was this American guy who approached me some time ago. He said, 'I bought this album artwork off of Thomas (Holm), who did the *Melissa* and *Don't Break the Oath* album covers. Now I can't use it.' He asked if I was interested in buying it and I said, 'Yes, I really like that. I'm sure that at some point I can use that cover for something.' Then I bought it. That was a few years back, so I have actually had it saved here on my computer. Then now with Denner Shermann, that was the perfect time to say, hey, I already have the cover, this old-school metal cover, an '80s style painted by the same artist who did *Melissa* and *Don't Break the Oath* and others as well, like some King Diamond albums. This is the perfect fit. It signals the musical style we're doing, and it is done by the same painter who did our classics. That's perfect—for this first EP, that's the perfect fit."

"I wrote to Thomas, who did the painting, and said, 'Hey Thomas, I just want to let you know that finally your cool painting is going to be released.' He said, 'Wow, cool,' and wished us all the best and all that. You can see that everything is pointing backwards. We have Brian Slagel, who's been supporting us for about 25 years. We have Thomas Holm, who did the early covers for Mercyful Fate and King Diamond. So, we have a lot of old, good friends putting into the band and who are around the band. We also have Mercyful Fate's manager, since we are in daily contact with him anyway. So, it feels pretty comfortable and smooth at the moment (laughs). You never know how things work out. We have a good relationship with Metal Blade and Mercyful Fate is still signed to them. Back in the '90s, we were doing a lot with Metal Blade when we were touring with Mercyful Fate. We have been out to California a lot to visit the record company, so that feels good. It's like a big family. Also, King Diamond is signed to Metal Blade. So, it's pretty cool; it feels good."

AN EPILOGUE

Indeed, this interesting happenstance of Mercyful still being signed to Metal Blade for one more record has got to have some role in King, Hank, Michael and Timi never publicly disavowing doing something, although as we've seen, Michael had said he'd step aside in place of Mike Wead (this curious comment would also resonate later).

As Hank confirms, "Initially, back in the mid-'90s we signed the recording contract and still we have one album left. King has been having some health issues lately though, like maybe the last four or five years with his back, his heart and whatnot. He's had to take care of himself. Also since the year 2000, I think he has been focusing and concentrating on work with his own band, the King Diamond band. As it looks now, it seems like they are going to tour Europe in 2016, playing festivals and stuff, and also are going to make a new album."

"Hopefully with Mercyful Fate, I'm sure that at some point, we will find a time when everybody is having time off to either record a new album or maybe do some select, exclusive shows—that could also be interesting. Hopefully we'll do it with the original lineup; that's what we talked about a few years ago. But suddenly there were a lot of other things happening with King and there are a lot of other things happening with us now. We just have to find the right time and see how that evolves. Of course, we haven't talked to any of the guys as such (laughs). It has been some years since King and I talked about maybe seeing what's going to happen. But since there are so many fans and followers of Mercyful Fate and everyone is still fit and playing live at least? Michael, King and I. Timi, the original bass player, is also pretty fit as a bass player; he just needs a little rehearsal and then he's good to go. The original drummer, Kim Ruzz, I haven't had so much contact with, but some of the other guys know that he's still drumming and stuff. Who knows?"

"Of course, from a fan perspective, everyone would like to see the original lineup. Like with Black Sabbath; of course, you want to have Bill Ward as the drummer and all that. Hopefully one day we can announce something. I mean, everyone is getting old here. King is doing really well with his own band, and we are about to start Denner Shermann and will see how that goes. Also, like I said, there are so many fans following King Diamond and Mercyful Fate. That's also a factor too as to what decisions we make in the future. King and I have talked about that at some point, that if we are going to record another album at this time of our career, then it has to be a masterpiece. That's the criteria; it has to be extraordinarily good—and we are very up for that task. The good thing is that the three of us are very active and things seem to be running well, rather than if everyone was retired and getting old and rusty."

After the EP and the full-length, in 2018, Denner Shermann called it a day, "due to different priorities within the band," said the band's website. "All members are continuing working on individual projects. Thanks to all our fans who supported our albums and our live shows."

Just when we might deem Michael Denner down for the count—remember the disconcerting dearth of songwriting across the projects and over the years—on November 15th, 2019, he snapped back with a new project called Denner's Inferno, brandishing a proudly retro-styled metal collection called *In Amber*. Accompanied mostly by unknowns, the drummer on the record is none other than Bjarne T. Holm.

The key to the album is embedded in the title, says Michael. "Yes, sometimes you can find amber on the beach with preserved insects a million years old. So, it's a valuable piece with something hidden from the past, visible inside of it. It's also a small tribute to Deep Purple *In Rock* (laughs), because for me, that's the blueprint for heavy rock. I don't want any comparisons with a legendary album like that, but I couldn't help it."

The tribute continues, with some deftly chosen obscure covers. Explains Denner, "'Loser' is a cover of Trapeze—Glenn Hughes, Mel Galley, Dave Holland. I've always been a fan of the obscure '70s hard rock and I have a huge collection of records. These obscure cover songs are more or less; I did my own versions and put some heavy riffing below some parts. I stretched the lead guitar pieces and added to some themes and added my own signatures guitar parts. It's a tribute to these more or less unknown bands to say thank you for inspiring me as a guitarist."

On covering "Taxman (Mr. Thief)," Michael says, "That might be a bit odd compared to the rest of the songs on the album, because Cheap Trick connects more with pop radio-oriented hits, 'Surrender' and so on. But for me, the very first Cheap Trick album is produced by Jack Douglas, and it's deeper and a bit heavier compared to what came afterwards. Also, the fact that before Cheap Trick, they had a band called Fuse, with one of my favourite albums. It's more Deep Purple/Uriah Heep type music. I've been a fan of Cheap Trick from the very beginning, and so I feel it was in its place to find a more obscure song by them and put it on the record as a tribute, my own version with my own signature stuff."

"The album shows clearly my taste in music and what I'm about," figures Michael in summary. "I do believe I've been on between 40 and 50 albums during my time, all kinds of different stuff, as a guest and as a performer. Many artists say, 'This is the best one,' but the new album is the best I've ever done (laughs). For me, it's even more personal because it's the closest to my own taste in music I've ever been, what I like to listen to and hear when I'm at home and relaxing and going through my old rare and obscure vinyl albums from the '70s—this is very much in the vein of these albums. And of course there's some inspiration from my base with Mercyful Fate, Force of Evil and Zoser Mez, to spice it up with my own history."

Catching up, on January 28, 2017, the original Mercyful Fate lineup, everybody except King, got together to receive an award in Copenhagen, bestowed upon them by the Danish Association of Music Critics. Also in 2017, King and Livia had a son, named Byron.

Although there was no mention of a new record, there was some major news on August 1st, 2019, when it was announced that there would be an unspecified number of Mercyful Fate shows conducted in 2020, at least in Europe. Given that bassist (in good standing) Timi Hansen was fighting cancer, Metal Blade utilitarian and all 'round good guy Joey Vera was announced as the band's thumper of the fat strings.

The rest of the lineup was slated to be King, Hank, Bjarne T. Holm and on second guitar... Mike Wead! Which meant that the internet went into overdrive at the travesty of Michael Denner not being involved, prompting folks to frame this not as a reunion but a continuation, albeit with a different bassist from Sharlee D'Angelo, who was there on *9*.

It turns out that Michael not being invited stems from a falling-out that he had with King, ostensibly over something pretty obscure.

"King and I lost contact some years ago now," Michael told me. This was after Hank and I did the Denner Shermann record. We had got this artist who did the original covers for *Melissa* and *Don't Break the Oath*, and he did a cover for the new stuff, the two albums. King saw them and got upset about it because they were too close to the originals. Somehow, I understand. I can understand, but there's no need to make a big issue out of it. I said, 'Hey, relax, man,' and he got very upset after that, and we lost contact. So, this is the price that he and I have to pay now for that small argument. It's a really sad, sad thing. The first two weeks after I got the news, I was in shock. I was sitting on my sofa just looking out... yeah (laughs), it was really tough. Because I didn't expect it. But I got used to the thing and now it's just time to move on. I have a great album out and a good band and feel good about myself. I'm in touch to be able to do touring and I've already started writing songs for the next Inferno album. So, I'm quite happy where I am. I just wish the guys the best of luck with what they're going to do. I mean... cool."

Speaking with Jimmy Kay from *The Metal Voice*, Michael elaborated that the hurt of it all was amplified by rumblings that the set lists for these 2020 shows was going to consist mostly of the band's classic '80s material.

"Yes, what surprised me—and I didn't know anything about this—it looked like it was supposed to be the original lineup with the songs from the first three albums. That totally caught me by surprise, because I was very much a part of these albums. If this is what Hank and King want to do, I can't force them to bring me in the band. So, I guess I wish them the best of luck. I just want to move on, doing my own stuff. I don't want to make a big deal out of this. I was part of Mercyful Fate history, a big part, but they didn't want to go that way and I cannot force them to change their mind. I'm at peace with this. It's okay."

One odd wrinkle in this is that Michael has a good relationship with Hank, having just had a band together. But at the same time, you would think this Denner Shermann cover art narrative surely involves Hank as well.

"Yeah, that was a big surprise in this," agrees Michael. "I didn't expect Hank to just keep quiet, because we always talked about private things and we had a good relationship as guitarists and composers. So that was a big shock in it. But I lost contact with King some years ago. We had some differences, small, small arguments about small things, so I didn't expect him to call me and say, 'Hey, Michael, let's start the band again' (laughs). But with Hank, it's a different story, because we were working very close together. He even helped me with the Inferno album. He did some of the guitar recordings and he helped with the artwork for the cover, so this was quite a big surprise."

Asked by Jimmy if he'd go along if they called him up tomorrow and said they changed their minds, Denner says, "It'd be very hard. It will not be enough just to give me that call. I would need some

An Epilogue

serious explanations. That's a hard question to answer because my feelings were a bit hurt when this happened three or four weeks ago. So now I'm healing (laughs). But it's perfect timing for my album to be released now. It could've easily been that I was not working. If I hadn't been active as a guitarist and composer and so on, then I would just disappear in all this. Now I'm a very big part of the whole family because I have a new album. I did my best and succeeded in not throwing mud in the face of the other guys. I've not said anything bad about these guys, even though they disappointed me."

At this juncture, Denner still held out hopes for Timi Hansen's recovery from his cancer. "He's doing better. I'm in close contact with Timi. We've been friends since we were 12 years old (laughs); played football together actually. He was in my first serious band, Starchaser, way back in 1976, I believe, and he lives just a mile down the road. He's been battling some serious things, but I do feel that things are going better for him. I think he's recovering. But I don't think he will ever play bass again, ever. He hadn't had a bass in over ten years now. He sold his bass. That's over ten years ago now. So, he's not active anymore."

As for original drummer Kim Ruzz... "Kim moved far away from here, Copenhagen. He lives, I think, on the southwest side of Zealand Island and he has two beautiful sons and a lovely wife, who is a lawyer by the way, and he works helping people with getting jobs. What do you call that? Where you go into this office and the guy will help you and see if he could find something for you. That's his job. He's a very well-respected man in the small town they live in. So, I'm very happy for him."

"There's a lot of crap going on and it's a little bit silly," reflected Snowy Shaw on the situation. "I called up Mike Wead when I heard about the reunion and I said, 'What's going on here? Since you are involved, Michael Denner isn't there. Who is playing drums?' It's Bjarne, who replaced me. 'Yeah, but okay, if it's a continuation of 9, is Sharlee going to be there?' 'No, we haven't contacted him either.' So, it's a bit sketchy, weird. The thing is that if they have some argument over an album cover with Denner Shermann, Hank has no problem with that and King has no problem with Hank, but Michael is out. I don't get it."

"Michael's been active through this whole thing, with Denner's Inferno and also Denner Shermann. So yeah, I don't know if they have some feud between each other. When I was at a King Diamond show in Copenhagen recently, I went to see Denner in his record store and he said, 'I won't go.' They're not even talking to each other. 'I'm not gonna go.' To me, you're old guys, bury the hatchet and move on. I mean, soon we're all dead (laughs)."

Adds "Metal" Mike van Rijswyck, there from even before the Roadrunner days, "I saw their manager, Ole Bang, a couple of months ago at the Summer Breeze festival and I gave him a hard time. I was swearing at him. Mercyful Fate reunion and they didn't even ask Michael Denner to join, so I was mad at him. I called him the manager of Mercyful Fake. He didn't agree with me. I said, come on, man. Then he said, 'Yeah, he hasn't toured for years, hasn't been on stage and within years he never plays.' I said, 'Well yeah he's on tour, with Denner Shermann all the time. I see him all the time touring and he's great.' But Hank Shermann knows about the reunion shows coming up and he's not allowed to tell Michael and he finds out via blah blah blah. So that puts a damper on that collaboration, you know what I mean? So, I was not happy. I'm always honest; I'm the guy that tells it like it is. So, I gave Ole Bang a hard time because of that 'cause I think it's not fair 'cause they're going to tour in the summer doing some festivals and only play stuff off the first two albums and the EP. The guy who was playing on all of that is not playing with them. That's not right."

"I understand Timi 'Grabber' Hansen because he has cancer and Kim Ruzz who except for some… a year in his own Kim Ruzz Band or something, they can't play, but at least Hank and Mike you should keep together. Although Mike Wead as another guitar player, he's a great guitar player. But don't you dare announce it without Michael Denner as part of it."

As for the reason cited by Michael, this issue with the Denner Shermann artwork, Mike says, "Yeah, I know, but that's the stuff you could easily put aside. Ole Bang just killing Michael off this reunion… maybe he rented some guys for a certain fee and not the guys who deserve to get paid. I dunno. It's always about money and business. I don't want to get involved with that. But for the fans, we already call it here the Mercyful Fake reunion."

Timi "Grabber" Hansen lost his battle with cancer, dying on November 4th, 2019, six days after his 61st birthday. Said King Diamond in a statement, "I just found out that I lost one of my dearest friends, who has been fighting cancer for a long time, in such an incredibly brave way. He was not just my roommate on the early Mercyful Fate tours, but he was always my favourite bass player of all times. I was fortunate to have been able to visit him at his apart-

AN EPILOGUE

ment with some other good friends, and we had a great afternoon that will never be forgotten. When I last talked to Timi on the phone on October 24th, I could understand that things had gotten tougher than they ever were, and yet he said, 'We fight on.' I feel so, so sad for his entire family; you have my absolute deepest sympathy. Rest in peace my dear, dear friend."

Also in 2019, Hank Shermann issues a bold and rumbling solo single called "The Bloody Theme" but no album follows. Meanwhile, King Diamond plays the summer festival circuit and on November 8th, he issues a new single, called "Masquerade of Madness," from a forthcoming album called *Institute* that never gets built. This is in the midst of a North American tour for the band, which represent the last King Diamond dates until 2024. Also, before the year is out, Mercyful Fate tour dates are announced for early 2020, with California rocker Joey Vera (Armored Saint, Fates Warning) announced as the band's new bassist. This promising reunion gets cancelled due to the worldwide pandemic.

In 2020, Hank is quoted as saying that there are six or seven songs written for a forthcoming Mercyful Fate album. Nothing happens for the balance of the year and all of 2021, but on June 2, 2022, Mercyful Fate play their first reunion show, at the Expo Plaza in Hannover, Germany, with a resplendent and elaborate stage set-up and frightening new costuming for Diamond, maybe his best look to date. The band consists of King, Hank, Bjarne, Mike Wead and Joey Vera. The short set debuts a new song called "The Jackal of Salzburg," which is long and proggy, fast and slow, heavy but with ballad bits. They go on to perform throughout the summer European festival season, with an isolated US show, in Las Vegas, August 21st, followed by a North American tour in October and November, supported by Midnight and Kreator and then two Mexican dates in December.

In 2023, all is quiet, save for some coloured vinyl reissues of four reunion-era Mercyful Fate albums in October. On January 16, 2024, the band announces its split with Joey Vera, and three days later, Becky Baldwin is announced as the Mercyful Fate's new bassist. Soon they are in South America for a couple of shows in Chile and Brazil, but other than that, things go dark once again. On October 15, King Diamond begins a North American tour, debuting a couple new songs in "Spider Lilly" and "Electro Therapy" but still there is no new album. "Spider Lilly" is issued as a single on December 17th, and it is avowed that the song is from the band's forthcoming

"Horror Trilogy," with the first instalment to be called *Saint Lucifer's Hospital 1920.*

Into 2025, Becky Baldwin reveals that a new Mercyful Fate album is in the demoing stages. Speaking with longtime Montreal metal champions *The Metal Voice*, Baldwin indicated that, "Instrumentally, it's mostly there. So, the next step is for King to work on it, but King also needs to put out the King Diamond album this year, hopefully. (That) should be this year and then he'll do a European tour. Then it's Mercyful Fate time."

"I'm not gonna give anything away," continues Baldwin. "I don't feel qualified to divulge that information. I haven't been told what I am and I'm not allowed to say (laughs). There's songs with names, there's concepts. I'm not going to sing you a little riff, but there are riffs (laughs)."

As for the story of her joining, Baldwin told *The Metal Voice* a year earlier that, "I guess the idea was floating around for a while, but it's quite recent still, the news that I was going to be permanent in Mercyful Fate. But I guess, as any band does when you've got a lot coming up and there's some... I don't want to say insecurity within the band, because it's not that. It was just a question about how busy Joey was, and I guess it was in the back of their minds. The way that the fans reacted when I did the tour was very positive. So, it was a natural progression, I guess."

"I think the main person for bringing me into the picture was Hank Shermann. So, he was the person who suggested me when they started looking at, 'Okay, well, actually, this whole list of male bass players that we're looking through, it doesn't have to be a guy. Who else do we know? Should we start looking somewhere else? Because there aren't any women on this list, and maybe that could be a thing, that could work out for Mercyful Fate.' Then I was at the top of Hank's list. When he showed King and the rest of the management and stuff some of my videos, it was literally the weekend of Bloodstock festival in the summer of 2022. They were, like, 'Okay, let's go. Let's go to Bloodstock. Let's ask her there.'"

On the topic of writing, Baldwin said, "I think the songwriting is still gonna be very much King Diamond and Hank Shermann heading up most of that, but definitely writing bass lines. I've studied all of Timi's bass lines very meticulously now, and so I really feel like I can bring some of that into the new bass lines for the next record."

As our story draws to an end, it's become quite surprising that the last Mercyful Fate album was 26 years ago, and that the last King

An Epilogue

Diamond album was 18 years ago. In any event, as a closing missive to our tale, King Diamond expresses a thank you to the fans for giving him this life, fully two prolific bands through which he can channel his views and scare the bejesus out of us at the same time.

"There's many factors," reflects Diamond. "Of course, it's the fans and people like you and radio stations and all those who support in sales. All these people keep the wheels turning. That's the main thing. Then there's the label support. The thing that's important for us with the label is what we've always had: artistic freedom. We've always had that, and that means a lot. We've always been able to compose and do everything straight from the heart. No one tells us to do things a certain way or to follow a certain trend. We've never followed the trend; we've never been a trendy band (laughs). Whatever came along then left, it's like we were driving along on a little back road on our own. We were never caught up on the big highway of going really fast and selling a lot of albums, because that highway comes to stops equally as fast and then another thing takes over. We just plough along on the side-street. We've created our own little niche, because of the freedom to do whatever we feel like."

"That has a lot to do with the longevity, I think. We were never in or out of any style. It becomes timeless, in some ways. It also puts a damper on your hopes of becoming a platinum seller (laughs). It comes with the territory, because you're never following the trends. But I don't regret anything. We never went along with what was selling the big numbers, and I can stand up proudly with anything I've been part of. It feels good to do that and to know that there are a lot of fans of King Diamond and Mercyful Fate that are very, very hardcore and loyal. They're very smart and they dig into the lyrics big time, especially with the stories on the records. It's such a pleasure to see. I often go on our fan club site and sit and see what they talk about. Sometimes I might stick a comment in. We definitely try to keep up with what the fans are thinking about the band and the music."

"I will never take directions from anyone, but sometimes I read some criticism that can be very good. Even though it might not be positive criticism, there are some times when you're so close to the music that you might not realise something until someone points it out. Then you think about it, and sometimes people are right. And other times you see people criticise and you think, 'You don't know because you weren't there.' What they're saying is just a guess, and it's a wrong guess. But having an open mind and listening to what people say is very useful."

A DANGEROUS MEETING: IN THE SHADOWS WITH MERCYFUL FATE

Commenting on the band's legacy, especially with respect to the black metal genre, King says that "It's a big honour to hear from a lot of those bands that we inspired them in some way. Whether we're black metal or not doesn't matter to me. It doesn't matter what we're called; it's so hard to put labels on music. But it's an honour to hear people say that they were inspired by us, in whatever way it might be. Whether it's for the live performance or the show or the musical parts, it's always an honour to hear."

"The funny thing is that King Diamond is so much blacker than Mercyful Fate ever was. Often people have a different opinion on that, but when you dig into it, I would say King Diamond is a lot more Satanic, if you want to put that word in there. It's very much about Satanic philosophy and horror, whereas Mercyful Fate is more about old myths and religion. That's the weird misconception, that Mercyful Fate is so much more Satanic than King Diamond. It's the other way around, if you really start thinking about it and dig into what the lyrics say. But I know that a lot of people say that Mercyful Fate is very dark and this and that. Venom was one of those early ones, too. They were playing when we started Mercyful Fate. Celtic Frost, too. There were a couple of bands that were quite dark at the time."

Fortunately for King, his recent heart problems did not result in forced retirement, or worse, death. Nor did it break him financially, which isn't out of the question, given the US health system.

"No, I've not thrown my money away on unnecessary things in my life, so I'm okay," laughs Diamond. "That was the not the things I was thinking of. I was thinking of trying to survive, first of all. The things that mattered to me were, it was a great thing to be able to lift a big glass of water, to be able to actually have strength to lift it. That was a big thing and a big step that mattered to me. It didn't matter if I got a check in for this or that. I never think like that."

"Those things are not... I don't need five cars in my garage to feel great. That's not what matters to me. Different things matter to me. Nowadays, yeah, I can tell you, a lot of good has come from that bad that happened. Of course, now I do what the doctors tell me, because I like being here. I got a second chance, I value it, I don't take tomorrow for granted, I don't take anything for granted. I appreciate when I do get some pay; those times when it still happens."

"I feel I have a lot more to give," continues King, "but there are other things where you pay attention to things. I feel like I'm in a house with 20 windows now compared to a house of ten windows in the past. I just see so many more things and pay attention to more things. So that whole thing with having this or that status symbols and shit like that, that's not really what it's about for me. It never really was. I didn't jump on the bandwagon somewhere or jump on a trend with a band—I can't do that. That's not honest. That's not me. I have to do things that I feel are right. That's what we have always done. I know that we are only here because our fans. We are not the super band that everybody has to buy because we're so great. It's a two-way street. It'll always be a two-way street. What's the fun to play with no one? Even if they pay you a million dollars? You're not going to get the thrill—I can guarantee that. Without each other it's no fun."

A DANGEROUS MEETING: IN THE SHADOWS WITH MERCYFUL FATE

DISCOGRAPHY

Pretty straight forward, the Mercyful Fate discography. That said, I've split out the compilations and then left the two EPs embedded in the sequence.

I've maintained the Side 1/Side 2 demarcation for releases from the vinyl years, mainly because doing so provides extra information as to how the band (and its extended family in management and perhaps the business office and over at the label) viewed and then sequenced these records. I've gone with European issues as the first editions for the '80s, but American for the '90s, given that at this point, the band becomes somewhat of an America-based act.

I've allowed myself a "Notes" section to mention in footnote form any fruity little foibles I found important or odd enough to mention (this section is not an exact science). I've not bothered with quote marks around songs—too messy: this section's virtually all songs. Also, in my "Notes" section, I've made known any alterations in band personnel from one album to the next.

The mission: it's a discography constructed more to provide a roadmap as to where, crucially, the songs come from. It's also an index of sorts to the book, a plot map, hopefully a reference tool useful in a number of ways.

I also thought it quite important to display who was writing which songs in terms of the music. Because King writes all the lyrics, I've abbreviated his lyric credit as "D" just to keep things tight; I've gone with Diamond for his music credits.

Mercyful Fate
(Rave-On RMLP-002, September 25, 1982)
Produced by: Jac Hustinx
Side 1: 1. *A Corpse Without Soul* (D, Shermann) 6:53; 2. *Nuns Have No Fun* (D, Shermann) 4:17
Side 2: 1. *Doomed by the Living Dead* (D, Shermann) 5:06; 2. *Devil Eyes* (D, Shermann) 5:48
Notes: Dutch issue only EP, also known as *Nuns Have No Fun*. King Diamond – vocals; Hank Shermann – guitars; Michael Denner – guitars; Timi Grabber – bass; Kim Ruzz – drums.

Melissa
(Roadrunner RR 9835, October 30, 1983)
Produced by: Henrik Lund
Side 1: 1. *Evil* (D, Shermann) 4:46; 2. *Curse of the Pharaohs* (D, Shermann) 4:00; 3. *Into the Coven* (D, Shermann) 5:35; 4. *At the Sound of the Bell* (D, Shermann) 5:20
Side 2: 1. *Black Funeral* (D, Shermann) 2:47; 2. *Satan's Fall* (D, Shermann) 11:21; 3. *Melissa* (D, Shermann) 6:40

A DANGEROUS MEETING: IN THE SHADOWS WITH MERCYFUL FATE

Don't Break the Oath
(Roadrunner RR 9898, September 7, 1984)
Produced by: Henrik Lund
Side 1: 1. A Dangerous Meeting (D, Shermann) 5:10; 2. Nightmare (D, Shermann) 6:20; 3. Desecration of Souls (D, Shermann) 4:54; 4. Night of the Unborn (D, Shermann, Denner) 5:03
Side 2: 1. The Oath (D, Diamond) 7:32; 2. Gypsy (D, Denner, Diamond) 3:07; 3. Welcome Princes of Hell (D, Shermann) 4:03; 4. To One Far Away (Denner) 1:32; 5. Come to the Sabbath (D, Diamond) 5:20

In the Shadows
(Metal Blade MBD-53892, June 6, 1993)
Produced by: King Diamond, Hank Shermann, Tim Kimsey
1. Egypt (D, Diamond) 4:52; 2. The Bell Witch (D, Shermann) 4:34; 3. The Old Oak (D, Shermann) 8:54; 4. Shadows (D, Diamond) 4:42; 5. A Gruesome Time (D, Denner), 4:31; 6. Thirteen Invitations (D, Diamond) 5:17; 7. Room of Golden Air (Denner) 3:06; 8. Legend of the Headless Rider (D, Shermann) 7:43; 9. Is That You, Melissa? (D, Diamond) 4:41; 10. Return of the Vampire... 1993 (D, Shermann) 5:08
Notes: Morten Nielsen replaces Kim Ruzz on drums. Nielsen is credited properly in print, but Snowy Shaw is pictured prominently as the band's drummer. Lars Ulrich is guest drummer on "Return of the Vampire... 1993."

The Bell Witch
(Metal Blade PCDS 53911, June 27, 1994)
1. The Bell Witch (D, Shermann) 4:34; 2. Is That You, Melissa? (D, Diamond) 4:38; 3. Curse of the Pharaohs (D, Shermann) 4:24; 4. Egypt (D, Diamond) 4:53; 5. Come to the Sabbath (D, Diamond) (6:48) 6. Black Funeral (D, Shermann) 3:40
Notes: Comprises two tracks from *In the Shadows* plus four live tracks recorded October 8th, 1993 at The Palace in Los Angeles. Bass on studio tracks by Timi Hansen; bass on live tracks by Sharlee D'Angelo.

Time
(Metal Blade P2 53942, October 25, 1994)
Produced by: King Diamond, Tim Kimsey; assistant producer: Hank Shermann
1. Nightmare Be Thy Name (D, Denner) 3:28; 2. Angel of Light (D, Diamond) 3:37; 3. Witches' Dance (D, Diamond) 4:47; 4. The Mad Arab (D, Shermann) 4:43; 5. My Demon (D, Diamond) 4:42; 6. Time (D, Diamond) 4:22; 7. The Preacher (D, Shermann) 3:29; 8. Lady in Black (D, Diamond) 3:49; 9. Mirror (D, Denner) 3:19; 10. The Afterlife (D, Shermann) 4:32; 11. Castillo del Mortes (D, Shermann) 6:13
Notes: Snowy Shaw replaces Morten Nielsen on drums. Sharlee D'Angelo replaces Timi Hansen on bass.

Into the Unknown
(Metal Blade P2 50586, August 20, 1996)
Produced by: King Diamond, Tim Kimsey
1. Lucifer (D, Diamond) 1:29; 2. The Uninvited Guest (D, Diamond) 4:14; 3. The Ghost of Change (D, Diamond) 5:41; 4. Listen to the Bell (D, Shermann) 3:56; 5. Fifteen Men (and a Bottle of Rum) (D, Denner) 5:04; 6. Into the Unknown (D, Shermann) 6:33; 7. Under the Spell (D, Diamond) 4:40; 8. Deadtime (D, Denner) 3:13; 9. Holy Water (D, Diamond) 4:31; 10. Kutulu (The Mad Arab, Part 2) 5:17
Notes: Bjarne T. Holm replaces Snowy Shaw on drums.

DISCOGRAPHY

Dead Again
(Metal Blade 3984-14159-2, June 9, 1998)
Produced by: Sterling Winfield, Mercyful Fate
1. Torture (1629) (D, Shermann) 5:03; 2. The Night (D, Shermann) 5:51; 3. Since Forever (D, Diamond) 4:39; 4. The Lady Who Cries (D, Diamond) 4:18; 5. Banshee (D, Diamond) 4:47; 6. Mandrake (D, Shermann) 6:06; 7. Sucking Your Blood (D, Diamond) 4:22; 8. Dead Again (D, Shermann) 13:41; 9. Fear (D, Diamond) 4:16; 10. Crossroads (D, D'Angelo) 5:42
Notes: Mike Wead replaces Michael Denner on guitars.

9
(Metal Blade 3984-14242-2, June 15, 1999)
Produced by: Kol Marshall, Mercyful Fate
1. Last Rites (D, Shermann) 4:12; 2. Church of Saint Anne (D, Shermann) 4:44; 3. Sold My Soul (D, Diamond) 5:04; 4. House on the Hill (D, Shermann) 3:43; 5. Burn in Hell (D, Diamond) 3:49; 6. The Grave (D, Shermann) 4:09; 7. Insane (D, Shermann) 3:01; 8. Kiss the Demon (D, Diamond) 3:53; 9. Buried Alive (D, Diamond) 4:53; 10. 9 (D, Wead) 4:31

Compilations

The Beginning
(Roadrunner RR 9603, June 24, 1987)
Side 1: 1. Doomed by the Living Dead (D, Shermann) 5:07; 2. A Corpse Without Soul (D, Shermann) 6:52; 3. Nuns Have No Fun (D, Shermann) 4:17; 4. Devil Eyes (D, Shermann) 5:48
Side 2: 1. Curse of the Pharaohs (D, Shermann) 3:50; 2. Satan's Fall (D, Shermann) 10:28; 3. Black Masses (D, Shermann) 4:30
Notes: Post-breakup compilation consisting of the *Mercyful Fate* EP, Tony Wilson-produced BBC live tracks and the non-LP "Black Masses" from the *Melissa* sessions.

Return of the Vampire
(Roadrunner RR 9184; May 12, 1992)
1. Burning the Cross (D, Petersen) 8:49; 2. Curse of the Pharaohs (D, Shermann) 4:28; 3. Return of the Vampire (D, Shermann) 4:51; 4. On a Night of Full Moon (D, Shermann) 6:40; 5. A Corpse Without Soul (D, Shermann) 8:12; 6. Death Kiss (D, Shermann) 5:53; 7. Leave My Soul Alone (D, Denner) 3:21; 8. M.D.A. (Denner/Denner) 4:21; 9. You Asked for It ((D, Shermann) 4:13
Notes: Compilation of early demos and rarities; various personnel. Subtitled *The Rare and Unreleased*.

The Best of
(Roadrunner RR 8339-2, 2003)
1. Doomed by the Living Dead 2. A Corpse Without Soul 3. Nuns Have No Fun 4. Evil 5. Curse of the Pharaohs 6. Into the Coven 7. Black Funeral 8. Satan's Fall 9. A Dangerous Meeting 10. Desecration of Souls 11. Gypsy 12. Come to the Sabbath 13. Burning the Cross 14. Return of the Vampire
Notes: There also exists *A Dangerous Meeting*, a 1992 compilation under the King Diamond banner that is roughly half King Diamond tracks, half Mercyful Fate tracks.

INTERVIEWS WITH THE AUTHOR

D'Angelo, Sharlee. July 14, 1999.
D'Angelo, Sharlee. October 5, 1999.
D'Angelo, Sharlee. February 4, 2006.
Denner, Michael. June 24, 2003.
Denner, Michael. September 24, 2019.
Diamond, King. October 14, 1996.
Diamond, King. September 15, 1999.
Diamond, King. December 13, 2001.
Diamond, King. October 2003.
Diamond, King. July 2007.
Diamond, King. 2009.
Drover, Glen. July 10, 2000.
Holm, Bjarne T. December 1, 2019.
Kimsey, Tim. September 27, 2019.
LaRocque, Andy. August 2000.
Marshall, Kol. November 5, 2019.
Shaw, Snowy. May 20, 2000.
Shaw, Snowy. October 29, 2019.
Shermann, Hank. June 26, 2003.
Van Rijswyck, Mike. October 8, 2019.
Wead, Mike. October 5, 1999.
Winfield, Sterling. November 4, 2019.

ADDITIONAL CITATIONS

Brave Words & Bloody Knuckles. Mercyful Fate: Masters of Musical Macabre! by Tim Henderson. Vol. 1, No.6. January/February 1995.
Brave Words & Bloody Knuckles. King Diamond: A Dangerous Meeting! by Alex Ristic. No.22. February/March 1998.
Brave Words & Bloody Knuckles. Mercyful Fate: Speak of the Devil by Scott Hefflon. No.31. June 1999.
Bravewords.com. King Diamond: Satan's Consummate Perfectionist by David Perri. May 20, 2008.
Cincinnati Enquirer, The. Mercyful Fate no longer on metal's cutting edge by Rob Hartzell. January 28, 1995.
Demonzine. Interview with King Diamond by Tony Oliver. 2001.
Dunn, Sam. Interview with King Diamond. 2009.
Evening Sun, The. Band cancelled from concert. December 6, 1984.
Hardradio. Interview with King Diamond by Sheila Rene. January 10, 1997.
Hit Parader. *Abigail* review by Andy Secher. No. 280. January 1988.
Hit Parader. King Diamond: Satan's Handyman by Winston Cummings. No. 281. February 1988.
Hit Parader. King Diamond: From the Dark Side by Andy Secher. No. 305. February 1990.
Hit Parader. *Voodoo* record review. No. 406. July 1998.
Hit Parader. *9* record review. No. 422. November 1999.
Kerrang!. Mercyful Fate: Gateway to Hell! by Malcolm Dome. No.40. April 21 - May 4, 1983.
Kerrang!. Fate Accompli! by Malcolm Dome. No.53. October 20 – November 2, 1983.
Kerrang! *In the Shadows* record review by Jason Arnopp. No.449. June 26, 1993.
Kerrang! Shadow King! By Don Kaye. No.452. July 17, 1993.
M&M. Fate: Melodic Hard Rock. January 31, 1987.

Metal-e-zine. An Interview with Mercyful Fate by RK. March 22, 1997.
Metal Forces. *Melissa* record review by Dave Constable. No.1, Autumn 1983.
Metal Forces. Mercyful Fate: Down to the Bones by Bernard Doe. No.2. 1983.
Metal Forces. King Diamond – Diamonds Are Forever by Bernard Doe. No.17. 1986.
Metal Forces. Us and Them by John Ricard. No.29. July 1988.
Metal Forces. Denner Sherman: Twinned by Fate by Anthony Morgan. October 2015.
Metal Hammer. Metallica: the story behind every *Garage Inc.* cover version by Chris Chantler. January 24, 2019.
Metal Maniacs. Mercyful Fate by Borivoj Krgin. Vol. 10, No. 2. June 1993.
Metal Rules. Interview with King Diamond by Lord of the Wasteland. July 17, 2005.
Metal Voice, The. Interviews with Becky Baldwin, Michael Denner, King Diamond and Hank Shermann by Jimmy Kay and Neil Turbin.
Morning Call, The. *In the Shadows* record review by Frank Pearn Jr. October 23, 1993.
MTV. Interview with Michael Denner and Hank Shermann by Vanessa Warwick. May 30, 1993.
MTV. Interviews with King Diamond. 1996.
Outcast, The. Interview with King Diamond by Mike Coles. October 12, 1999.
Pittsburgh Post-Gazette. Satanic rock band cancelled at Mosque by Mark Madden. December 5, 1984.
Plain Dealer, The. Reveling in the black arts by Jane Scott. January 27, 1995.
Record, The. As Fate would have it by Brian Aberback. October 1, 1999.
Robb's Metal Works. Interview with Hank Shermann by Robb Chavez. October 16, 1999.
Sick Drummer magazine. Snowy Shawy interview Continuation by Noel Smart & Craig Sternberg. Issue No.7. June 7, 2009.
Terrorizer. Journey into the Unknown: An Interview with King Diamond. No.34. September 1996.
Wormwood Chronicles. King Diamond: In His Satanic Majesty's Service by Dr. Abner Mailty.

ABOUT THE AUTHOR

At approximately 7900 (with over 7000 appearing in his books), Martin has unofficially written more record reviews than anybody in the history of music writing across all genres. Additionally, Martin has penned approximately 135 books on hard rock, heavy metal, classic rock, progressive rock, punk and record collecting. He was Editor-in-Chief of the now retired *Brave Words & Bloody Knuckles,* Canada's foremost heavy metal publication for 14 years, and has also contributed to *Revolver, Guitar World, Goldmine, Record Collector,* bravewords.com, lollipop.com and hardradio.com, with many record label band bios and liner notes to his credit as well.

Additionally, Martin has been a regular contractor to Banger Films, having worked for two years as researcher on the award-winning documentary *Rush: Beyond the Lighted Stage,* on the writing and research team for the 11-episode *Metal Evolution* and on the ten-episode *Rock Icons,* both for VH1 Classic. Additionally, Martin is the writer of the original metal genre chart used in *Metal: A Headbanger's Journey* and throughout the *Metal Evolution* episodes.

Then there's his audio podcast, *History in Five Songs with Martin Popoff* and the YouTube channel he runs with Marco D'Auria and Grant Arthur, called *The Contrarians.* Martin currently resides in Toronto and can be reached through martinp@inforamp.net or martinpopoff.com.

A MARTIN POPOFF BIBLIOGRAPHY

2025: A Dangerous Meeting: In the Shadows with Mercyful Fate, A Million Vacations: The Max Webster Story, Guns N' Roses at 40, Hallowed by Their Name: The Unofficial Iron Maiden Bible, Blockbuster! The Sweet Story

2024: Judas Priest: Album by Album, Behind the Lines: Genesis on Record: 1978 – 1997, Entangled: Genesis on Record 1969 - 1976, Run with the Wolf: Rainbow on Record, Van Halen at 50, Honesty Is No Excuse: Thin Lizzy on Record, Pictures at Eleven: Robert Plant Album by Album, Perfect Water: The Rebel Imaginos

2023: Kiss at 50, The Electric Church: The Biography, Dominance and Submission: The Blue Öyster Cult Canon, The Who and Quadrophenia, Wild Mood Swings: Disintegrating The Cure Album by Album, AC/DC at 50

2022: Pink Floyd and The Dark Side of the Moon: 50 Years, Killing the Dragon: Dio in the '90s and 2000s, Feed My Frankenstein: Alice Cooper, the Solo Years, Easy Action: The Original Alice Cooper Band, Lively Arts: The Damned Deconstructed, Yes: A Visual Biography II: 1982 – 2022, Bowie @ 75, Dream Evil: Dio in the '80s, Judas Priest: A Visual Biography, UFO: A Visual Biography

2021: Hawkwind: A Visual Biography, Loud 'n' Proud: Fifty Years of Nazareth, Yes: A Visual Biography, Uriah Heep: A Visual Biography, Driven: Rush in the '90s and "In the End," Flaming Telepaths: Imaginos Expanded and Specified, Rebel Rouser: A Sweet User Manual

2020: The Fortune: On the Rocks with Angel, Van Halen: A Visual Biography, Limelight: Rush in the '80s, Thin Lizzy: A Visual Biography, Empire of the Clouds: Iron Maiden in the 2000s, Blue Öyster Cult: A Visual Biography, Anthem: Rush in the '70s, Denim and Leather: Saxon's First Ten Years, Black Funeral: Into the Coven with Mercyful Fate

2019: Satisfaction: 10 Albums That Changed My Life, Holy Smoke: Iron Maiden in the '90s, Sensitive to Light: The Rainbow Story, Where Eagles Dare: Iron Maiden in the '80s, Aces High: The Top 250 Heavy Metal Songs of the '80s, Judas Priest: Turbo 'til Now, Born Again! Black Sabbath in the Eighties and Nineties

2018: Riff Raff: The Top 250 Heavy Metal Songs of the '70s, Lettin' Go: UFO in the '80s and '90s, Queen: Album by Album, Unchained: A Van Halen User Manual, Iron Maiden: Album by Album, Sabotage! Black Sabbath in the Seventies, Welcome to My Nightmare: 50 Years of Alice Cooper, Judas Priest: Decade of Domination, Popoff Archive – 6: American Power Metal, Popoff Archive – 5: European Power Metal, The Clash: All the Albums, All the Songs

2017: Led Zeppelin: All the Albums, All the Songs, AC/DC: Album by Album, Lights Out: Surviving the '70s with UFO, Tornado of Souls: Thrash's Titanic Clash, Caught in a Mosh: The Golden Era of Thrash, Rush: Album by Album, Beer Drinkers and Hell Raisers: The Rise of Motörhead, Metal Collector: Gathered Tales from Headbangers, Hit the Lights: The Birth of Thrash, Popoff Archive – 4: Classic Rock, Popoff Archive – 3: Hair Metal

2016: Popoff Archive – 2: Progressive Rock, Popoff Archive – 1: Doom Metal, Rock the Nation: Montrose, Gamma and Ronnie Redefined, Punk Tees: The Punk Revolution in 125 T-Shirts, Metal Heart: Aiming High with Accept, Ramones at 40, Time and a Word: The Yes Story

2015: Kickstart My Heart: A Mötley Crüe Day-by-Day, This Means War: The Sunset Years of the NWOBHM, Wheels of Steel: The Explosive Early Years of the NWOBHM, Swords and Tequila: Riot's Classic First Decade, Who Invented Heavy Metal?, Sail Away: Whitesnake's Fantastic Voyage

2014: Live Magnetic Air: The Unlikely Saga of the Superlative Max Webster, Steal Away the Night: An Ozzy Osbourne Day-by-Day, The Big Book of Hair Metal, Sweating Bullets: The Deth and Rebirth of Megadeth, Smokin' Valves: A Headbanger's Guide to 900 NWOBHM Records

A DANGEROUS MEETING: IN THE SHADOWS WITH MERCYFUL FATE

2013: The Art of Metal (co-edit with Malcolm Dome), 2 Minutes to Midnight: An Iron Maiden Day-by-Day, Metallica: The Complete Illustrated History, Rush: The Illustrated History, Ye Olde Metal: 1979, Scorpions: Top of the Bill - updated and reissued as Wind of Change: The Scorpions Story in 2016

2012: Epic Ted Nugent, Fade To Black: Hard Rock Cover Art of the Vinyl Age, It's Getting Dangerous: Thin Lizzy 81-12, We Will Be Strong: Thin Lizzy 76-81, Fighting My Way Back: Thin Lizzy 69-76, The Deep Purple Royal Family: Chain of Events '80 – '11, The Deep Purple Royal Family: Chain of Events Through '79 - reissued as The Deep Purple Family Year by Year books

2011: Black Sabbath FAQ, The Collector's Guide to Heavy Metal: Volume 4: The '00s (co-authored with David Perri)

2010: Goldmine Standard Catalog of American Records 1948 – 1991, 7th Edition

2009: Goldmine Record Album Price Guide, 6th Edition, Goldmine 45 RPM Price Guide, 7th Edition, A Castle Full of Rascals: Deep Purple '83 – '09, Worlds Away: Voivod and the Art of Michel Langevin, Ye Olde Metal: 1978

2008: Gettin' Tighter: Deep Purple '68 – '76, All Access: The Art of the Backstage Pass, Ye Olde Metal: 1977, Ye Olde Metal: 1976

2007: Judas Priest: Heavy Metal Painkillers, Ye Olde Metal: 1973 to 1975, The Collector's Guide to Heavy Metal: Volume 3: The Nineties, Ye Olde Metal: 1968 to 1972

2006: Run for Cover: The Art of Derek Riggs, Black Sabbath: Doom Let Loose, Dio: Light Beyond the Black

2005: The Collector's Guide to Heavy Metal: Volume 2: The Eighties, Rainbow: English Castle Magic, UFO: Shoot Out the Lights, The New Wave of British Heavy Metal Singles

2004: Blue Öyster Cult: Secrets Revealed! (updated and reissued in 2009 with the same title; updated and reissued as Agents of Fortune: The Blue Öyster Cult Story in 2016), Contents Under Pressure: 30 Years of Rush at Home & Away, The Top 500 Heavy Metal Albums of All Time

2003: The Collector's Guide to Heavy Metal: Volume 1: The Seventies, The Top 500 Heavy Metal Songs of All Time

2001: Southern Rock Review

2000: Heavy Metal: 20th Century Rock and Roll, The Goldmine Price Guide to Heavy Metal Records

1997: The Collector's Guide to Heavy Metal

1993: Riff Kills Man! 25 Years of Recorded Hard Rock & Heavy Metal

See martinpopoff.com for complete details and ordering information.